Tax Guide 404

HOME SALES UNLIMITED

by

Holmes F. Crouch
Tax Specialist

Published by

Allyear Tax Guides
20484 Glen Brae Drive
Saratoga, CA 95070

ISBN-13: 9780944817827
ISBN-10: 0944817823

LCCN 2006930824

Printed in U.S.A.

Series 400

Owners & Sellers

Tax Guide 404

HOME SALES UNLIMITED

For other titles in print, see page 224.

The author: **Holmes F. Crouch**
For more about the author, see page 221.

PREFACE

If you are a knowledge-seeking **taxpayer** looking for information, this book can be helpful to you. It is designed to be read — from cover to cover — in about eight hours. Or, it can be "skim-read" in about 30 minutes.

Either way, you are treated to **tax knowledge** . . . *beyond the ordinary*. The "beyond" is that which cannot be found in IRS publications, the IRS web site, IRS e-file instructions, or tax software programs.

Taxpayers have different levels of interest in a selected subject. For this reason, this book starts with introductory fundamentals and progresses onward. You can verify the progression by chapter and section in the table of contents. In the text, "applicable law" is quoted in pertinent part. Key phrases and key tax forms are emphasized. Real-life examples are given . . . in down-to-earth style.

This book has 12 chapters. This number provides depth without cross-subject rambling. Each chapter starts with a head summary of meaningful information.

To aid in your skim-reading, informative diagrams and tables are placed strategically throughout the text. By leafing through page by page, reading the summaries and section headings, and glancing at the diagrams and tables, you can get a good handle on the matters covered.

Effort has been made to update and incorporate all of the latest tax law changes that are *significant* to the title subject. However, "beyond the ordinary" does not encompass every conceivable variant of fact and law that might give rise to protracted dispute and litigation. Consequently, if a particular statement or paragraph is crucial to your own specific case, you are urged to seek professional counseling. Otherwise, the information presented is general and is designed for a broad range of reader interests.

The Author

INTRODUCTION

The term "Section 121" refers to a particular portion of the Internal Revenue Code (administered by the IRS) titled: ***Exclusion of Gain from Sale of Principal Residence.*** Without more information than this, the implication is that all capital gain from the sale of your home is excluded from being reported on your personal income tax return. No; this is not the case at all. Only up to certain amounts are excluded. For single persons, the exclusion of gain is up to $250,000; for married persons filing jointly, the exclusion doubles to $500,000. If your home sells for the excluded amounts or less, then all gain is indeed excluded.

What happens to the capital gain amounts excluded? They are all TAX FREE money: the IRS can **not** come after you for it. You can use it for whatever purpose serves your interests. Among your options are:

1. Blow it at a gambling casino;
2. Pay off your credit cards, then go on vacation;
3. Buy a fancy car or other vehicle;
4. Make a higher down payment on your next home;
5. Buy a second home for time off with the kids;
6. Buy rental property and become a landlord;
7. Invest in the stock market to make a million;
8. Give it to needy family members or to charity; or
9. Save it for your own retirement, because you **will** live longer than you now think.

How many exclusions can you claim?

Answer: As many times as you can tolerate buying a home and moving in, fixing it up, then selling it and moving out. There is just one catch. You must own and use each home as your principal residence for two years or more in a five-year period ending on date of sale. We'll explain this requirement in much detail herein.

Otherwise, there is no limit to the number of exclusions you can claim. There is no age limit. There is no dollar limit on the price of a home sold. There is no limit on the size of a home sold; it can be a small condo or a large mansion. There is no limit on the kind of home you sell. You could buy a duplex, live in one unit and rent the other unit. When you sell, you will have sold two properties: one as your residence, the other as investment property. The investment property does not participate in the exclusion benefits. In short, except for the minimum 2-year ownership and use rule, there is no limit to the number of exclusions you can claim. There is, however, a special 5-year ownership/use requirement should you acquire a residence via a Section 1031 (like-kind) exchange. We'll address this matter in due course.

Meanwhile, as a purely hypothetical example, suppose you were a homeowner for 40 years of your lifespan. If you sold your home every 2$^+$ years, that would be potentially 19 exclusions! [40 ÷ 2$^+$ ≈ 19.] If you sold your home every five years or so, that would be eight exclusions. For this number of exclusions, can you not imagine the accumulation of potentially between $1,000,000 ($1 million) and $2,000,000 ($2 million) **tax free**?

How do you compute — and claim — the amount of capital gain exclusion that is tax free?

The short answer is that you have to report the actual sales price on your personal income tax return (Form 1040 in most cases). Then you have to enter your *cost or other basis* (from your records). Subtract the latter from the former (sales price – cost basis) to get your total gain. At this point, you subtract your allowable exclusion amount. Any excess gain is taxable . . . at a **highly favorable** 15% rate (Federal).

There is also a long answer. It is too long for citation here. This is because there are approximately 15 **special rules** that modify the short answer above. We cover them all herein.

What happens if, instead of a capital gain, there is a capital loss? Sadly, we must tell you that said loss is NOT TAX RECOGNIZED. It is simply a loss/loss. You still must report the sale, then report the loss as "zero."

Fortunately, the unlimited frequency of exclusion of gain opportunities provides ample time to make up for the loss in one or more subsequent sales. We say this because we believe that Section 121 is perhaps the most taxpayer friendly rule of all time.

CONTENTS

1

BASIC LAW EXPLAINED

> Any Individual Who Owns And Occupies His Or Her Principal Residence For 2 Years Or More (In A 5-Year Period) Can TAX EXCLUDE Up To $250,000 Of Capital Gain When Such Residence Is Sold Or Exchanged. This Is NOT A One-Time Exclusion. It Is An EVERY SALE Exclusion Every 2 "Plus" Years. No Rollover Of The Exclusion To A Replacement Residence Is Required. Each Sale Is An INDEPENDENT Exclusion Event On Its Own. Age Of The Seller Is Not A Factor. If One Starts Early Enough, And Is Fiscally Prudent, He Or She Can Amass A Substantial Nest Egg Of $1,000,000 Or More . . . Completely TAX FREE!

Section 121 of the Internal Revenue Code as currently in effect is an unusual tax law. It is so in several respects. Foremost are its simplicity and straightforwardness. It addresses the benefits of one owner at a time, when a personal residence is sold. It is more taxpayer friendly than other tax rules associated with the sale of real property. It consists of multiple qualifying elements which are separable and readily definable. It separates every home sale from every other home sale, whether past, present, or future. Every home sale, therefore, becomes a separate tax accounting event of its own. This one feature alone greatly simplifies recordkeeping.

And . . . the "icing on the cake" is a $250,000 *per owner* exclusion of gain on **every home sale** throughout one's occupational life. The frequency of home sales in one's lifetime opens up truly intriguing opportunities for building up a substantial nest egg . . . TAX FREE! We can't wait to explain to you how these opportunities can arise.

As tax laws go, Section 121 is quite lengthy. Its full statutory text comprises about 1,800 words (more or less). Of this count, three particular subsections (of about 140 words) comprise the basic features of the general law itself. These subsections are 121(a): *Exclusion*, 121(b)(1): *Limitations, in General* and 121(b)(3): *Application*. In this introductory chapter, we want to extract from these three subsections the fundamental essence of Section 121 that you can rely on when selling a home that exceeds $250,000 in value. For sale prices of $250,000 or less, Section 121 does not apply. Nevertheless, the sale may need to be reported.

Our position is that, if we can carve out and present to you the important basics of Section 121, you will be able to memorize them on your own. You will then be able to use these features when planning your next and future home sales. In subsequent chapters, we'll present various refinements to these basics.

The Title Words

The official title of Section 121 is: *Exclusion of Gain from Sale of Principal Residence*. This is a total of just eight words. Ordinarily, the words in a title of a tax law do not constitute the law itself. Title words are for indexing purposes only. The caption words highlight what the law is supposed to be about. Much too often, caption titles in the Internal Revenue Code tend to be misleading or tend to have some political agenda associated with them. Not so for Section 121. The title words are straightforward and simple in meaning.

Take the very first word: *Exclusion*, for example. What does this word mean?

If you look in an ordinary dictionary, the word is defined as: *a thing excluded; a thing kept out*. A legal dictionary defines the term more precisely as:

*An amount that otherwise would constitute a part of **Gross Income** but that under a specific provision of the **Internal Revenue Code** is excluded from gross income.*

There you have it. An exclusion is an authorized omission from gross income. Anything in gross income, as you surely know, after adjustments and deductions, winds up being taxed. If it is not in gross income, it is not taxed. Therefore, if it is not taxed, it must be tax free. Right? Right.

What is it that is tax free?

Answer: It is a certain amount of **gain** from the sale of a principal residence that is tax free. The amount of gain must be established before any exclusion can be claimed.

The Section 121 title does not include the word "certain" as it more properly should. Without it, a reader gets the impression that all gain — capital, short-term, long-term, ordinary — is tax free when selling a home. This is NOT true. Only certain gain is tax free. As you'll see later, only a certain (limited) amount of capital gain is tax free. If there is a capital loss — instead of gain — Section 121 does not apply. Any loss on the sale of a personal residence is a "loss/loss" . . . **not** tax recognized.

Principal Residence Defined

The eight title words cited above end with the words: *Principal Residence*. What does the term "principal residence" mean? Nowhere in the 1,500 statutory words of Section 121 is it defined. Consequently, we have to resort to citing for you IRS Regulation § 1.121-1(b)(2): *Principal residence*.

This regulation reads in full as—

*In the case of a taxpayer using more than one property as a residence, whether property is used by the taxpayer as the taxpayer's principal residence depends upon all the facts and circumstances. If a taxpayer alternates between 2 properties, using each as a residence for successive periods of time, the property that the taxpayer **uses a majority of the time during the year** ordinarily will be considered the taxpayer's principal residence. In addition to the taxpayer's use of the property, relevant factors in determining a taxpayer's principal residence, include, but are not limited to—*

(i)   The taxpayer's place of employment;

> *(ii)*   *The principal place of abode of the taxpayer's family members;*
> *(iii)* *The address listed on the taxpayer's federal and state tax returns, driver's license, automobile registration, and voter registration card;*
> *(iv)* *The taxpayer's mailing address for bills and correspondence;*
> *(v)*   *The location of the taxpayer's banks; and*
> *(vi)* *The location of religious organizations and recreational clubs with which the taxpayer is affiliated.*

Property used by the taxpayer as the taxpayer's principal residence does not include personal property that is not a fixture under local law.

Whew! A lot of words (about 170). But what is the essence that comes through? Is it not the concept of a *personal dwelling* — no matter where, what kind, or one of many — that is used *a majority of the time during the year*? So, what is a dwelling?

An ordinary dictionary defines a "dwelling" as: *a place to live in*; *residence*; *home*; *abode*. An "abode" is: *a place where one lives or stays*; *a residence that is more than temporary*.

Barron's Dictionary of Legal Terms defines a "dwelling" as—

One's residence; a structure or apartment used as a home for a family unit; a house in which the occupier and his family reside; the home address to which the family always intends to return for prolonged periods; it includes everything attached to or considered an accessory to the main building, such as a garage or barn, and may consist of a cluster of buildings.

In other words, a principal residence is where you (and your family) spend most of the year living; where your family mail is sent; where you vote; and from where you mail your income tax returns. In a series of multiple residences which you may occupy periodically throughout the year, it is that primary one you occupy most of the year. Instead of "most," the IRS regulation above states: *majority of the time during the year*. This, we submit, ordinarily means more than six months for any given year. As you'll see later, one may "aggregate" the occupancy years.

The implication above is that one can have any number of personal residences at any time. But only one counts as the **principal** residence when claiming the exclusion of gain under Section 121.

A Stroke of Genius

Here it is; the stroke of genius. Section 121(a), the general rule: *Exclusion*, reads precisely as—

Gross income shall not include gain from the sale or exchange of property if, during the 5-year period ending on the date of the sale or exchange, such property has been owned and used by the taxpayer as the taxpayer's principal residence for periods aggregating 2 years or more.

There are 48 words here. Count them. Better yet, memorize them. Or, at least memorize the gist of them: "2-out-of-5 years ownership and use."

Where is the genius? It is not in the 48 words themselves. It is what the words do **not** say that establishes their creativity and ingenuity. The leadoff words are direct and straightforward: *Gross income shall not include . . .* (etc.).

There is no reference to, or any restriction based on, a prior home sale or sales. Nothing is said about age of the owner at time of sale. So long as he/she is of legal age at time of sale, one could be 19 years old . . . or 99 years old. Other than being of legal age under state law for validating real estate contracts, there is no age limitation whatsoever. Nothing is said about there being a one-time exclusion. Any number of exclusions can be claimed by any one person, so long as the 2-out-of-5-year rule is followed. Nothing is said about requiring a replacement residence, in order to claim the exclusion. In fact, one does not have to get a replacement residence at all. He/she can choose to rent for the rest of life. Or he/she can move into a second home, into a vacation home, into residential property that is owned but previously rented to another family, into inherited property, or into a retirement home. This brings us to the basic underlying premise of Section 121(a). The premise is that each exclusion-qualified home sale is independent of every other home sale throughout one's entire occupational life!

There are just two restrictions that apply in order to claim the Section 121(a) exclusion-of-gain benefits. One is the 2-out-of-5-year requirement; the other is the principal residence requirement. We have already covered the principal residence requirement.

As for the 2-out-of-5-year requirement, we depict its quantitative features for you in Figure 1.1. For simplicity of depiction, we are treating a year as consisting of 365 days, irrespective of whether a leap year (366 days) intervenes or not. Note that the 5-year period *ends* on date of sale. Thus, a 5-year period covers consecutively 1,825 days (365 d/yr x 5 yrs). While ownership and use of a principal residence may precede five years before date of sale, it is only the 5-year period ending on date of sale that counts. The precise statutory wording on point is—

. . . during the 5-year period ending on the date of the sale . . .

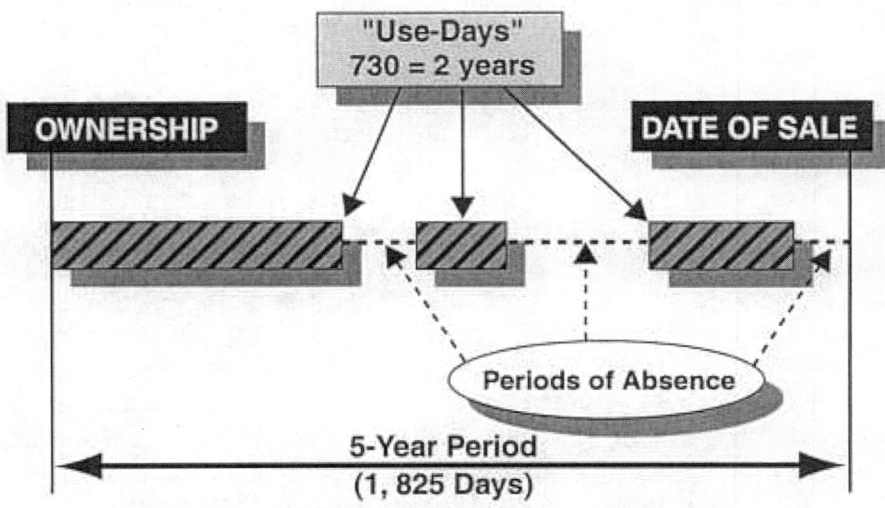

Fig. 1.1 - The "2-Out-of-5" Use Rule of Section 121

As Figure 1.1 indicates, ownership is implied throughout the 5-year measuring period. The focus is on use days. The required minimum period of *use* days is 730 days (365 d/yr x 2 yrs). The statutory language says—

. . . for periods [plural] *aggregating 2 years or more . . .*

In other words, one does not have to live in his home for two (or more) consecutive years in order to claim the exclusion. He (and his family) only have to live in it for an *aggregate* of two years or more (or two years plus one day, to be safe). Reasoning in reverse, Section 121(a) provides that one may be absent from his principal residence for 1094 days (365 d/yr x 3 yrs – 1 day) and still have the sale qualify for the exclusion of gain. This is an extremely liberal tax law. We know of no other like it in the entire Internal Revenue Code.

For "24 Full Months"

The 2-out-of-5-year requirement of Section 121(a) is called the "ownership and use test" for the exclusion qualification. This requirement is expressly addressed in IRS Regulation § 1.121-1(c): *Ownership and use requirements.* We wish to cite this regulation in its entirety.

Accordingly, the test regulation reads—

*The requirements of ownership and use for periods aggregating 2 years or more may be satisfied by establishing ownership and use for **24 full months** or for 730 days (365 x 2). The requirements of ownership and use may be satisfied during nonconcurrent periods if both the ownership and use tests are met during the 5 years ending on the date of the sale or exchange. In establishing whether a taxpayer has satisfied the 2-year use requirement, occupancy of the residence is required. However, short temporary absences, such as for vacation or other seasonal absence (although accompanied with rental of the residence) are counted as periods of use.*

In your mind, what is the most significant testing application of this regulation? Would it not be the **24 full months of ownership**

and occupancy during five years of noncurrent periods? What does "24 full months" mean?

When a regulation is this specific within a tax law that is liberal, be forewarned that a trap is set. You have nearly three full years in a 5-year span of time in which to accommodate both foreseeable and unforeseeable nonoccupancy contingencies. Therefore, expect no additional latitude or leniency whatsoever. Instead, plan on and prepare to meet precisely the "24 full months" requirement.

First of all, each day in a full month must be a full 24-hour day. If you occupy your residence at 11:00 a.m. on day 1, say, your first full 24-hour day is day 2. Conversely, if you move out at 2:00 p.m. on the 30th day of a 30-day month (having moved in the night before the 1st of the month), you would have occupied the residence only 29 days. This is not a full month if it were a 30-day month.

February is a 28-day month three out of every four years, and a 29-day month every 4th year (2000, 2004, 2008, etc.). Every other month is either 30 days or 31 days. Consequently, a full month is 672 hours (28 d x 24 hr/d) for a 28-day month, 696 hours for a 29-day month, 720 hours for a 30-day month, and 744 hours for a 31-day month. Obviously, not all months in an aggregate of 24 full months will have the same number of days. Consequently, when there are periods of occupancy and nonoccupancy in one's principal residence in a 5-year measuring span, great care is required to establish the true months of occupancy. How can this be done?

The best way is to establish and maintain an *Occupancy Log* on the residence you anticipate selling. See our representation of such in Figure 1.2. When you move into the residence and start or resume family living, make a written entry into whatever form of record you wish to keep. Enter the time of day, day of the week, day of the month, and, of course, the year. Similarly, when you move out . . . be it for temporary purposes or other.

Ideally, each move-in and move-out should be documented with an official notice to the U.S. Postal Service. Presumably, you would be giving instructions on holding or forwarding your mail. Other types of verification — such as a witnessing signature by a neighbor, instructions to utility service providers, receipts by moving companies, etc. — can be used. For each occupancy period, attach a preprinted calendar for the applicable year(s) and month(s). Cross-hatch each batch of consecutive full 24-hour days. If you do these things in a timely and conscientious manner, your occupational log will be accepted by the IRS.

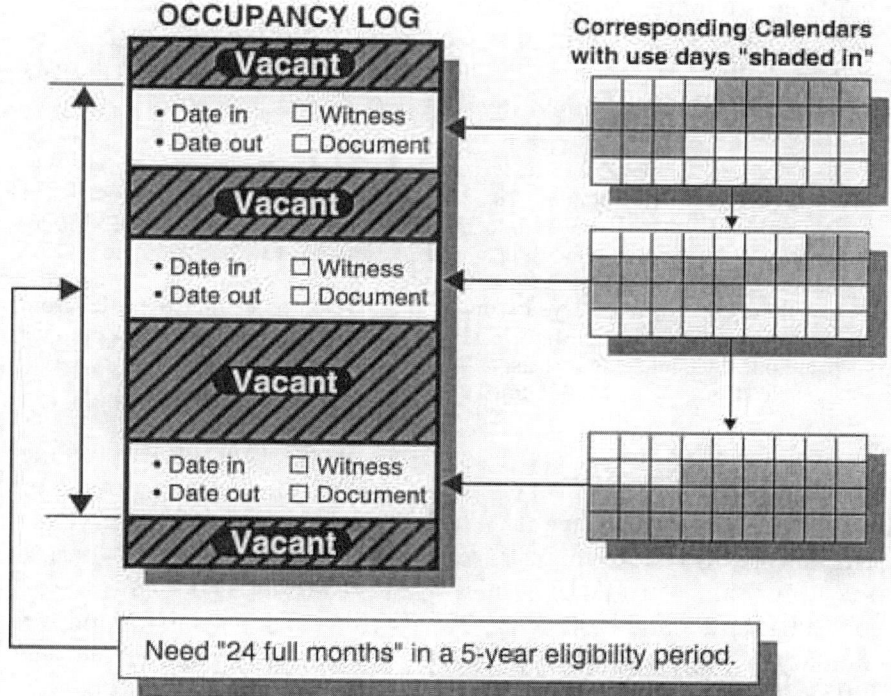

Fig. 1.2 - Sec. 121 (a) "Occupancy Log" Amid Sporadic Vacancies

Regulatory Examples

IRS Regulation § 1.121-1(c)(4): *Examples*, presents **5** different occupancy illustrations of compliance and noncompliance with the 2-out-of-5-year rule. From the official five examples, we'll select three and critique them in our own words. Except for the dates used, we'll cite each example verbatim

Example 1. Taxpayer A has owned and used his principal residence since 1997. On January 31, 2004, A moves to another state. A rents his house to tenants from that date until April 18, 2005, when he sells it. A is eligible for the section 121 exclusion because he has owned and used the house as his principal residence for at least 2 of the 5 years preceding the sale.

In Example 1, the 5-year measuring period started on April 18, 2001 (five years preceding date of sale). A lived continuously in the house from April 18, 2001 through January 31, 2004. This is a qualifying ownership-use period of two years (2002 and 2003), eight months (May through December 2001), and 31 days in January 2004. Because the full 24-month requirement was continuous, no occupational log was necessary.

Example 3. Taxpayer C lives in a townhouse that he rents from 1999 through 2002. On January 18, 2003, he purchases the townhouse. On February 1, 2004, C moves into his daughter's home. On May 25, 2006, while still living in his daughter's home, C sells his townhouse. The section 121 exclusion will apply to gain from the sale because C owned the townhouse for at least 2 years out of the 5 years preceding the sale (from January 19, 2003 until May 25, 2006) and he used the townhouse as his principal residence for at least 2 years during the 5-year period preceding the sale (from May 25, 2001 until February 1, 2004).

Official Example 3 presents an interesting twist to the ownership-and-use rule. The period of ownership and period of use **need not be concurrent**. The two can be separated in time, so long as both requirements are confined to the 5-year period preceding sale. In this example, the 5-year period began on May 25, 2001 and ended on May 25, 2006. The ownership period (January 18, 2003 to May 25, 2006) covered two years (2004 and 2005), 11 months in 2003, and four months in 2006. The use period (May 25, 2001 to February 1, 2004) covered two years (2002 and 2003), seven months in 2001, and one month in 2004. In this case, use preceded ownership. But it could be the other way around: ownership could precede use. So important is this concept of ownership and use, and their separation, that we must depict it for you in Figure 1.3. This figure supports our earlier premise of the genius of Section 121(a).

Example 5. Taxpayer E purchases a house on February 1, 2004, that he uses as his principal residence. During 2004 and 2005, E leaves his residence for 2-month summer vacations. E sells the house on March 1, 2006. Although, in the 5-year period preceding the date of sale, the total time E used his residence is less than 2 years (21 months), the section 121 exclusion will apply to gain from the sale of the residence because, under paragraph (c)(2) of this section, the 2-month vacations are short temporary absences and are counted as periods of use in determining whether E used the residence for the requisite period.

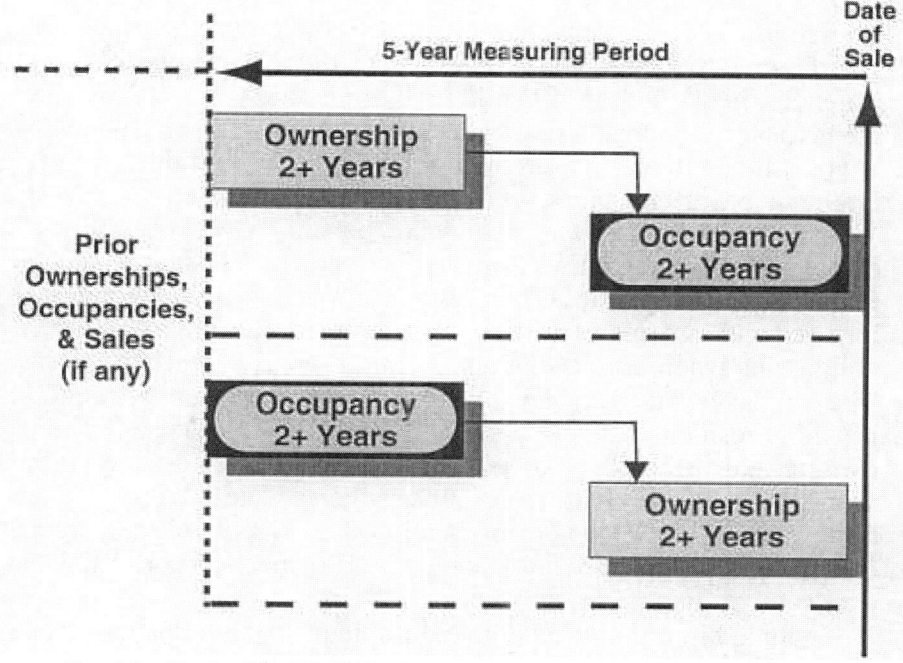

Fig. 1.3 - Exclusion Eligibility When Noncurrence of Ownership & Use

In Example 5, the residence was owned for a total of two years and one month (25 months: February 1, 2004 through February 28, 2006). It was used as such for only 21 months. You can be sure that the IRS is going to want some solid third-party documentation of the date of purchase, date of sale, and some evidence of date of departure (to where) and date of return (from where) of the two 2-month vacation periods. On page 1-7, we cited 11 lines of Regulation § 1.121-1(c) requiring 24 full months of occupancy. But then the last three lines say—

However, short temporary absences, such as for vacation or other seasonal absence . . . are counted as periods of use.

Now you know why we went to some length in Figure 1.2 to display the importance of an occupancy log.

Who is "The Taxpayer"?

Section 121(a), previously cited, uses the terms: *the taxpayer* and *the taxpayer's principal residence.* Nowhere in subsection (a) is gender mentioned or implied. Nothing is said (thus far) whether the taxpayer is married, divorced, widowed, or not. Marital status is **not** a fundamental requirement for the exclusion right. So, who is "the taxpayer" for purposes of Section 121(a)?

The answer is: Every *individual* person who owns, or part-owns, and uses a dwelling as his or her principal residence for the requisite period of time. The presumption is that such person is of his/her legal age and is sufficiently competent to understand legal obligations when purchasing and selling property. In other words, "the taxpayer" is a person who has purchased or acquired a principal residence at some point in time and who has sold it after owning and using it for more than two years in a test-measuring span of five years. It is irrelevant whether he/she is 100% owner, 50% owner, 35% owner, or some other fractional percentage owner. He/she is entitled to each owner's respective portion of the exclusion of gain.

Included in the above is the requirement that a taxpayer be one who prepares and files **Form 1040:** *U.S. Individual Income Tax Return.* This rules out corporations (which file Form 1120), partnerships (which file Form 1065), and trusts (which file Form 1041). A Form 1040 filer must either be a U.S. citizen (regardless of where he/she may reside throughout the world) or a U.S. resident (regardless of whatever country he/she may be a citizen of). It also follows that a Form 1040 filer may own and sell his principal residence in **any** of the 50 states within the United States. No U.S. state imposes a restriction on Section 121(a).

As to the ownership and sale of a *foreign* principal residence by a U.S. taxpayer, the benefits of Section 121(a) would appear to apply. However, there are other twists. Real property located in a foreign country is subject to the tax laws and property laws of that country. This may subject the homeseller to a "double taxation" effect. In such case, one must seek recourse to any Tax Treaty between the U.S. and the host country. At present, the U.S. has tax treaties with 60 independent countries throughout the world.

Eligible Every 2 "plus" Years

Subsection 121(b)(3) is titled: *Application to only 1 sale or exchange every 2 years*. This subsection reads in full as—

*(A) **In General**—Subsection (a) shall not apply to any sale or exchange by the taxpayer, if, during the 2 year period ending on the date of such sale or exchange, there was any other sale or exchange by the taxpayer to which subsection (a) applied.*

*(B) **Pre-May 7, 1997 Sales not taken into account**— Subparagraph (A) shall be applied without regard to any sale or exchange before May 7, 1997.*

Section 121(a), recall, is the general 2-out-of-5-year rule to which the exclusion of gain applies. Subsection (b)(3)(A) says, in effect, that once the 2-out-of-5-year rule has been met, a sale or exchange thereafter may be repeated every 2+ years. We add the "+" to the two years as a safety factor. Trying to cut too close to exactly two years ("24 full months") is simply not prudent when a very liberal tax benefit is at stake. Our safety rule is 25 full months of ownership and occupancy (including regular vacations).

Subsection (b)(3)(B) above is self-explanatory. Section 121 was enacted into law on May 6, 1997. We discuss any changes since then in upcoming Chapter 2.

For hypothetical excitement, let us ask ourselves: How many eligible sales could be made in a 40-year period? We consider 40 years to be an ordinary lifetime of home ownership and sales. This corresponds to an occupational span of from age 30 (a likely first home sale) to age 70 (a likely final home sale).

Back to our question. In 40 years of principal residence ownership, how many eligible sales under Section 121(a) could be made? Assume a sale or exchange every 25 months.

Answer: 40 yrs x 12 mo/yr = 480 months. Therefore, the number of sales =

480 mo ÷ 25 mo/sale = <u>19 sales</u>!

IF —and this is a big "if" — such a number of sales were actually made by a taxpayer, each and every one would qualify for the exclusion-of-gain benefits. Except for the 2-year rule, there is no limit to the number of sales or exchanges that can be made. As we depict in Figure 1.4, each event stands entirely on its own. There is no "tax interlock" between them. This is truly an advantage when job changes cause the home sales.

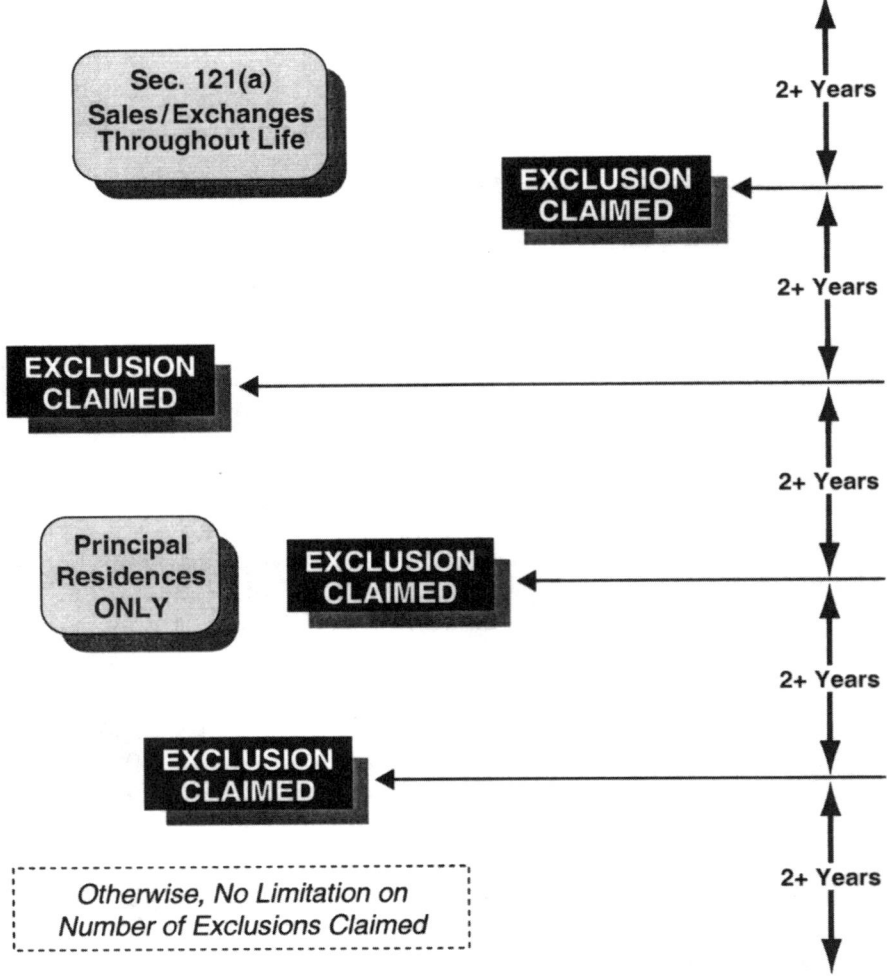

Fig. 1.4 - Each Sale/Exchange Event Stands Alone: No "Tax Interlock"

[There is, however, a 5-year exception when your residence is acquired in a "like-kind" exchange. Otherwise, you'd get two tax benefits for one transaction.]

Common sense suggests that some practical limit will prevail. Moving one's self, his family, and his household furniture and effects every 25 months is not everyone's cup of tea. For career military personnel and upwardly mobile corporate executives, moving this frequently is quite common. More generally, though, the average job-seeking, job-keeping person makes — on average — between about five and eight home sales in a lifetime. The sales are more frequent (about five) in the early occupational years (ages 30 to 50) and less frequent (about three) in the later occupational years (ages 50 to 70).

Meaning of "Sale or Exchange"

Selected wording from the previously cited-in-full Section 121(a) says—

*Gross income shall not include gain from the **sale or exchange** of property if, . . . ending on the date of the **sale or exchange**, such property has . . .* [Emphasis added.]

Believe it or not, the term *sale or exchange* is used a total of **24 times** in the 1,500-word Section 121. When a plain language term is used this frequently, we have to ask: What is the meaning of "sale or exchange"?

The very first judicial ruling on the term "sale or exchange" goes back to around 1920. In *K.A. Spalding*, 7 BTA 588, Dec. 2601 (Acq.), the court held that—

*To constitute an exchange, there must be a **reciprocal transfer of properties** as distinguished from the transfer of property for money.* [Emphasis added.]

Editorial Note: The letters "BTA" above are Board of Tax Appeals: the predecessor to the present U.S. Tax Court. The "Dec." is Decision Number. The "(Acq.)" means acquiescence or consent (or acceptance) by the IRS.

This early ruling makes it quite clear that a "sale" is the transfer of property for money, whereas an "exchange" is the transfer of property for other property (other than money). The term "other property" includes not only a replacement residence (if desired), but also such items as debt relief, installment notes, title to land, works of art, bullion coins, etc. Other property is whatever the property seller/exchanger is willing to accept in "money's worth" at its fair market value. It makes no difference for Section 121 purposes. Either transaction is tax reportable.

The Two 2-Year Rules

Because our emphasis in this chapter is on fundamental matters, we need to clarify what could be two confusing eligibility requirements for the Section 121 exclusion. In case you've missed it, there are TWO 2-year requirements. They are not one and the same. Each serves a different qualifying purpose: one *before* sale, the other *after* sale.

For common identification, let us call the before-sale 2-year rule the "aggregation of 2 years." Similarly, let us call the after-sale 2-year rule the "subsequent sale 2 years." The two 2 years are **not** measured the same.

The "aggregation of 2 years" pertains solely to the ownership and occupancy requirement within a 5-year measuring period. As we have pointed out earlier, the 5-year period ends on date of sale. This permits one's principal residence to be vacated or rented to others for intermittent periods aggregating less than 3 years.

The exact statutory words in Section 121(a) are—

*owned and used . . . for periods **aggregating** 2 years or more.*

Note the use of the plural: "periods." The use of this plural permits noncontinuous occupancy by the owner before the residence is sold.

The "subsequent sale 2 years" has nothing to do, per se, with ownership and occupancy. It is simply a limitation period before a second residence sale can qualify for another exclusion. Such is the significance of Section 121(b)(3): ***Application to Only 1 Sale or Exchange Every 2 Years***. Another way of looking at this second 2-year rule is as a "frequency-of-sale" rule. This was the message that we were trying to get across to you in Figure 1.4.

Still another way of distinguishing between the two 2-year rules is in terms of measuring them. The aggregation of two years must be for *24 full months . . . within* a 5-year period. In contrast, the subsequent-sale two years is a period of *continuous* 24 months. The only documentation needed is the closing escrow statement on the preceding sale. We summarize in Figure 1.5 the contrast between these two 2-year periods.

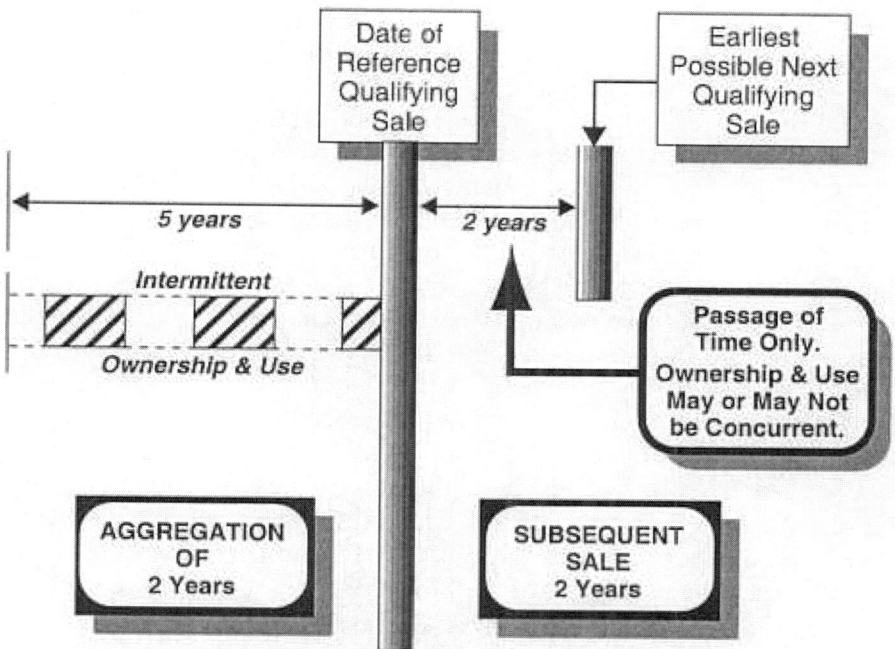

Fig. 1.5 - Distinction Between the Two 2-Year Rules

The $250,000 "Per" Icing

We have made reference repeatedly to the phrase: "Exclusion of gain." How much is the exclusion? Is there any dollar limitation that can be claimed tax free?

Section 121(b)(1): *Limitations; In General*, answers both questions. It reads in full—

The amount of gain excluded from gross income under subsection (a) with respect to any sale or exchange shall not exceed $250,000.

From this tax law, three observations can be made. One, the reference to subsection (a) means that the dollar limitation is **per** *taxpayer person* (who is owner and user). If there is more than one owner/user when a residence is sold, each person gets his or her own exclusion. The second observation is that the dollar limitation pertains to **any** sale or exchange (primarily within the U.S.). There is no tax interlock between sales. Each sale or exchange is an exclusion event entirely on its own. The third observation is: *shall not exceed* $250,000 per sale. Obviously, if the amount of gain on a sale is only $150,000, that's the exclusion amount: **not** $250,000. If there are three owners, for example, and the total gain is $150,000 on the sale, each owner gets a $50,000 exclusion: **not** $150,000 and certainly not $250,000.

In the ultimate sense, the exclusion limitation is a **per** *homesale event* (regardless of whether there is one owner, two owners, or even three owners). It is an exclusion of GAIN (capital gain) which is derived from the marketability of the home: not of the owner(s).

Realizing that each home sale is a separate exclusion-of-gain event, let us postulate a hypothetical example. Suppose, as an unmarried person, you made eight home sales in your lifetime. And, further, suppose that you could time each sale so that the average gain per sale was $125,000. How much money tax free would you have at the end of the 8th sale?

Answer: **$1,000,000**. That is, 8 sales x $125,000 exclusion of gain per sale = $1 million.

As a person, suppose you were prudent, fiscally conservative, and did not refinance foolishly. After each sale, you plunked the $125,000 exclusion-of-gain amount into a tax-free municipal bond account yielding 3% per annum. YES, such accounts are available; consult your own broker. If you did so, at the end of the 8th sale, with the compounding of interest tax free, you would have accumulated approximately $1,800,000 (1.8 million). This all would be TAX FREE! This is not a fictitious nor fanciful possibility. It is potentially achievable.

2

POST-ENACTMENT UPDATES

It Takes From 5 To 10 Years After A New Tax Law Goes Into Effect To Remedy Its Ambiguities, Inconsistencies, And Omissions. It Is An Updating Process Involving Revisions By Congress, Judicial Interpretations, Administrative Rulings, And The Adoption Of Formal Regulations (After Public Notice And Hearing). The More Significant Results To Date Are: (1) Clarification Of Reduced Exclusion Fractions; (2) Suspension Of The 5-Year Period For Military Families; (3) Extending The 2-Year Period To 5 Years For "Tax Free" Exchanges; (4) Treatment Of "Relocation Sales" By Employees; And (5) The Role Of Adjacent Land In Qualifying Sales.

IRC Section 121: *Exclusion of Gain from Sale of Principal Residence*, was enacted on May 6, 1997. This meant that all home sales closing after that date, if otherwise qualified, could derive their tax-free benefits. To do so required the self-interpretation of approximately 1,500 words of statutory text, arranged into subsections (a) through (g). Not all of the 1,500 words were clear and specific, though many were. Those that were not, raised questions and presented ambiguities that could not be resolved by the good faith efforts of homesellers themselves. In such situations, the IRS will always interpret against the taxpayer, then leave it up to Congress and to the courts to clarify the issues raised.

As a result of this traditional IRS stance, various interpretation clarifications and updates have been adopted. As of mid-2006, some 500 new statutory words have been added to Section 121;

approximately 12,000 words of regulations have been adopted; about 1,600 words of legislative intent have been issued; and some 2,500 words of judicial and administrative rulings have been made. Obviously, as an affected homeseller, you need to know the gist of these updates and whether they are targeted to your situation or to others in special situations.

As initially enacted, Section 121 was christened: P.L. (Public Law) **105-34**: *Taxpayer Relief Act of 1997*. Since then, five other public laws have included wording that either alters or adds to specific portions of Section 121. In this chapter, we want to tell you about these altering aspects and how they will aid your understanding of the chapter texts that follow. No tax law remains fixed in forever time, though, surprisingly, the fundamentals of Section 121 are quite stable. This attests to the sensibility of Section 121 and its inclusion of tax litigation experiences with home sales going back as far as 1964.

The First Clarification Act

One of the first taxpayer–IRS disputes arising from Section 121 pertained to its subsection (c): *Exclusion for Taxpayers Failing to Meet Certain Requirements*. The intent behind subsection (c) was that a reduced exclusion would be allowed based on the *fraction* of ownership and use that had occurred when a home was sold due to change of employment, health and safety reasons, or unforeseen circumstances. The allowable fraction would be the actual months of ownership and use compared to the 2-year (24-month) statutory requirement of subsection 121(a) that we covered in Chapter 1.

For example, suppose a taxpayer owned and used his residence for 15 months when a change of employment occurred. The fraction recognized under subsection 121(c)(1)(B) would be 15/24ths or 62.5%. Does this fraction apply to the amount of actual capital gain realized, or does it apply to the maximum amount of exclusion allowed ($250,000 per owner person)?

Answer: The reduced exclusion fraction applies to the "up to" $250,000 amount. Congress so ruled in a tack-on provision to P.L. 105-206: *IRS Restructuring and Reform Act of 1998*. Congress then was reviewing other complaints against the IRS.

As recorded in Congressional documents, the clarifying intent was expressed as—

The ['98 Act] *clarifies that an otherwise qualifying taxpayer who fails to satisfy the two-year* [24 month] *ownership and use requirements is able to exclude an amount equal to the fraction of the $250,000 ($500,000 if married filing a joint return),* **not the fraction of the realized gain.** . . . *In addition, the bill provides that if a married couple filing a joint return does not qualify for the $500,000 maximum exclusion, the amount of the maximum exclusion that may be claimed by the couple is the sum of each spouse's maximum exclusion* [of $250,000] *determined on a separate basis.*

This intent wording by Congress makes it clear that reasonable interpretations are to be made. The insistence by Congress on reasonableness, we believe, is a form of rebuke to the IRS for its too often strident stance against well-meaning taxpayers. There is no prohibition against the IRS relying on Congressional intent.

Synopsis of Other Acts

The '98 Act above was enacted on July 7, 1998. Subsequent thereto four other Acts were created, namely: the '01 Act, the '03 Act, the '04 Act, and the '05 Act. These Acts of Congress did not exclusively address Section 121; they included tack-on provisions to clarify certain nuances therewith. These four Acts are Public Law (P.L.) titled as follows:

'01 Act — Economic Growth and Tax Relief Reconciliation Act of 2001: P.L. 107-16 (enacted 6-07-01).

'03 Act — Military Family Tax Relief Act of 2003: P.L. 108-121 (enacted 11-11-03).

'04 Act — American Jobs Creation Act of 2004: P.L. 108-357 (enacted 10-22-04).

'05 Act — Gulf Opportunity Zone Act of 2005: P.L. 109-135 (enacted 12-21-05).

The '01 Act extends the exclusion of gains benefits to estates, trusts, and heirs of a decedent who owned and used the residence for two or more years before his or her demise. If a decedent's heir occupies the property before its sale, the decedent's period of ownership and occupancy can be added to the heir's ownership and occupancy to claim the applicable maximum exclusion. Subsection **121(d)(11): Property Acquired from a Decedent**, was added to Section 121 (Special Rules) to accommodate this Act. Weirdly, it goes into effect *after* year 2009.

The '03 Act enables military and uniformed services members to *elect to suspend* the 5-year test period (for ownership and occupancy) to up to 10 years. The election to suspend is valid only if active duty is more than 50 miles away, and is pursuant to official orders compelling residence elsewhere for more than 90 days or for an indefinite period. Subsection **121(d)(9): *Members of Uniformed Services and Foreign Service***, was added to accommodate this Act. Also, a 500-word Regulation § 1.121-5: *Suspension of 5-year period for certain members of the uniformed services*, was added. This regulation prescribes the manner for making the election. A year of sale return is required, but the amount of gain then realized is not shown. The gain is not computed nor is the exclusion claimed until the elected suspension period expires.

The '04 Act provides that the exclusion of gain benefits do not apply if one's principal residence was acquired via a Section 1031 like-kind (tax free) exchange in which no gain was tax recognized. For Section 121 to apply, the exclusion qualifying test period is increased from 2 years to 5 years after the exchange residence is acquired. This 5-year requirement is formulated quite succinctly by the addition of subsection **121(d)(10): *Property Acquired in Like-Kind Exchange***.

The '05 Act sought to further clarify the '04 Act as it applied to gulf coast hurricane victims re Katrina (8-24-05), Rita (9-22-05), and Wilma (10-22-05). Emphasis was placed on proper **basis adjustments** for properties acquired via Section 1031 (like-kind exchanges), Section 1033 (involuntary conversions), and Section 1034 (rollover of gain, under prior law to Section 121). Amended wording was added to subsection 121(d)(5): *Involuntary Conversions*, to subsection 121(d)(10): *Like-kind Exchanges*, and to subsection 121(g): *Rollovers under Section 1034.* Unfortunately, these intended clarifications are not as clarifying as Congress had hoped.

Judicial Rulings Few

Ordinarily, for 10 years or so after a new tax law goes into effect, there is a rash of court cases testing the interpretation or validity of certain words and phrases therein. With respect to the '97 Act version of Section 121, there have been only two types of disputable issues settled in Federal courts. One issue pertains to the rights of a bankruptcy estate to the exclusion of gain benefits upon the sale of a debtor's principal residence. The other significant issue pertains to which of three residences in three different states — each treated as the petitioner's "home" — constitutes one's "principal residence" for Section 121 purposes.

The "bankruptcy rights" issue was heard in the landmark case of *L. Popa*, BC-DC Ill., 98-1 USTC ¶ 50,276. The *Popa* federal judge applied the rules of IRC Section 1398: ***Relating to the Bankruptcy of Debtor Individuals***. Particular attention was paid to subsection 1398(g): [Bankruptcy] ***Estate Succeeds to Tax Attributes of Debtor***.

The IRS (as respondent) argued that the eight tax attributes listed in subsection 1398(g) do not expressly identify Section 121 as one of the attributes of the bankruptcy estate. The estate (as petitioner) argued, and the court agreed, that—

> The bankruptcy estate was liable for the same tax, and entitled to the same exclusion as the debtor would be on the sale of the residence because it succeeded to the holding period and "character" of the property and was to be "treated as the debtor" for purposes of subsection 1398(g)(8): ***Other Attributes***. Because of the exclusion of gain benefit under Section 121, there was substantial equity in the estate to permit a payment to the creditors.

The "principal residence" issue was resolved by comparing the facts and circumstances of three residences in three separate states: Wisconsin, Georgia, and Arizona. The published ruling on point is: *J. M. Guinan v. U.S.*, DC Ariz., 2003-1 USTC ¶ 50,475. The plaintiffs, Mr. and Mrs. Guinan, sold their Wisconsin home on September 15, 1998 and claimed the $500,000 marital exclusion of gain under Section 121. They presented five years of ownership and occupancy records showing 847 days in the Wisconsin home, 563 days in the Georgia home, 375 days in the Arizona home, and 40 days of travel in between the three homes (for a total of 1,825 days: 5 years x 365 days per year).

The *Guinan* court analyzed the situation as though there were just two homes: Wisconsin and Georgia/Arizona. The court did this by focusing narrowly on the phrase: *majority of time **during the year***, that appears in Regulation 1.121-1(b)(2): ***Principal residence defined***. The court thereupon concluded that the Georgia/Arizona home was occupied for 938 days (563 + 375) whereas the Wisconsin home was occupied for 847 days. Thus, the Wisconsin home was **not** the Guinan's principal residence at the time of its sale. The Section 121 benefits were therefore denied. The denial was so ORDERED on April 10, 2003.

IRS Rulings More Frequent

In the *Guinan* case above, note the time lapse between the taxable event (sale of residence) and the judicial order thereon. The residence was sold on September 15, 1998; the Order disqualifying the sale for Section 121 benefits was made on April 10, 2003. That's a span of four years and eight months. In other words, judicial decisions never come fast. This is because such decisions must take into account and weigh all of the "facts and circumstances" therewith.

To reduce the *wait time* (as it were), between event and decision, the IRS has developed a series of public notices, letter rulings, revenue procedures (Rev. Proc.), and revenue rulings (Rev. Rul.). These administrative rulings focus on a narrow point of tax law. As such, the IRS can express its position well ahead of any judicial process. Its expressed position can generally be relied on for interpretive guidance by taxpayers. A few examples are instructive in this regard.

Subsection 121(c)(2)(B) uses the term: *unforeseen circumstances*, as a premise for allowing reduced exclusion benefits. In its *Notice 2002-60*, the IRS included: "Taxpayers **affected by** the September 11, 2001 terrorist attacks "may qualify for the reduced exclusion." In *Letter Ruling 1-16-04*, the IRS indicated similarly for sales necessitated by: "**Intolerable, vehement, and hostile protests** by neighbors" who objected to a family member (of the homeseller) being under house arrest while receiving rehabilitation treatment (as a sex offender).

Rev. Proc. 2005-14 addresses like-kind exchanges by requiring that the properties be held and used: "**consecutively or concurrently** as a home and as a business." *Rev. Rul. 1988-29* points out that: "Gain realized from the **relinquishment of rights** in a rent-controlled apartment complex" does not qualify for Section 121 as ownership is not conferred by such relinquishment. *Rev. Rul 1983-50* rules that the: "Gain realized when a taxpayer **sells the land under his home** and moves the home to another lot," does not qualify under Section 121. *Letter Ruling 9-11-00* acknowledges that: "An individual who **creates a revocable trust** that held title to his residence," is the owner of the residence (for Section 121 purposes) when it is sold.

You get the idea, don't you? A narrow point of tax law is addressed, on which the IRS takes a position. Usually, these administrative rulings self-obsolete in about five years. This is about the time it takes for the IRS to corral its positions into formal regulations (after public comment).

Rev. Rul. 2005-74: The Latest

As of this writing, the latest IRS ruling applicable to Section 121 is: *Rev. Rul. 2005-74* (adopted December 8, 2005). It addresses three relocation assistance programs offered to employees by employers, when an employee sells his/her/their home in order to move to a job at another location. The "assistance" is via an intermediary called an RMC (Relocation Management Company). The RMC purchases the residence temporarily as a non-grantee (non-occupant), then resells it to a third party buyer who becomes the occupying grantee (bona fide owner). Three versions of this scenario are possible, and are depicted in Figure 2.1 for visualization purposes. An employer's "assistance" covers only the RMC contracted expenses.

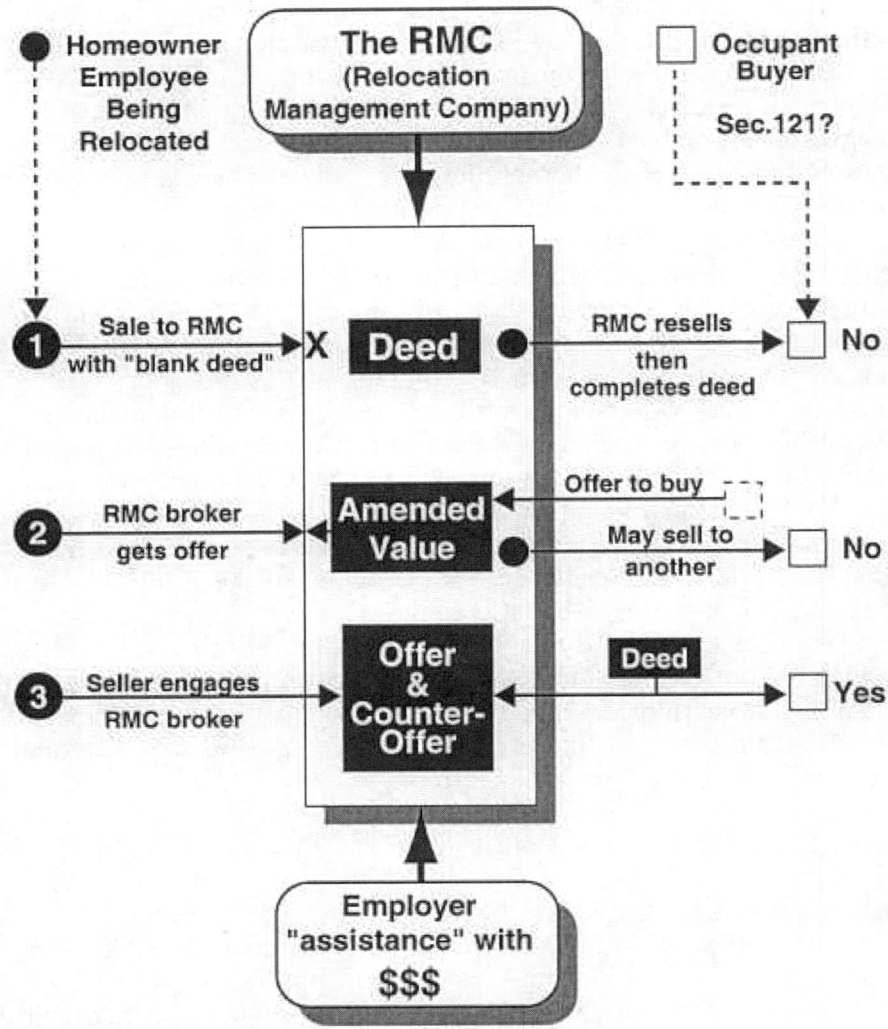

Fig. 2.1 - Options for Treatment of Employee Relocation Assistance

Version 1 is the ***Blank deed*** approach. The RMC "purchases" the employees home at a competitive fair market value. When the employee accepts the price offered, he executes a *grant deed* conveying title to an unnamed (blank space) grantee/buyer. When the RMC resells to a bona fide third party, the deed is then recorded in official county records for property tax purposes.

According to the IRS, this constitutes two sales, neither of which qualifies under Section 121. There are selling price and selling expense discrepancies between the two sales.

Version 2 is the *Amended value* approach. The employee himself lists the home with a real estate broker (on a list maintained by the RMC). When a third party buyer makes a bona fide offer, the RMC matches or exceeds the offering price to the employee. When the employee accepts the RMC's revised offer, a blank grant deed is conveyed to the RMC. No selling price or selling expense discrepancies occur. There are still two sales for federal tax purposes. The RMC is not obligated to resell to the bona fide offerer. He may resell to another offerer.

Version 3 is the *Employee maintains control* approach. That is, the employee retains the right to approve or disapprove any offer or counter offer made in the course of negotiations between the RMC and the ultimate third party buyer. In this manner, no blank deed is involved. The employee, with the monetary assistance paid to the RMC by the employer, grant deeds directly to the ultimate buyer as the grantee. This is one sale. As such, it now qualifies for the Section 121 benefits.

Our point here is this. A well-analyzed administrative ruling — as *Rev. Rul. 2005-74 exemplifies* — can provide much needed guidance on those matters where a tax law, judicial order, or formal regulation is conspicuously silent.

Formal Regulation § 1.121

Although Section 121 was enacted on May 6, 1997, it was not until December 23, 2002 that formal regulations were adopted. This interpretive "grey area" of time spanned a period of five years and seven months. This is about the average length of time for a new tax law to be supplemented with administrative (IRS) regulations. Regulation § 1.121 is mirror titled exactly the same as Section 121, namely: *Exclusion of Gain from Sale of Principal Residence*. The difference is that the regulation has greater word count than the law it purports to clarify.

We'll tell you right off that IRS Regulation § 1.121 consists of approximately 12,000 words in contrast to the 2,000 words of Section 121. In its official text, these regulatory words are presented in 18 pages of print. Obviously, all we can do is to highlight (in this chapter and others that follow) those portions that truly augment the provisions of Section 121. No tax law is completely self-explanatory on its own. Therefore, when legitimate questions arise concerning the correctness of a taxpayer's position, good faith reference must be made to any applicable regulation thereon. In the *Guinan* court case above, the federal judge based his Order on the wording he found in subregulation § 1.121-1(b)(2): *Principal residence defined.*

The quickest way to glean the gist of the regulatory coverage of Section 121 is to read through our listing of the many subregulations in Figure 2.2. Note particularly that there is a total of 28 such subregulations. There are also subparagraphs and subsubparagraphs to many of the subregulations.

In addition to its interpretive coverage, Regulation § 1.121 is helpful in another respect. When citing a subregulation that is not self-explanatory on its own, specific practical examples are given in the regulation. Whenever an example is cited in a tax regulation, that example is to be treated as the IRS's official position on the facts and circumstances illustrated in that example.

For example, the 43rd example follows subregulation § 1.121-4(e): ***Sales or exchanges of partial interests.*** The official example thereunder reads:

> *In 1991 Taxpayer A buys a house that A uses as his principal residence. In 2004 A's friend B moves into A's house and A sells B a 50% interest in the house realizing a gain of $136,000. A may exclude the $136,000 of gain. In 2005 A sells his remaining 50% interest in the home to B realizing another gain of $138,000. A may exclude $114,000 ($250,000 – $136,000 gain previously excluded) of the $138,000 gain from the sale of A's remaining interest.*

Thus, our message is that regulations often bring to light a point of view that you may not have previously considered. This is why we want you to be aware that Regulation § 1.121 covers many more points than we introduced to you in Chapter 1.

IRS REGULATION 1.121: EXCLUSION OF GAIN; PRINCIPAL RESIDENCE

Reg. 1.121-1: Exclusion of gain from sale of principal residence

(a) General rule - 2 out of 5 years
(b) Principal residence - defined
(c) Ownership and use requirements
(d) Depreciation taken after May 6, 1997
(e) Property used in part as principal residence

Reg. 1.121-2: Limitations: maximum exclusion amounts

(a) Dollar limitations: $250,000 single; $500,000 married
(b) Only one sale or exchange every 2 years
(c) Effective dates on or after 12/24/2002

Reg. 1.121-3: Reduced maximum exclusion for certain taxpayers

(a) General rule - when less than 730 days or 24 months
(b) Primary reason for sale or exchange
(c) By reason of change in employment
(d) By reason of health - doctor recommended
(e) By reason of unforeseen circumstances
(f) Qualified individual - defined
(g) Computation of reduced maximum exclusion

Reg. 1.121-4: Special rules: other

(a) Property of deceased spouse
(b) Property of spouse or former spouse
(c) Tenant-stockholder in cooperative housing
(d) Involuntary conversions
(e) Sales or exchanges of partial interests
(f) No exclusion for expatriates
(g) Election to have section not apply
(h) Residences acquired in rollover under Sec. 1034
(j) Election to apply regulations retroactively

Reg. 1.121-5: Suspension of 5-year period

(a) For uniformed services of the U.S.
(b) Manner of making election
(c) Application of election to closed years
(d) Illustrative 8-year example

Fig. 2.2 - Listing of the Subregulations to Section 121

Role of Adjacent Land

Regulation § 1.121-1(b)(3): *Vacant land,* treats such land as part of one's principal residence when it is immediately adjacent to the land containing the dwelling unit. Such land is "part and parcel" of the dwelling unit when used more or less regularly as part of the landscape and enjoyment of the dwelling owner. When buying a personal residence, one is not limited strictly to only that amount of land which contains the residence. He may buy adjacent land in any size or shape that he wants. Such land is treated as an outdoor extension of one's residence . . . like another dwelling area of its own. It must be truly used as such.

The term "vacant land" is understood to be of sufficient size and shape that it would be attractive to a potential buyer in and of itself. If sold separately from the dwelling unit, the land sale must occur either within two years before or within two years after the residence sale. Otherwise, if sold more than two years before the dwelling unit, or more than two years after the dwelling unit sale, the vacant land becomes a separate capital transaction of its own. As such, the land is **not treated** as part of the principal residence sale for Section 121 exclusion purposes.

If otherwise qualified, the sale of a dwelling unit and its adjacent vacant land is treated as one transactional event. As a consequence, only one maximum exclusion amount can be claimed. Even if two separate sales of the dwelling unit and land are involved, there is only one exclusion. For a single-person owner, the maximum exclusion is $250,000. For a married couple filing a joint return, the maximum exclusion is $500,000. In any case, the exclusion applies first to the dwelling unit. If any unused portion of the exclusion remains, it applies to the vacant land. This means that, if the land and dwelling are sold in separate taxable years, the dwelling unit gets first priority. After all, the $250,000/$500,000 exclusion of gain pertains to the sale of one's principal residence: **not** to the many acres of vacant land that may be surrounding it.

If the sale of vacant land occurs before the sale of the dwelling unit (in different taxable years), no exclusion applies to the land. The event is no different from that of any other sale of valuable land. The full capital gains tax must be computed and paid.

If, subsequently, within the following two years, the dwelling unit is sold, the vacant land return may be amended. The land sale proceeds may then be folded into the dwelling unit sale proceeds to form one grand total. By doing so, the two separate sales are treated as one, for purposes of the $250,000/$500,000 exclusion.

In Figure 2.3, we try to depict the consequences of two sales versus one sale when vacant land adjacent to a dwelling unit is an issue. Note that the land may be sold "before" or "after" the residence sale. Note also: "Not more than two years" before or after. Unless the land sale is within these two time frames, the land enjoys no exclusion benefits whatsoever. Our suggestion is that, should vacant land be sold prior to the dwelling unit sale, the land sale be contingent upon the dwelling unit sale following within two years.

Depreciation after May 6, 1997

Property used in a trade or business, or for rental purposes, is subject to a deduction allowance called: "depreciation." This allowance is for the wear and tear on a building structure — could be a principal residence — that is used for business purposes. The proper amount allowable annually is ascertained from the well-established rules of IRS Sections 167: *Depreciation* and 168: *Accelerated Cost Recovery*. Depreciation is a deduction against the gross income of an enterprise which, in turn, reduces its taxable income . . . for **each year** of business use.

With the above in mind, Regulation § 1.121-1(d): *Depreciation taken after May 6, 1997*, takes on a separate role from the exclusion-of-gain allowance under Section 121. More particularly, the regulation reads—

*The Section 121 exclusion **does not apply** to so much of the gain from the sale or exchange of property as does not exceed the portion of the depreciation adjustments . . . attributable to the property for periods after May 6, 1997.*

Suppose, for example, that you rent or use a portion of your residence for business purposes. You've done so for several years and have claimed a total of $25,000 in allowable depreciation deductions. After living in the residence well over two years, you sell it, realizing $85,000 in total gain. The excludable amount of gain is $60,000 ($85,000 – $25,000). The $25,000 is nonexcludable and therefore taxed at regular capital gain rates.

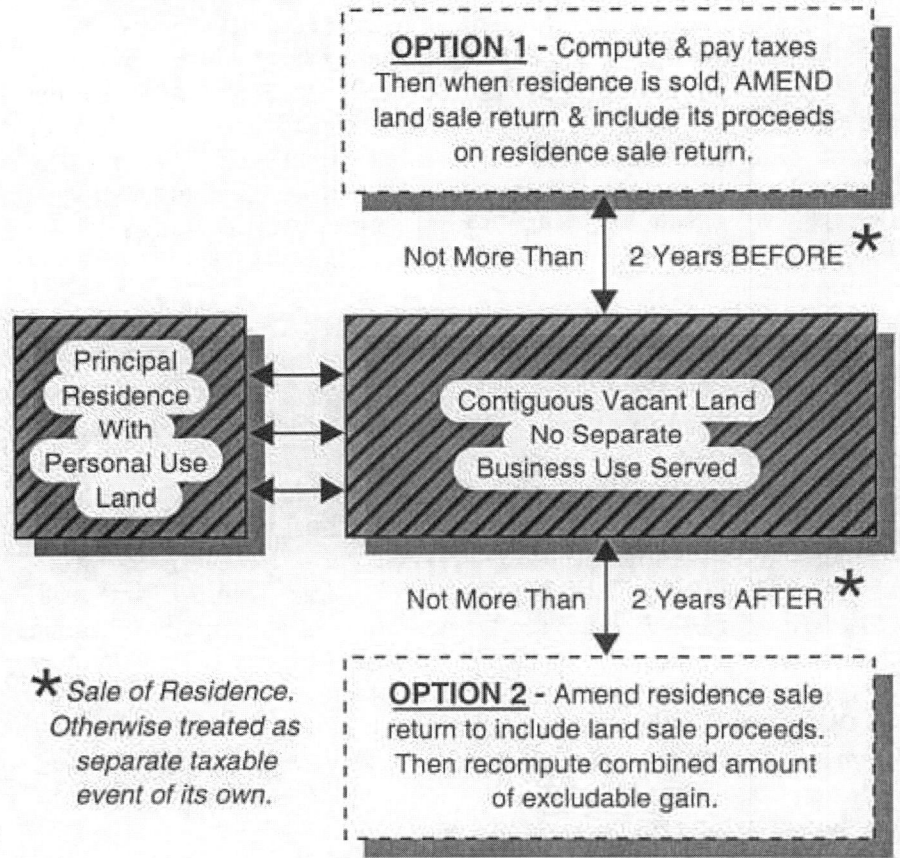

OPTION 1 - Compute & pay taxes Then when residence is sold, AMEND land sale return & include its proceeds on residence sale return.

Not More Than | 2 Years BEFORE **✱**

Principal Residence With Personal Use Land

Contiguous Vacant Land No Separate Business Use Served

Not More Than | 2 Years AFTER **✱**

✱ *Sale of Residence. Otherwise treated as separate taxable event of its own.*

OPTION 2 - Amend residence sale return to include land sale proceeds. Then recompute combined amount of excludable gain.

Fig. 2.3 - Options With Vacant Land Contiguous To Principal Residence

The illustrated situation is called: *depreciation recapture.* The idea is that, since you've taken one tax benefit (a deduction against business income), you are not entitled to two tax benefits (depreciation *plus* exclusion) for the same property.

If you use adjacent vacant land for business purposes in lieu of, or in addition to, your dwelling unit, you are not using the same property any more. You are using two properties: nonresidential and residential. The nonresidential property (when used for business purposes) does not participate in the Section 121 exclusion-of-gain benefits. The net result is that you have to *allocate* the property between its business (nonresidential) and personal (residential) use portions.

When "Allocation" is Required

The term "allocation" applies to the tax accounting separation when property owned by the same person (or persons) is used for two or more different purposes. In our case, we are addressing two different kinds of allocation. One allocation is the separation of nonresidential use from residential use where the nonresidential (business use) property is vacant or other land adjacent to the residential property (dwelling unit). The second allocation is within the dwelling unit itself. Within a dwelling unit, a portion — generally a minority portion — often is used for business purposes. Because of the regulatory distinction between these two allocation concepts, we depict the distinction for you in Figure 2.4. Note that one concept is marked WITHIN and the other is marked NOT WITHIN the dwelling unit.

Be introduced now to Regulation § 1.121-1(e): *Property used in part as a principal residence; Allocation required.* This regulation consists of just four sentences. Sentences 1 and 2 address nonresidential property which is separate from the dwelling unit: the NOT WITHIN portion. Sentences 3 and 4 address residential property which is within the dwelling unit: the WITHIN portion. We'll cite Sentences 1 and 2, then follow with our own comments. We'll do so separately for Sentences 3 and 4.

Sentences 1 and 2 of Regulation § 1.121-1(e) read primarily as:

Section 121 will not apply to the gain allocable to any portion (separate from the dwelling unit) of property sold or exchanged with respect to which the taxpayer does not satisfy the [personal/residential] *use requirement. Thus, if a portion of the property was used for residential purposes and a portion of the property (separate from the dwelling unit) was used for nonresidential purposes, only the gain allocable to the residential portion is excludable under Section 121.*

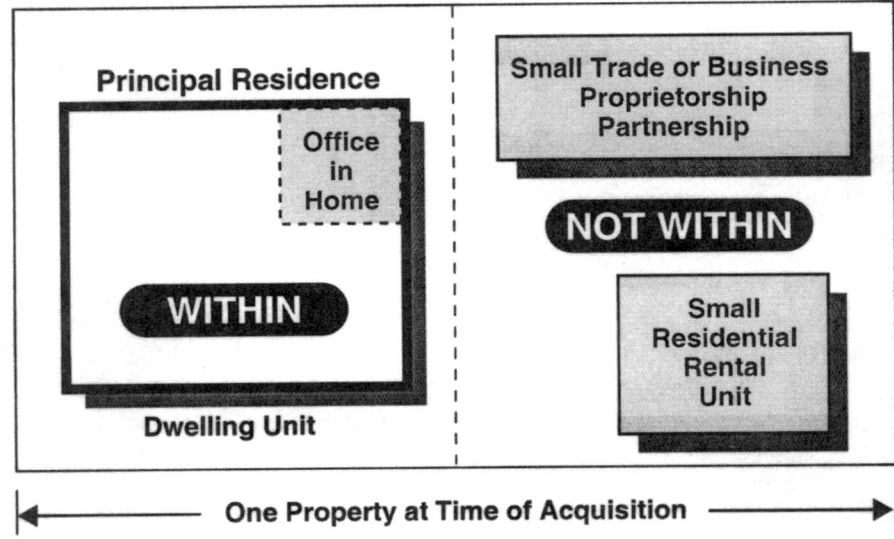

Fig. 2.4 - The "Within" and "Not Within" Allocation Concepts

Here, the term "the property" refers to both the dwelling unit and its adjacent vacant land or adjacent vacant building(s). By allocating proportionately all acquisition costs, improvements, use, etc. of the property, it will have been tax separated into two portions: nonresidential and residential. As two separate properties, the nonresidential portion does not participate in the Section 121 benefits. At the time of its sale or exchange, any gain realized is treated as ordinary capital gain (provided the nonresidential portion was held at least one year before its sale). This is the NOT WITHIN concept depicted in Figure 2.4.

Sentences 3 and 4 of Regulation § 1.121-1(e) read:

No allocation is required if both the residential and non-residential portions of the property are within the same dwelling unit. However, Section 121 does not apply to the gain allocable to the residential portion of the property to the extent provided by [Reg. § 1.121-1(d): **Depreciation taken** . . . etc.].

In other words, if you claim an office-in-home depreciation allowance, only the cumulative depreciation amount taken as a deduction is recaptured as ordinary capital gain. Otherwise, the sale of the residence-with-office is treated as a principal residence sale under Section 121. There is just one property sale: the WITHIN concept previously depicted in Figure 2.4.

Limitation on Excluded Amounts

Always keep in mind that Section 121 addresses only the amount of capital gain exclusion that is allowable when a qualified principal residence is sold or exchanged. In general terms, there are two separate and specific maximum dollar amounts allowed. Both are identified in Regulation § 1.121-2(a): *Dollar limitations*. The first exclusion limitation is $250,000 of capital gain for a single person filing his or her personal income tax return (Form 1040 with attachments). The second exclusion limitation is $500,000 of capital gain for married taxpayers filing a joint return as husband and wife. These are *maximum amounts* for each qualified residence sale. Furthermore, these maximums can be claimed no more frequently than every 2-plus years.

If the net sale proceeds produce capital gains which exceed $250,000/$500,000, the excess capital gains are taxed under ordinary capital gain rules. If the net sale proceeds result in less capital gain than these maximum amounts, the lower amounts become the maximum amount excludable. If the gross sale proceeds are $250,000/$500,000 or less (including capital gains), there are no tax consequences whatsoever caused by the sale. It should be self-evident, therefore, that only "higher end" real property comes within the provisions of IRC Section 121 . . . and IRS Regulation § 1.121.

Even so, variations of the maximum exclusion allowable can arise. Consider, for example, that, upon the sale of a principal residence, $380,000 in capital gain was realized. If it were a single owner of that residence, his or her allowable exclusion would be $250,000. The remaining $130,000 of capital gain ($380,000 – $250,000) would be taxable. On the other hand, suppose there were two single persons, A and B, co-owning the property 50/50. In this case, Owner A could claim $190,000 ($380,000 x 50%) as excludable, as could Owner B.

But, suppose A owned 75% of the residence and B owned 25%, what then?

Answer: Owner A's 75% of the above $380,000 gain would be $285,000. Since his maximum exclusion is limited to $250,000 he would pay capital gain tax on $35,000 ($285,000 – $250,000). Owner B's 25% of the same $380,000 gain would be $95,000. Since this is less than $250,000 as a single taxpayer, the entire $95,000 would be excludable to Owner B. Because Owner B is not able to use his maximum exclusion of $250,000 ($155,000 is unused), there could be temptation by Owner A to "shift" his taxable gain of $35,000 to Owner B. This would be tax legal, **if**, on or before date of sale closing, A and B agreed to reconstitute their ownership arrangement from 75/25 to 65.8/34.2. Owner B could then claim 34.2% of $380,000 or $130,000 ($95,000 + $35,000) as excludable capital gain.   Owner A's $250,000 exclusion would be unaffected (65.8% of $380,000 = $250,000).

There is a further limitation on the exclusion amount if any part of the residence is used for business purposes. As previously explained on page 2-13, a depreciation deduction on the business-use portion(s) is allowed. That which is claimed as depreciation annually is cumulatively "recaptured" at time of sale as ordinary capital gain: not of the Section 121 type.

For married persons, there are numerous special rules which we prefer to tell you about in Chapter 3. The principles above apply but with many more twists: pre-marriage, marriage, divorce, post-marriage, and death.

3

MARRIED PERSON RULES

For Joint Return Filers (Husband And Wife Only), There Are 5 Sets Of Exclusion Rules. Rule 1 Addresses "Certain" Joint Filers Who Did Not Purchase A Residence Together. Rule 2 Addresses The Separate Sales Of Two Residences. Rule 3 Addresses The Repeat Sales Of The Joint Residence. Rule 4 Addresses Deceased Spouse Situations. And Rule 5 Addresses Divorce Situations. The Idea Is To Encourage Qualification For As Much Of The $500,000 Exclusion As Possible. Each Spouse Is Treated As Entitled To His/Her Own $250,000 Exclusion, But There Is No Exclusion-Swapping Between Spouses.

In Chapter 1, our focus was on an individual (unmarried) taxpayer who owned and occupied a principal residence for the requisite exclusion-of-gain time. For a single-person owner, the maximum exclusion is $250,000 of capital gain when the residence is sold. This exclusion amount cannot be exceeded even though, in prosperous housing markets, gains can well exceed $250,000. If the gain on sale were $600,000, for example, a single owner/seller would be allowed a $250,000 exclusion. The $350,000 excess gain would be taxable.

Suppose, now, in a $600,000 gain-on-sale example, the taxpayer were a married person. If his spouse also qualified for the ownership and occupancy test (two years or more), she, too, would be entitled to a separate $250,000. If married on date of sale, the combined exclusion would be $500,000. Thus, in a $600,000-gain sale, the taxable amount would be only $100,000. Obviously, then, there is a definite tax saving when married . . . and filing a joint return for the year-of-residence sale.

As we'll see in this chapter, the flexibility of the exclusion requisites is more than just adding two exclusions together. For example, a man and woman living together unmarried (for two years or more) decide to get married the day before their residence is sold. Do they qualify for one exclusion or two exclusions? Answer: Two exclusions. You'll see why more clearly as we discuss the married person rules of Section 121. There is also the concept of *interspousal gifting* that plays a role in married person matters, including their estates.

For our purposes, let us clarify what we mean by the term "married person." Firstly, such a person is one who is legally married, or has been legally married. A married person is one who may be living with his spouse, or who may be living separately from his spouse. They may have one house, two houses, or possibly even three houses. A married person, for Section 121 purposes, also includes a person who is divorced, widowed, or remarried. The dates of these happenings are very important for year-of-sale **and** end-of-year purposes.

In short, the married person rules of Section 121 embrace a broad range of marital relationships and human endeavor. This is another feature that attests to the genius of Section 121. It preserves the individuality of each spouse as an economic unit.

Joint Return: Special Rules

On page 1-17 of Chapter 1, we introduced you to paragraph (1) of subsection 121(b): *Limitations.* Paragraph (1) set the exclusion-of-gain limitation at $250,000 for each individual owner/seller of a home. There is also paragraph (2): *Special rules for joint returns.* Paragraph (2) has two subparagraphs, namely: (A) *$500,000 limitation for certain joint returns*, and (B) *Other joint returns*. Thus, clearly, paragraph (2) of subsection 121(b) focuses expressly on joint returns.

We want to digress from subsection 121(b)(2) for a moment, to give you a little background on why there is something very special about joint returns.

To file a joint return (Form 1040), the parties must be legally married as of the close of the taxable year. They do not have to live together; they just have to be legally married. The determination of when one is legally married is prescribed by Section 7703: **Determination of Marital Status**. Its subsection (a) consists of two paragraphs that read—

(1) The determination of whether an individual is married shall be made as of the close of his taxable year; except that if his spouse dies during his taxable year such determination shall be made as of the time of such death; and

(2) an individual legally separated from his spouse under a decree of divorce or of separate maintenance shall not be considered as married.

In other words, if a man and woman get married before midnight December 31 for a given taxable year, they are tax treated as married for the entire calendar year: starting January 1. Conversely, if a couple gets divorced before midnight December 31, they are tax treated as unmarried (single) for the entire year starting on January 1.

Another tidbit of tax law that we should tell you about is Section 2523: **Gift to Spouse**. Its subsection (a): **Allowance of Deduction**, reads in full as—

Where a donor transfers during the calendar year by gift an interest in property to a donee who at the time of the gift is the donor's spouse, there shall be allowed as a deduction in computing taxable gifts for the calendar year an amount with respect to such interest equal to its value.

The concept behind Section 2523 is called: *interspousal gifting*. Ordinarily, if one person transfers property or money over $11,000 to another person not his or her spouse, a gift tax return is required. If the transfer is between spouses, there is no gift tax regardless of the amount transferred. This means that if a husband or wife owns separately a principal residence, he or she can give to the other spouse one-half ownership interest in that residence without any income tax or transfer tax consequences. If the residence is worth $800,000, for example, by adding to its title the other spouse's name as co-owner, the donee spouse would be treated as owner of $400,000 thereof, at time of sale. Even without the name add-on, there is implication of co-ownership when married . . . in community property states.

Keep Sections 7703 (Marital status) and 2523 (Gift to spouse) in mind as we unfold the married person rules of Section 121. The results will turn out to be far more tax favorable than you could ever have imagined.

"Either Spouse" Ownership

Let us go back now to paragraph (2) of subsection 121(b): *Special rules for joint returns.* This and its subparagraph (A): *Certain joint returns*, read—

In the case of a husband and wife who make a joint return for the taxable year of the sale or exchange of the property—

(A) Paragraph (1) shall be applied by substituting "$500,000" for "$250,000" if—

*(i) **either spouse** meets the **ownership** requirements of subsection (a) with respect to such property;*

*(ii) **both spouses** meet the **use** requirements of subsection (a) with respect to such property; and*

*(iii) **neither spouse is ineligible** for the benefits of subsection (a) with respect to such property by reason of paragraph (3)* [only 1 sale every 2 years]. [Emphasis added to (i), (ii), and (iii).]

Clause (i) — *either spouse ownership* — is the "certain" feature of the special rules for joint returns. It is a special concession to newly marrieds or remarrieds where only one spouse has owned the home for the requisite time before its sale. This is **Rule 1** that we enumerated in the head summary to this chapter.

Let us examine clauses (i) and (ii) more closely. Particularly note that clause (i) addresses the *ownership* requirement exclusively, whereas clause (ii) addresses the *occupancy* requirement exclusively. This takes us back to the nonconcurrence of ownership and use requirements that we depicted in Figure 1.3 (on page 1-11). Both clauses are preceded by the requirement that husband and wife file a joint return for the taxable year of the sale or exchange. If they do so, they get a $500,000 exclusion . . . if (i) *either spouse* meets the ownership requirement and (ii) *both spouses* meet the occupancy requirement. Clause (i) is definitely a liberalization of the ownership and use rule.

Let us put clauses (i) and (ii) into a more everyday adult perspective. Person A (an unmarried man) owns and lives in his principal residence for five years. Some two years after purchasing his residence, person B (an unmarried woman who owns no residence) moves in. A and B take on cohabitational living. They plan on getting married after person A sells his house, and they will then buy another house as husband and wife. A's house is worth $800,000, though, with his purchase and improvements, his capital basis in the house is $300,000. With Section 121(b)(2)(A) in mind, what should the couple do?

First thing, they should get married **before** person A sells his home. Suppose the house had been previously put on the market for sale (net sale price after commissions and costs: $800,000). It sold and was scheduled to close on December 30. A and B get legally married on December 28th. The very next day, December 29th, they instruct the escrow closing agent to add B's name to the closing statement papers (and, perhaps also, to the title of the house), thus showing it as owned by husband and wife. The sale legally closes on December 30th as originally scheduled. Spouses A and B now qualify for joint tax filing.

When filing their joint return for the year of sale, they would report as follows:

Section 121 sale	$800,000
less cost basis	<300,000>
Realized gain	$500,000
less joint exclusion	<500,000>
Taxable gain	ZERO

Had A and B not married before the sale, $250,000 would be taxable gain to A. At a 20% federal capital gains rate, that would be $50,000 in tax. Why pay this amount of tax unnecessarily? They could always marry and divorce the following year.

Confirmed by Regulation

If the above example sounds too good to be true, take heed. It **is** allowable. It is allowable because of two married-taxpayer subtleties behind Section 121(b)(2)(A). The two behind-the-scenes factors are Section 7703 (Marital status) and Section 2523 (Gift to spouse). Those subtleties also permeate other rules pertaining to married persons with principal residences.

The above married-before-sale example was a true life situation that took place in December 2000. An unmarried man bought a home after going through divorce. Two years later, a woman moved in and they lived together as unmarried man and unmarried woman for 10 years. In a civil ceremony, they married on the day before the sale. Such an arrangement is confirmed by Regulation § 1.121-2(a)(3): *Special rule for joint returns*. This particular regulation reads—

A husband and wife who make a joint return for the year of the sale or exchange of a principal residence may exclude up to $500,000 of gain if—

(i)   *Either spouse meets the 2-year ownership requirements;*

(ii)   *Both spouses meet the 2-year use [occupancy] requirements, and*

(iii) *Neither spouse excluded gain from a prior sale or exchange of property . . . within the last 2 years.*

This regulation is a restatement of the statutory requirements in Section 121(b)(2)(A). But look how much more straightforward it is. Ordinarily you do not find this kind of clarity in IRS regulations. The "either spouse ownership" clause is truly a refreshing addition to common sense in tax laws. So important is the flexibility of this concept that we try to depict it in Figure 3.1. We call it: Rule 1 — Singles Together.

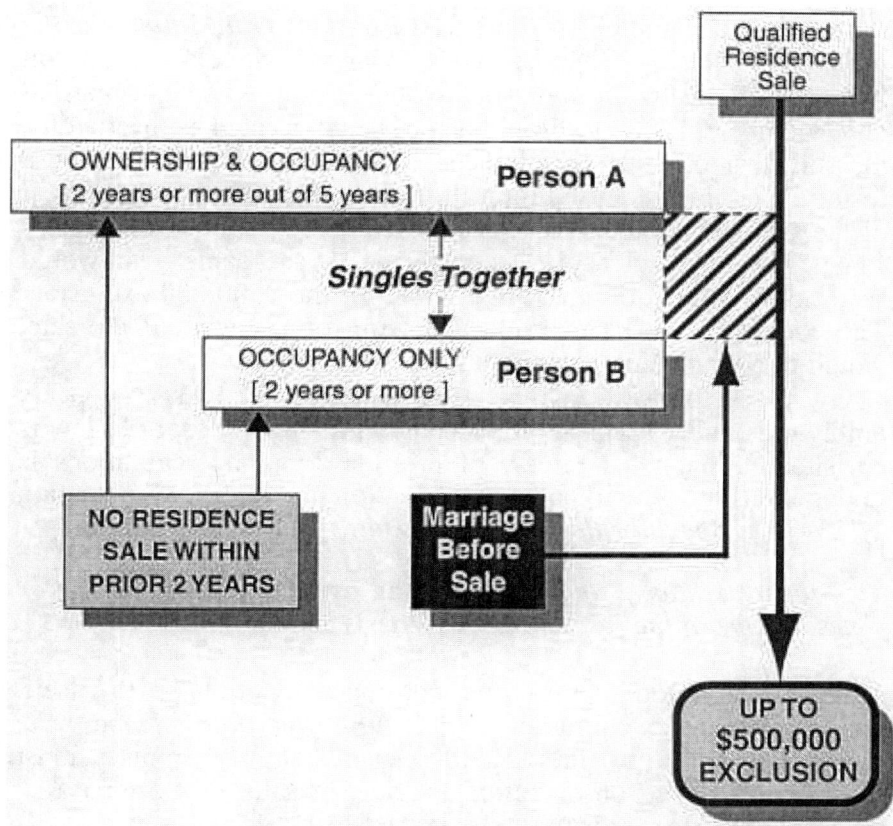

Fig. 3.1 - The Exclusion for Singles Together Who Marry Before Sale

Marital Status: Date of Sale

The fundamental requirement for a $500,000 exclusion-of-gain benefit is that two persons (man and woman) be married on the date that the residence is sold. Whether they are married one day before sale, one month before, cne year before, two years before, or ten years before — it makes no difference.   The regulation simply says . . . *make a joint return for the year of the sale or exchange.* Only a husband and wife can file a joint return. Thus, if two persons marry on December 10th and the house is sold on December 20th of the same year, they are married for the "year of the sale."   Earlier, we illustrated the monetary benefit of such a marriage. Previously married persons often do so.

How much "stretch" is there in the phrase: *joint return for the year of the sale*? Suppose a principal residence was sold on January 1, 2006 by an unmarried owner. Suppose he got married on December 31, 2006. Would he not be tax treated as married for the full year of 2006 (recall Sec. 7703)? Yes, he would. As a result, he could file a joint return for the year 2006. Is not the year of the sale also 2006? Yes. Therefore, selling a home on January 1 and getting married on December 31 of the same year would seem to make the arrangement eligible for the $500,000 exclusion. The couple would be husband and wife for the *year* of the sale, would they not? Yes . . . it would seem so. But . . .

It is customary practice that, when a new law appears ambiguous under specific circumstances, its predecessor old law is revisited. That is, a review of prior law and its regulations is undertaken. For the hypothetical situation above, prior Regulation 1.121-5(f): *Special rule* [re] *marital status*, stands out. It reads—

Marital status is to be determined as of the date of sale or exchange of the residence. [Emphasis added.]

This regulation supports the wording of Section 121(a) itself. The exclusion is computed as of: *on the date of the sale.* Consequently, to get the $500,000 exclusion, the spouses must have been married on or before the date of sale: not after it . . . even though afterwards might be in the "year" of sale.

Prior Sales "Look Back"

On any joint return claiming a $500,000 exclusion of gain, there is always a "look back" requirement re prior sales. This is the substance of clause (iii) in the above cited Regulation §1.121-2(a)(3). The precise words cited were:

Neither spouse excluded gain from a prior sale or exchange of property under section 121 within the last 2 years . . . [Emphasis added.]

This is a restatement of the "only 1 sale every 2 years" rule that we made a point of in Chapter 1. As an adjunct to this rule, Regulation § 1.121-2(b)(1) goes on to say—

For purposes of this paragraph (b)(1), any sale or exchange
before *May 7, 1997 is* **disregarded.** [Emphasis added.]

Why May 7, 1997? Because the "new" Section 121 was
enacted into law on May 6, 1997. It repealed all "old law" aspects
pertaining to the sales and deferment of gain of principal
residences. Hence, you may treat May 7, 1997 as *start clean* date
for keeping track of ALL of your future residence sales. If you
sold your first home after this date, you are in for an exciting tax
venture . . . providing you keep good records.

In view of the above, we urge that you start tracking all of your
home sales in an orderly manner. You have a whole lifetime ahead
in which every sale may qualify for the Section 121 exclusion.
While every sale may not qualify for the maximum $500,000
exclusion-of-gain allowed (to joint filers), it should at least qualify
for some amount. By cumulatively tracking — and **saving** — your
exclusion over 20, 30, 40, or 50 years,you could build up a quite
substantial nest egg. How? By using the earlier year exclusions to
reduce the mortgage principal on your replacement home(s).
When there is no longer any mortgage, your subsequent sale
exclusions could be stashed into tax-free money market accounts.

In Figure 3.2, we offer one arrangement of how your nest egg
records might be kept. Bear in mind that whatever system you use,
it should be formulated as a LIFETIME VENTURE.

Note (in Figure 3.2) our portrayal of a "Section 121 Exclusion
Treasure." This is all tax-free money. Suppose that after 50 years
of home sales you accumulated $2,000,000 (2 million) in this
account. How would you prove to the IRS that it was truly tax-free
money? Without clear and convincing records, you could not do
so. Without records, you could be accused of a "willful pattern of
tax evasion." The IRS could then max tax you on the $2,000,000
at, say, a 35% rate; then add the 75% civil fraud penalty (Sec.
6663); then add 6% per annum interest for 50 years. Altogether,
your tax, penalty, and interest could amount to—

Tax	= $2,000,000 x 35% max rate	= $ 700,000
Penalty	= $ 700,000 x 75% fraud rate	= 525,000
Interest	= $2,000,000 x 6% p.a. x 50 yrs	= 6,000,000

Total Assessment = $7,225,000!!

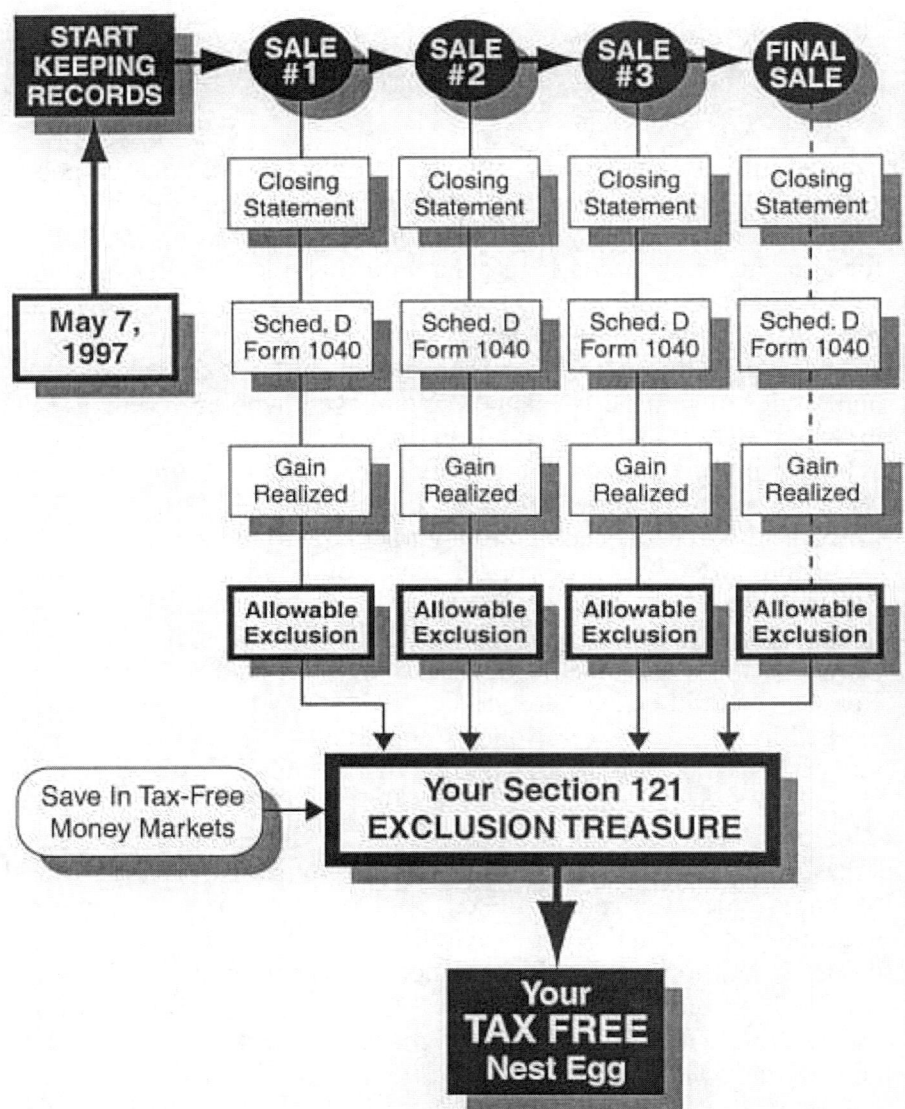

Fig. 3.2 - Documenting Your Home Sales from "Start" to "Final"

When the IRS accuses one of willful tax evasion, it goes all out to destroy that person . . . or persons. Better take heed now and go all out to protect your Section 121 Exclusion Treasure. We can foresee the time — 10, 20, 30 years or so downstream — when the

IRS will be cracking down on "abusive exclusions" from frequent home sales. If you have the records that we depict in Figure 3.2, you'll absolutely stun the IRS.

What If "Within 2 Years"

Suppose that some prior sale was closed within two years of the current reportable sale. This could come about, for example, if X was formerly married to W, who sold that residence with X's name still on the title. X would have no control over, and may not even know, the date of W's prior sale. What if X later married Y and filed a joint return claiming a $500,000 exclusion? Without knowing other facts, said exclusion could be disqualified.

To make matters worse, suppose W's sale (with X's name on the title) closed escrow 23 months and 23 days before the X and Y sale closed. The exclusion claimed by W in X's name was $35,000 — say. With these facts (assumed for illustration purposes), X and Y would definitely lose their claimed $500,000 exclusion. Losing a $500,000 exclusion for some inadvertent (and uncontrollable) prior sale for which only $35,000 was excluded is a heavy price to pay. The same disqualification would apply if Y (or Y's name on title) was associated with a prior sale. What can X and Y do?

Be introduced now to Section 121(f): ***Election to Have Section Not Apply***. This subsection (f) reads—

[Section 121] *shall not apply to any sale or exchange to which the taxpayer elects not to have this section apply.*

In other words, X and Y as joint filers have the option of negating any prior exclusion claimed on either spouse's behalf. For the facts presented in X's case, this would require that an ***Amended Return*** (Form 1040X) be filed for the year of W's sale (with X's name on the title). The amended return would have to identify W as X's former spouse. X would have to indicate the sale particulars, disclaim any exclusion for the $35,000 gain, and pay his prorata share of tax on the $35,000 amount. The amended return would require the signature of both X and Y, even though Y was not a participant in W's sale. X will have to pay W's share of the amended tax because W gets no benefit from the election.

For the above situation, Regulation § 1.121-4(g): *Election*, etc., says (in pertinent part, as edited) that—

*The taxpayer makes the election to have Section 121 not apply, by filing a return for the taxable year . . . that **includes** the gain from the sale . . . **in** the taxpayer's gross income. A taxpayer may [do so] . . . at any time **before** the expiration of the 3-year period . . . for filing the return for the taxable year in which the sale occurred.* [Emphasis added.]

Other Joint Returns

Moving onto other married person situations, we now address Section 121(b)(2)(B): *Other joint returns*. This subparagraph (B) reads in full—

If such spouses do not meet the requirements of subparagraph (A) [Certain joint returns], *the limitation under paragraph (1)* [$250,000] *shall be the **sum** of the limitations under paragraph (1) to which each spouse would be entitled if such spouses had not been married.*

This is the married person **Rule 2** that we enumerated in the head summary to this chapter. You can think of this rule as two separate sales by separately qualifying home owners. The end result would be the same whether the two owners were married or not, or were married but were filing separately.

What is this subparagraph (B) citation getting at? It is for those cases where, instead of a married couple selling one home jointly, each spouse sells a qualifying home separately in the joint return filing year. These are persons A and B who are now married, but who were not previously married to each other when each acquired and occupied a former qualifying residence. The two separate homes may not be of like value, nor of like gain. Doesn't matter: each sale qualifies for its own single-person exclusion. As per Regulation § 1.121-2(a)(3)(ii), the joint exclusion effect is—

*the **sum** of each spouse's limitation amount determined on a separate basis **as if** they had not been married.*

Regulation § 1.121-2(a)(4): *Examples*, illustrates subparagraph (B) above as follows:

Example 3 During 2004, married taxpayers H and W each sells a residence that each had separately owned and used as a principal residence before their marriage. Each spouse meets the ownership and use tests for his or her respective residence. Neither spouse meets the use requirement for the other spouse's residence. H and W file a joint return for the year of [both] sales. The gain realized from the sale of H's residence is $200,000. The gain realized from the sale of W's residence is $300,000. Because the ownership and use requirements are met for each residence by each respective spouse, H and W are eligible to exclude up to $250,000 of gain from the sale of each of their residences. However, W may not use H's unused exclusion [$50,000] to exclude gain in excess of her exclusion amount. Therefore, H and W must recognize [and pay tax on] $50,000 of the gain realized on the sale of W's residence.

We illustrate the above [Rule 2] in Figure 3.3.

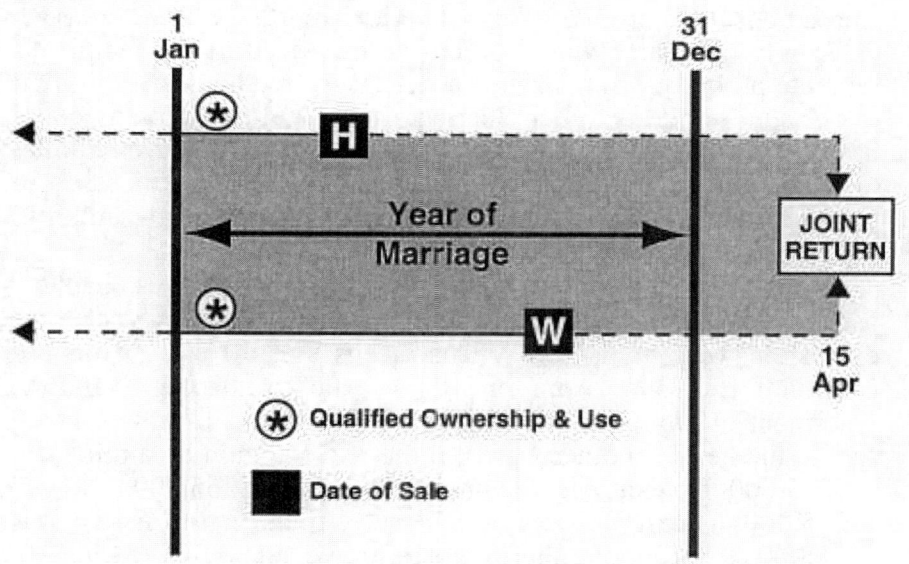

Fig. 3.3 - Separate Qualified Home Sales in Year of Marriage

Rule 3: Joint Sales

If a couple has been married for many years and they move around for employment, children, or lifestyle upgrade purposes, every qualifying sale reported on a joint return is eligible for the $500,000 exclusion. This is so, whether both spousal names are on the house title or not. This is the implication in Section 121(d)(1): *Joint Returns*: *General rule.*

Section 121(d)(1) expressly reads—

*If a husband and wife make a joint return for the taxable year of the sale or exchange of the property, subsections (a) and (c) shall apply if **either spouse** meets the ownership and use requirements of subsection (a) with respect to such property.* [Emphasis added.]

On its surface, this is not a particularly earth-shaking tax law. For persons who have been married for many years, and living together throughout this time, the general joint return rule is common sense. Ordinarily, for mortgage company reasons, the lender wants both names of husband and wife on the title deed. But suppose the property were inherited mortgage free. In such case, only one name would be on the title deed as the recipient's separate property. Similarly, if a mortgage-free house were gifted to one spouse by his or her elderly parents. Or, the property could have been placed in trust for one or both spouses who are required to live in the residence for the qualifying time before its sale. In our view, the generality of subsection (d) is further attestation to the genius of Section 121.

From what we have said in this and the two previous chapters, it should be self-evident that every joint home sale is a separate exclusion event of its own. This means that there is no unused exclusion carryover from one home sale to the next, and no deferment of any gain in excess of the exclusion from one home sale to the next. In other words, if the realized gain on a joint sale is $235,000, for example, the unused portion of $265,000 (500,000 – 235,000) is lost forever. Conversely, if the gain on sale was $650,000, for example, the excess gain over $500,000 ($150,000) cannot be tax deferred in any beneficial manner. In the majority of cases, these "technicalities" seldom arise.

The above three rules, as well as Rules 4 and 5 to come, are summarized in Figure 3.4. We believe that these rules cover virtually every conceivable variant of residence ownership and sale from singles together, to marrieds, to divorced persons, to remarrieds, to married persons living separately, and to surviving spouse situations.

Rule	Characteristics	Exclusion	Code Section
1	"Certain" Joint Returns 1 owner 2 users	$500,000 if married before sale	121 (b) (2) (A)
2	"Other" Joint Returns 1 owner/user 1 owner/user	2 separate $250,000 exclusions	121 (b) (2) (B)
3	"General" Joint Returns Joint owner/users	$500,000 for each sale event	121 (d) (1)
4	"Deceased" Joint Return Year of death sale only	$500,000 Otherwise $250,000	121 (d) (1), (d) (2)
5	"Divorced" Return Any qualifying year (separate)	$250,000 with O & U tack-ons	121 (d) (3) (A), (d) (3) (B)

Fig. 3.4 - Married Person Homesale Rules Summarized

When a Spouse Dies

For married persons, a question that invariably arises is: What happens when a spouse dies and the residence is sold? Is there one exclusion or are there two exclusions?

The answer depends on when the residence is sold, assuming, of course, that it otherwise qualifies for the exclusion. If sold by the surviving spouse in the *year of death* of the decedent spouse, the $500,000 exclusion (two exclusions) applies. If sold (by the surviving spouse) in *any year following* the year of death, only one exclusion applies (the $250,000). The obvious reason is that a single person can never claim more than one exclusion. See Rule 4 in Figure 3.4.

Regulation § 1.121-2(a)(4): *Examples*, cites the following two examples to support the above. Its *Example 5* reads—

> Married taxpayers H and W have owned and used their principal residence since 1998. On February 16, 2004, H dies. On September 21, 2004, W sells the residence and realizes a gain of $350,000. Pursuant to Section 6013(a)(3), W and H's executor make a joint return for 2004. All $350,000 may be excluded.

This year-of-death-sale example is the equivalent of two exclusions at $175,000 each (175,000 x 2 = 350,000). One exclusion for the decedent spouse applies because his executor joins with the surviving spouse to file a joint return. The principle here goes back to the tax concept of marital status of Section 7703 (cited earlier). The year of death is treated as a full year of marriage . . . for that year only.

The above point is made clear in *Example 6* of the cited regulation. Said example reads—

> Assume the same facts as *Example 5* except that W does not sell the residence until January 15, 2005 [the year after year of death]. Because W's filing status for the taxable year of the sale is single, the special rules for joint returns . . . do not apply and W may exclude only $250,000 of the [$350,000] gain.

Note that Example 5 above references Section 6013(a)(3). What is this section all about?

Section 6013(a) is titled: ***Joint Returns of Income Tax by Husband and Wife***. Its essence is that a single joint return may be filed (for the taxable year) . . .

> *even though one of the spouses has neither gross income nor deductions.*

In many surviving spouse cases, the survivor is also the executor of the decedent spouse's estate. This means that when a joint return is filed for the year of death, the surviving spouse signs the return as "taxpayer" and signs also as "executor for the estate" (two signatures).

As rule 5 in Figure 3.4 indicates, when spouses divorce, the Ownership and Use (O & U) rules are quite different (from those above). We'll address these differences in Chapter 9.

4

REDUCED EXCLUSION RULES

For Good Cause Shown, A Home Seller Is Allowed A Lesser Amount Of Exclusion Than $250,000/$500,000. The Recognized Causes Are: (1) Change In Place Of Employment, (2) Serious Health Conditions, And (3) Unforeseen Circumstances. The Lesser/Reduced Amount Is A Prorata Fraction Of The Maximum Allowable. The NUMERATOR Of The Fraction Is "The Shortest Of" THREE Measuring Times, Namely: (1) Ownership, (II) Occupancy/Use, Or (III) The Period Between Sales. The DENOMINATOR Is 730 Days (Which Is 24 Months, Or 2 Years). Guidance Must Be Sought On Other Short-Period Sales.

In Chapters 1 (single returns) and 3 (joint returns), the focus was strictly on the maximum allowable exclusion of gain on any qualified home sale. The single person maximum was $250,000; the married persons maximum was $500,000. Aside from the variants of marital arrangements, there were just two basic requirements that had to be met. These two requirements were:

1. Ownership and use aggregating 2 years or more in a 5-year period ending on date of sale. This is the "at-least-2-year-ownership-and-use" requirement: 2 years' ownership concurrent (or nonconcurrent) with 2 years' occupancy.

2. No more than 1 sale every 2 years. Disregarding Chapter 2, this is the 2-year-frequency-of-sale limitation.

Not every qualified home sale will realize a capital gain in excess of $250,000 (single person) or $500,000 (married persons). Obviously, if the gain realized is only $200,000, for example, whether single or joint, the excludable gain is $200,000. If the realized gain were $765,000, for example, for a joint return, the maximum exclusion would be $500,000. The amount of excess gain would be $265,000. This excess gain is taxable. These are the consequences of Sections 121(a) and 121(b).

Now, suppose that, for whatever reason, Requirement 1 is not met, when Requirement 2 is met. What happens? Well . . . it depends. It depends on what the particular reason is for not meeting Requirement 1.

Conversely, what would happen if Requirement 1 were met when Requirement 2 were not met? The same answer applies: It depends. It depends on what the reason is, and whether there is any accommodation somewhere within the 1,800 words of Section 121. There are times when "accommodation" is not intended.

When **either** Requirement 1 or Requirement 2 is not met, the reduced exclusion rule *may* apply. Said rule is expressly set forth in Section 121(c). This rule, after we explain it to you herein, is another one of those elements of genius and generosity of Section 121. This section overall tries to accommodate most practical variants of human nature and turmoil with respect to principal residence sales.

Section 121(c) Overview

Section 121(c) consists of approximately 190 words. Its official title is: ***Exclusion for Taxpayers Failing to Meet Certain Requirements***. The immediate implication is that, if you fail to meet "certain" requirements, at least some amount of the exclusion may apply. For example, instead of the $250,000 maximum allowable for a single person, maybe "only" a $100,000 exclusion of gain under Section 121(c) would apply. The amount applicable is determined from paragraphs (1) and (2) of Section 121(c).

Paragraph (1) tells you how to establish the prorata fraction to be used, whereas paragraph (2) tells you what circumstances must prevail before paragraph (1) is effective. Because of its prerequisite importance, let us first address paragraph (2).

Paragraph (2) of Section 121(c) is titled: ***Sales and exchanges to which subsection (c) applies***. Pertinent excerpts from this 70-word paragraph are—

(i)   *a failure to meet the ownership and use requirements of subsection (a),* ***or***

(ii) [a failure to meet the requirements of] *subsection (b)(3)*[only 1 sale every 2 years], ***and***

(iii) *such sale or exchange is by reason of a change in place of employment, health, or, to the extent provided in regulations, unforeseen circumstances.*

The requirement(s) of "subsection (a)" — that is, Section 121(a) — is the 2-year-ownership-and-use rule. This we have identified above as Requirement 1. The requirement(s) of subsection (b)(3) — that is, Section 121(b)(3) — is the 2-year-frequency-of-sale rule. This we have identified above as Requirement 2.

There is also a third requirement which has not been succinctly identified. We call it Requirement 3: "Good-cause reason for premature sale." As item (iii) above indicates, there are three such reasons, namely: (1) change in place of employment, (2) health, and (3) unforeseen circumstances. While subsection 121(c)(2)(B) identifies these reasons, it does not adequately describe them. Hence, we must resort to the appropriate IRS regulation thereon.

The "Good Cause" Regulation

The companion regulation covering Section 121(c) is Regulation § 1.121-3. It consists of about 960 words and is titled: ***Reduced maximum exclusion for taxpayers failing to meet certain requirements***. As these title words imply, the focus is on **reducing** the maximum exclusion: not on altering it in any other way. The circumstances for doing so are set forth expressly in subregulations § 1.121-3 . . .

(b) *Primary reason for sale or exchange.*
(c) *Sale by reason of change in place of employment.*
(d) *Sale or exchange by reason of health.*

(e)   *Sale by reason of unforeseen circumstances.*

These four subregulations are preceded by Regulation § 1.121-3(a): *In general.* The generality is that—

. . .. *a reduced maximum exclusion **may be available** for a taxpayer who* . . . [qualifies as below].

The first "as below" qualification is subregulation (b): *Primary reason for.* In its 300-word text, the term "safe harbor" pops up in the following two sentences:

*If a taxpayer qualifies for a **safe harbor** described in this section, the taxpayer's primary reason* [for a short-period sale or exchange] *is deemed to be a change in place of employment, health, or unforeseen circumstances. If the taxpayer does not qualify for a **safe harbor**, factors that may be relevant in determining the taxpayer's primary reason* . . . *include (but are not limited to)* . . .

In other words, there are three safe harbors and one nonsafe harbor for qualifying a premature residence sale for reduced exclusion benefits. A safe harbor is a regulatorily prescribed set of circumstances which, if met in good faith, the IRS will not challenge. A nonsafe harbor leaves the door open for other valid circumstances, not expressly covered by regulations. A qualified nonsafe harbor primarily means that more facts and documents must be produced to convince the IRS that a reduced maximum exclusion is equitable and fair.

For summary purposes, we present in Figure 4.1 a depiction of the safe harbors for qualifying early principal residence sales for reduced exclusion benefits.

The 50-Mile Safe Harbor

Regulation § 1.121-3(c): ***Sale by reason of change in place of employment***, establishes a distance safe harbor of "at least 50 miles." Clearly, a change in place of employment by this distance or greater is one of the more practical reasons for allowing a reduced exclusion. The 50 miles is one way. Commuting 50 miles from home to work, and another 50 miles from work to home again is stressful, nonproductive, and time consuming. Whether your commute is by car, train, rapid transit, or bus, there is another three to four hours added to an ordinary 8-hour workday.

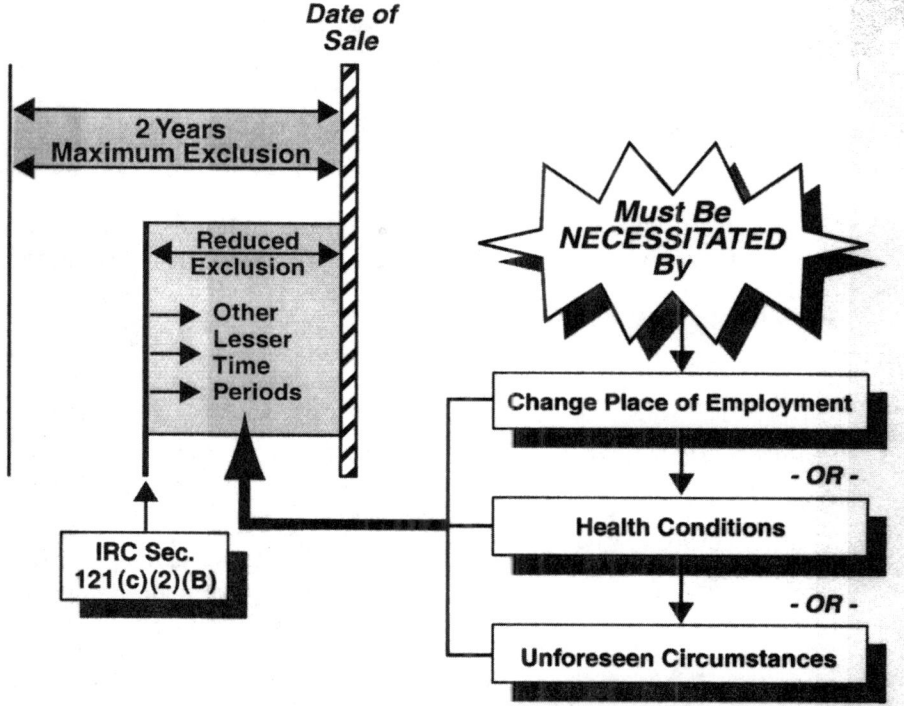

Fig. 4.1 - The Three Safe Harbors for "Reduced Exclusion" Benefits

The at-least-50-mile distance is determined as follows:

1. Number of miles from **old home** to **new workplace** _____
2. Number of miles from **old home** to **old workplace** _____
3. Subtract line 2 from line 1 _____

If line 3 is at least 50 miles or more, you meet the distance safe harbor test. The only other requirement is that you be a "qualified individual." As per subregulation § 1.121-3(f), such an individual is a worker who is: (1) the taxpayer, (2) the taxpayer's spouse, (3) a co-owner of the residence, or (4) any other person or family member whose occupational income is the principal financial source for mortgage payments and household maintenance.

What happens if you do not quite meet the 50-mile safe harbor test? Suppose the verifiable distance change was 46 miles instead of 50 miles. What then?

Answer: This is where the **primary reason** rationale comes in. Subregulation § 1.121-3(c)(1) uses the clause—

If . . . the primary reason for the sale . . . is a change in the location of the individual's employment.

This regulatory clause precedes, and is separated from the 50-mile distance safe harbor clause. This arrangement implies that there could be some acceptable variance to the preciseness of the 50 miles. The IRS cites a specific example in this regard.

Example 4 under Regulation § 1.121-3(c)(4) reads—

In July 2003, D buys a condominium that is 5 miles from her place of employment, and uses it as her principal residence. In February 2004, D, who works as an emergency medicine physician, obtains a job that is located 51 miles from D's condo. D may be called in to work at unscheduled hours and, when called, must be able to arrive at work quickly. Therefore, D sells her condo and buys a townhouse that is 4 miles from her new place of employment. Because D's new place of employment is only 46 miles [51 − 5} farther from the condominium than is D's former place of employment, the sale is not within the safe harbor [of 50 miles]. **However,** D is entitled to claim a reduced maximum exclusion . . . because, under the facts and circumstances, the primary reason for the sale is the change in D's place of employment.

Sale by Reason of Health

Regulation § 1.121-3(d) safe harbors that a premature sale is by reason of health—

if the primary reason . . . is to obtain, provide, or facilitate the diagnosis, cure, mitigation, or treatment of disease, illness, or injury of a qualified individual . . ., or to obtain or provide medical or personal care for [such] individual suffering from a disease, illness, or injury. A sale . . . that is merely beneficial to the general health or well being of the individual is not a sale by reason of health.

There you have it! Clearly, the health reason must be serious and ongoing. A temporary illness or short hospital stay would not qualify the sale for the reduced exclusion. The IRS's expectation, we believe, would be some incurable disease (Parkinson's, for example), some terminal condition (cancer, for example), or some permanent disability brought on by an on-the-job accident or by a near-fatal auto accident. Possibly other health misfortunes that cause substantial financial hardship and stress would also qualify. A good-bet safe harbor would be a specific recommendation (in writing) by a physician for a change of residence based on described health conditions.

Regulation § 1.121-3(d)(3) gives five examples of how the reason-of-health rule can be applied. We cite just two of the five examples, namely:

Example 2. H's father has a chronic disease. In 2003 H and W purchase a house that they use as their principal residence. In 2004, H and W sell their house in order to move into the house of H's father so that they can provide the care he requires as a result of his disease. Because . . . the primary reason for the sale of their house is the health of H's father, H and W are entitled to a reduced maximum exclusion.

Example 5. In 2003 H and W purchase a house in Michigan that they use as their principal residence. H's doctor tells H that he should get more exercise, but H is not suffering from any disease that can be treated or mitigated by exercise. In 2004, H and W sell their house and move to Florida so that H can increase his general level of exercise by paying golf year-round. Because the sale of the house is merely beneficial to H's general health, the sale of the house is not by reason of H's health. H and W are not entitled to claim a reduced maximum exclusion.

Unforeseen Circumstances?

Regulation § 1.121-3(e): *Sale by reason of unforeseen circumstances*, stresses that the sale must be caused by an event that could not be anticipated *before* buying and occupying the residence. Changes in place of employment and chronic health conditions are a form of unforeseens, but this is not what the IRS is getting at. Unforeseen circumstances are truly those which could not be reasonably envisioned by ordinary and prudent homebuyers. There are two categories of such unforeseens: (1) safe harbor types, and (2) nonsafe harbor types. An overview of the distinction between these two is presented in Figure 4.2. Note that safe harbors are *specific events* (sudden and unforeseen), whereas nonsafe harbors are various forms of *gradual changes* after owning and occupying the residence.

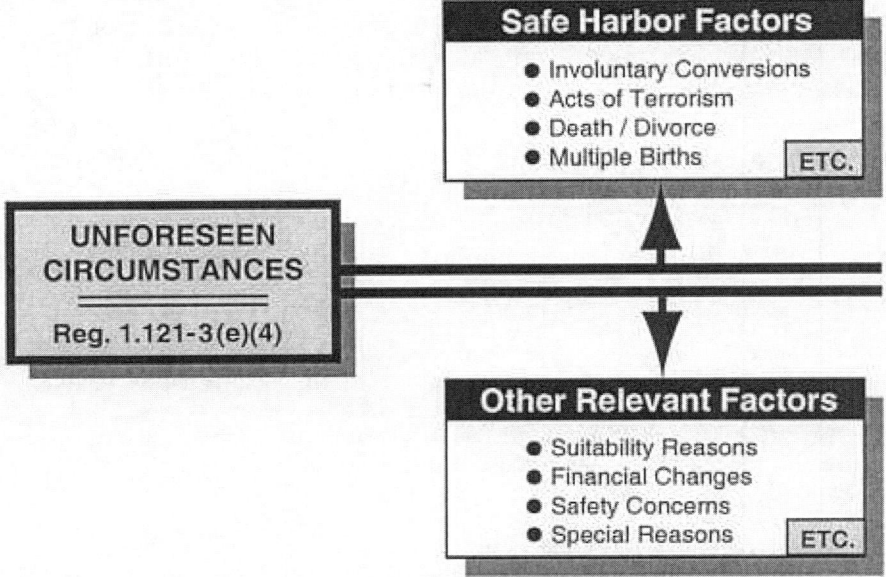

Fig. 4.2 - The Two Versions of Unforeseen Circumstance Sales

Paragraph (2) of subregulation 3(e) is designated: *Specific event safe harbors*. Such specific events may be:

(i) Involuntary conversion of the residence (by fire, flood, hurricane, earthquake, etc.);
(ii) Man-made disasters or acts of war or terrorism;
(iii) Death of an owner-worker paying the mortgage;
(iv) Divorce or legal separation of a married couple;
(v) Multiple births resulting from the same pregnancy; or
(vi) Any other event determined by the IRS to be an unforeseen circumstance.

Regulation § 1.121-3(e)(4) *Examples*, gives six examples of what the IRS considers to be unforeseen circumstances. They address such issues as: (1) earthquakes, (2) spousal job loss, (3) birth of twins, (4) fee increases, (5) noisy traffic, and (6) canceled weddings. We'll cite only two of these official examples. You'll get the safe harbor idea from each of our selected citations.

> *Example 2.* H works as a teacher and W works as a pilot. In 2003 H and W buy a house that they use as their principal residence. Later that year, W is furloughed from her job for 6 months. H and W are unable to pay their mortgage during the period W is furloughed. H and W sell their house in 2004. The sale is within the safe harbors [above and, therefore,] H and W are entitled to claim a reduced maximum exclusion.

> *Example 5.* In 2003 C buys a house that he uses as his principal residence. The property is located on a heavily trafficked road. C sells the property in 2004 because the traffic is more disturbing than he expected. C is **not** entitled to claim a reduced maximum exclusion . . . because . . . under the facts and circumstances, the traffic was not an unforeseen circumstance.

Even the IRS cannot foresee all conceivable unforeseeables. It is always possible that some adversity (such as a lawsuit, tax audit, or calamity) will strike when least expected.

Other Relevant Factors

As Figure 4.2 depicts, there are two distinct versions of the unforeseen circumstances test. The more dominant (and perhaps most common) version comprises specific (safe harbor) unforeseen events as enumerated above. The less dominant version has to do with the deterioration of circumstances while living in one's principal residence. The deteriorating factors are based on the premise that they could not be reasonably foreseen when a home is purchased and used. This is where the thrust of Regulation § 1.121-3(b): *Primary reason for sale or exchange*, comes in. The term "primary reason" implies the weighing of all relevant factors that induce the premature sale.

The primary reason regulation reads in part as—

*If the taxpayer does not qualify for a safe harbor, **factors that may be relevant** in determining the taxpayer's primary reasons for the sale . . . include the extent to which—*

(i)   The **suitability** of the property as the taxpayer's principal residence materially changes;

(ii)   The taxpayer's **financial ability** to maintain the property materially changes;

(iii) The circumstances giving rise to the sale were not **reasonably foreseeable** when the taxpayer began using his principal residence;

and so on.

In other words, there could be all kinds of nonsafe harbor reasons — rash of neighborhood burglaries, nonfatal accidents (loss of limbs), loss of employment, loss of life savings through investment fraud, lawsuit judgment awards causing inability to continue paying housing costs, personal bankruptcies, pending foreclosures, imprudently running up heavy gambling losses, carrying 2nd, 3rd, and 4th mortgages exceeding the home's fair market value . . . and on and on. These are not sudden and unforeseen events. They are *deteriorating* circumstances (mostly financial), some of which may, and others which may not, qualify the homeseller for a reduced maximum exclusion.

Let us cite two more examples from IRS Regulation § 1.121-3(e)(4): **Examples**. This time, we select—

> *Example 4.* B buys a condominium in 2003 and uses it as his principal residence. B's monthly condo fee is $X. Three months after B moves into the property, the condo association decides to replace the building's roof and heating system. Six months later, B's monthly condo fee doubles. B sells his condo in 2004 because he is unable to pay the new condo fee along with his monthly mortgage payment. [While not a safe harbor situation] . . . under the facts and circumstances, the primary reason [for the sale] . . . entitles B to claim a reduced maximum exclusion.

> *Example 6.* In 2003, D and her fiancé E buy a home and live in it as their principal residence. In 2004 D and E cancel their wedding plans and E moves out of the house. Because D cannot afford to make the monthly mortgage payments alone, D and E sell the house in 2004. [While not a safe harbor situation] . . . under the facts and circumstances, the primary reason [for the sale] . . . entitles D and E **each** to claim a reduced maximum exclusion.

The Proration Fraction

The premise underlying a reduced exclusion is the proration concept. That is, the amount of nonqualifying time is compared with the amount of required qualifying time (2 years) to arrive at a proration fraction. The maximum exclusion times the proration fraction establishes the reduced exclusion. For those sales where the gains are less than the maximum exclusion amounts, the prorata fraction is unchanged.

For computing the fraction, you are allowed to use days or months, whichever is more appropriate. We think for accuracy purposes, days are preferred. It is easier to document days of ownership, use, and sale than it is to document in months and fractions of months. Let us illustrate.

Suppose you owned and used your home for 250 days, after which you were transferred to a new place of employment. What would be your applicable prorata fraction? (Recall that 2 years = 730 days, ordinarily.)

Answer: 250 days ÷ 730 days = 0.3424

For a leap year, the answer would be

250 days ÷ 731 days = 0.3419

(For fractional computations involving large dollar amounts, the practice is to express the fraction in four decimal places.)

If we were to use months instead of days, how many months would 250 days be? Assume that the 250 days are consecutive.

The answer would depend on which particular months are involved. For 250 days (non-leap year) commencing January 1st, the period would end on September 8th. That would be 8 months and 8 days (8/30th of a month) or 8.2666 months. If the 250 days started on April 1st, the period would end on December 7th. That would be 8 months and 7 days (7/31st of a month) or 8.2258 months. The corresponding prorata fractions would be

8.2666 months ÷ 24 months = 0.3444 (from Jan 1st)

8.2258 months ÷ 24 months = 0.3427 (from Apr 1st)

As you can see, the by-month fractions are not too different from the by-day fractions. It is just that it is easier to think and document in days rather than in months and fractions of months.

Using our by-day fractions above, what would be allowable reduced exclusion amounts? Answer:

Single Returns

$250,000 x 0.3424 = $ 85,600
$250,000 x 0.3419 = $ 85,475 (leap year)

Joint Returns

$500,000 x 0.3424 = $171,200
$500,000 x 0.3419 = $170,950 (leap year)

Nothing is expressly mentioned in Section 121(c) about a leap year computation. However, subsubparagraph 121(c)(1)(B)(ii) expressly uses the term *2 years* as the denominator of the fraction. This would imply that if one of your two years included a leap year, and your computing time was in days, you would be expected to take the leap year into account (731 days).

Use Smallest Fraction

What Congress was trying to do in subsection 121(c) is admirable. If there were circumstances beyond a taxpayer's control which required him to sell his home before meeting the minimum 2-year ownership and use period, Congress wanted to allow him at least some exclusion of gain, rather than have him lose the entire exclusion and pay full (capital gains) tax. Just how the allowable reduced exclusion amount is computed is where Regulation § 1.121-3(g): *Computation of reduced maximum exclusion*, comes in very handy. This 150-word regulation reads in full as—

The reduced maximum exclusion is computed by multiplying the maximum dollar limitation of $250,000 ($500,000 for certain joint filers) by a fraction. The numerator of the *fraction is **the shortest of the period of time** that the taxpayer **owned** the property during the 5-year period ending on the date of the sale or exchange; the period of time that the taxpayer **used** the property as the taxpayer's principal residence during the 5-year period ending on the date of the sale or exchange; **or** the period of time between the date of a prior sale or exchange of property for which the taxpayer excluded gain under Section 121 and the date of the current sale or exchange. The numerator of the fraction may be expressed in days or months. The denominator of the fraction is 730 days or 24 months (depending on the measure of time used in the numerator).* [Emphasis added.]

Particularly note that this regulation identifies *three* 2-year periods. In abbreviated form, the three periods are—

R-(i)   the 2-year ownership period,
R-(ii)   the 2-year use period, and
R-(iii)   the 2-years-between-sales period.

To put these three periods in perspective, we present Figure 4.3. The net effect is that you must use the **shortest of** the three periods to compute the allowable prorata fraction for the reduced exclusion. Particularly note in Figure 4.3 that we designate the letter "R as meaning: Reduced Exclusion Numerator. Let us illustrate how it works. Suppose the applicable time periods are:

R-(i) - - - - 485 days
R-(ii) - - - - 285 days
R-(iii) - - - 385 days

Clearly, the shortest time period is 285 days. The resulting prorata fraction (smallest) becomes

285 days ÷ 730 days = 0.3904

In contrast, the largest fraction would be

485 days ÷ 730 days = 0.6643

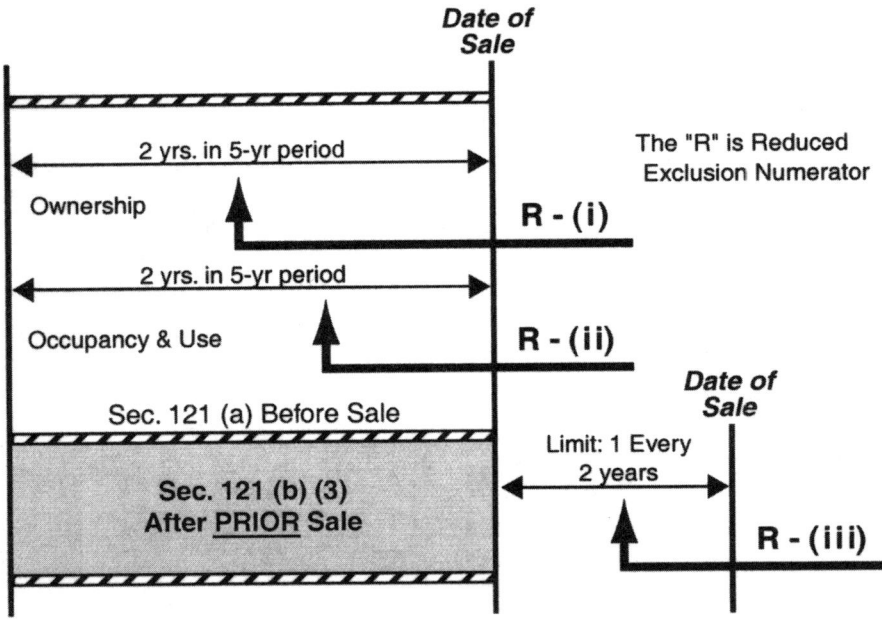

Fig. 4.3 - Three Time Periods of Measure: Use "Shortest of"

From a taxpayer point of view, you'd like to be allowed the largest fraction. As such, your reduced exclusion (single person) would be $166,075 ($250,000 x 0.6643). Instead, you are directed to use the smallest fraction (shortest measuring time period). For such case, your reduced exclusion would be $97,600 ($250,000 x 0.3904). This certainly is better than zero exclusion.

Regulatory Examples

Regulation § 1.121-3(g)(2): ***Examples***, presents two illustrative examples. We'll cite both of them, then follow each with our own critique. Neither of the official examples goes into the fine points that we have discussed above.

Example 1. Taxpayer A purchases a house that she uses as her principal residence. Twelve months after the purchase, A sells the house due to a change in her place of employment. A has not excluded gain under Section 121 on a prior sale or exchange of property within the last 2 years. A is eligible to exclude up to $125,000 of the gain from the sale of her house (12/24 x $250,000).

This, of course, is an oversimplified example. It does, however, raise an important point. Even though the ownership and occupancy periods are concurrent, one still has to address the issue of the recency of a prior sale where there has been an exclusion of gain. This is essential in order to establish "the shortest of" the three time periods. In this particular example, the R-(iii) time period (prior exclusion of gain) is not applicable.

Example 2. (i) Taxpayer H owned a house that he used as his principal residence since year 2000. On January 15, 2004, H and W marry and W begins to use H's house as her principal residence. On January 15, 2005, H sells the house due to a change in W's place of employment. Neither H nor W has excluded gain under Section 121 on a prior sale or exchange of property within the last 2 years.

(ii) Because H and W have not each used the house as their principal residence for at least 2 years during the 5-year period preceding its sale, the maximum dollar limitation amount that may be claimed by H and W will **not** be $500,000, but the sum of each spouse's limitation amount determined on a separate basis as if they had not been married.

(iii) H is eligible to exclude up to $250,000 of gain because he meets the requirements of Section 121. W is not eligible to exclude the maximum dollar limitation amount. Instead, W is eligible to claim a reduced exclusion. Because the sale of the house is due to a change in place of employment, W is eligible to exclude up to $125,000 of the gain (365/730 x $250,000). Therefore, H and W are eligible to exclude up to $375,000 of gain ($250,000 + $125,000) from the sale of the house, even though they filed jointly for the year of sale.

This illustrates a very common occurrence these days. Two wage earners married, but having different ownership and occupancy times. Again, there is no prior sale exclusion at issue. Nevertheless, the message here is that the reduced exclusion amounts are computed as though the two individuals were not married. This aspect, again, attests to the wisdom and practicality of Section 121. Even though individuals are married at time of sale, each may be treated as a separate homeseller where there are any differences in common ownership, use, and prior sale matters.

No tax law can cover every conceivable variant of human activity. Therefore, what is a serious-minded taxpayer to do when faced with a situation not expressly covered in Section 121(a), (b), (c), and others?

Answer: He searches for "appropriate guidance." Such guidance includes information on tax forms, their instructions, IRS administrative rulings, court rulings, and other relevant sources. Ideally, the best guidance in an ambiguous situation is a recent court ruling on point. The first such post-May 1997 "test" was that of *S.C. St. Francis*, 99-1 USTC ¶ 50,495.

The ambiguity was a bankruptcy case in which the husband filed for bankruptcy protection, but the wife did not. The residence was purchased in 1988 in joint title. Consequently, one-half of the house went into the bankruptcy estate for trustee administration. The trustee sold the house on August 19, 1997 for $928,000. One-half of the gain on the sale amounted to $265,300. The bankruptcy trustee claimed $250,000 as an exclusion. The IRS disallowed this exclusion claim because the house was not sold by the taxpayer. The Federal court ruled against the IRS.

The *St. Francis* court, in its own search for guidance, relied on IRC Section 1398(g): [Bankruptcy] *Estate Succeeds to Tax Attributes of Debtor.* [An "attribute" is a quality, character, or distinctive feature ascribed to a person, entity, or property.] Thus, the court held that the trustee succeeded to the holding period and "character" of the debtor's asset as a principal residence. Thereupon, the court ORDERED that—

The Trustee has no additional administrative tax liability to the [IRS].

Subsequently, the IRS acquiesced in the court's order.

5

SPECIAL SITUATION RULES

> **Not All Home Sales Will Qualify For Exclusion Of Gain Under The "Regular Rules." If Special Conditions Are Met, Other Full-Exclusion Rules May Apply. Examples Are Sales: (1) During Out-Of-Residence Care; (2) After Spouse Is Deceased; (3) Of Life-Expectancy Remainder Interests; (4) By Tenant-Stockholders In Co-Op Housing; (5) Under Equity Sharing Arrangements; (6) Of Reacquired Residences; (7) Of Property Involuntarily Converted (Due To Destructive Forces And Condemnation Powers); And (8) Under Bankruptcy Protection. The Exclusion Is Denied Expatriates Unless Tax Avoidance Was Not A Principal Motivation.**

A "special situation" is a set of unusual circumstances associated with one's residence sale, which affects relatively few other sellers, compared to the vast majority of home sales throughout the U.S. Our belief is that these rare circumstances affect no more than about 3% to 5% of all home sales in a given year. Obviously, if *you* happen to be one of the 3-to-5% special-situation sellers, the applicable rules are very important to you. We do not intend to demean the importance of such rules.

These are **not** variants of the reduced-exclusion rules in Chapter 4. They are maximum exclusions permitted under special circumstances. The special circumstances are prescribed by statute (Section 121(d) and (e), and other tax code sections). The special rules therewith employ the tack-on principle to enable qualification under the regular ownership-and-use (occupancy) rule, and on fractional ownership principles. The special situation rules are still further evidence of the generosity and all-inclusiveness of the intent of Congress when it enacted Section 121 on May 6, 1997.

For example, one unusual type situation has to do with what we class as "out-of-residence care" sales. These are sales prompted solely by elderly sellers becoming physically and mentally incapable of self-care. The homes are sold primarily to produce money for paying for long-term nursing home care. We think the number of this type of sale would hold constant at about 2% of all home sales each year. This is a national socio-medical problem of widespread concern. Fortunately, one special situation rule definitely applies [Sec. 121(d)(7)].

Or, take the case of a single individual or married couple who give up their U.S. citizenship and move abroad for 10 years or more. They are tax treated as expatriates. The home-sale exclusion of gain and other capital gain rules do not apply [Sec. 121(e)]. Realistically, how many expatriates are there likely to be each year? Probably one-tenth of 1%. There are always more immigrants *to* than emigrants from the U.S.

Accordingly, in this chapter we want to pull together all of the special situation rules that may potentially apply. We present them only once. We do so because we regard this chapter as a repository of such rules. Who knows, in one's lifetime of home sales, any one of these rules could apply when least expected. If you are affected, this chapter becomes a place you can come back to. Otherwise, all subsequent chapters are devoted to ordinary (qualified) home sales where preparation for, and claiming, the exclusion become truly major tax accounting tasks.

Out-of-Residence Care

As we've already hinted at, a truly special situation occurs when an ill or elderly person becomes physically or mentally incapable of self-care. This is not a health or accident emergency, but a major lifestyle change requiring long-term nursing care. If the nursing care is out of one's personal residence, subsection 121(d)(7) comes into play. The focus is on what qualifies as the ownership and use period for the 2-out-of-5-year requirement of Section 121(a).

Subsection 121(d)(7) is titled: ***Determination of Use During Periods of Out-of-Residence Care***. This reads in most part as—

*In the case of a taxpayer who— (A) becomes physically or mentally incapable of self-care, and (B) owns and uses property as the taxpayer's principal residence during the 5-year period described in subsection (a) for periods aggregating **at least 1 year**, then the taxpayer shall be treated as using such property . . . [when he] **resides in any facility (including a nursing home)** licensed by a State or political subdivision to care for an individual in the taxpayer's condition.* [Emphasis added re nursing homes.]

What is this rule saying? It is saying that one year of actual residence in one's home counts as two years, if the owner resided in a licensed out-of-residence care facility at any time during the four years his/her own residence was not occupied. Apparently, one's residence in the out-of-residence care facility must equal one year or more (to make up for the missing one year in one's own home). Furthermore, as long as the patient is alive, he/she does not need to be actually living at home when it is sold.

There is an interesting ancillary feature to subsection 121(d)(7). The maximum exclusion amount of $250,000 for any one individual is **not prorated** in any manner. If one enters a duly licensed care facility at any qualifying time before the sale of his home, he can claim up to the full exclusion amount. If his spouse is not in a care facility, but otherwise qualifies, the $500,000 joint return exclusion can be claimed.

Property of Deceased Spouse

In spousal ownership and use situations at time of sale, there is a fundamental point always to keep in mind. Whatever the circumstances, each spouse must separately meet the 2-out-of-5-year requirement on his or her own. Where a special situation rule may apply to one spouse, it does not automatically apply to the other spouse. That is, each spouse is entitled to claim his or her own $250,000 exclusion potential independently of the other.

Two frequently asked questions are:

"If my spouse dies (for whatever reason) and I subsequently sell our home, do I get one exclusion amount or two? What if we both owned and used the residence more than two years at time of sale?"

No matter how you rationalize, your marital status for Section 121 purposes is determined at the time of sale or exchange of your residence. If your spouse dies before the sale, you are an *unmarried* person. That is, you are one individual: not two. What appears to be a tax contradiction is that, for the year in which your spouse dies, you can file a joint return. But you can't claim a joint $500,000 exclusion. The best you can do is to treat your deceased spouse's ownership and use time as part of your own. To help you visualize this "death of spouse" feature, we present Figure 5.1.

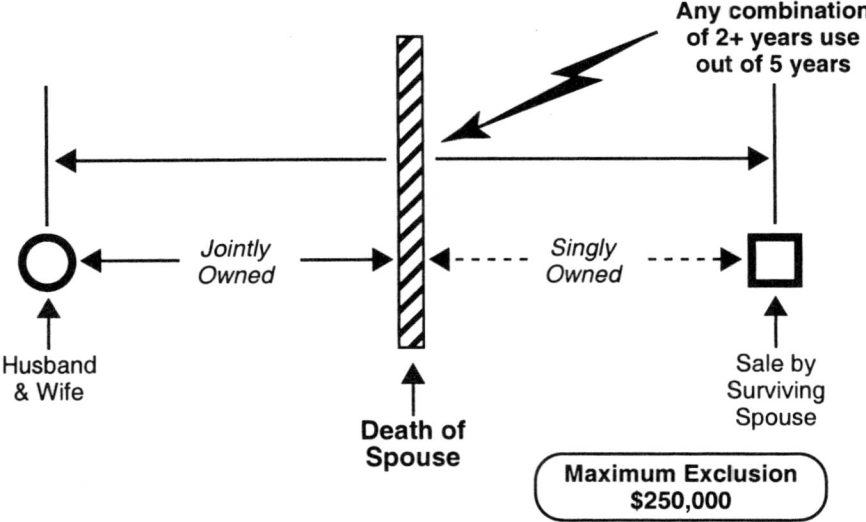

Fig. 5.1 - Ownership and Use When Residence Sold by Surviving Spouse

Section 121(d)(2) addresses Figure 5.1 specifically. It is titled: ***Property of Deceased Spouse***, and reads as—

*For purposes of this section, in the case of an unmarried individual whose spouse is **deceased on the date of the sale** or exchange of property, the period such unmarried individual owned and used such property **shall include** the period such* *deceased spouse* owned and used such property before death. [Emphasis added.]

For example, suppose you were a divorced, widowed, or single (never married) person. You married a person who owned and lived in her own home three years. You lived there for one year, after which time your spouse was killed in a fatal auto accident. The home was sold. Do you get an exclusion?

Answer: No. Why not? Because you didn't own the home at time of sale. Your name as a spouse was not added to the property prior to the time of death. Plans were to do so, but the accident occurred before you and she got around to it.

On the other hand, suppose your name were added to the property title as husband and wife. You lived there one year before its sale. What now?

Yes, you get one exclusion (up to $250,000) for yourself only. This is because subsection (d)(2) has the effect of *tacking on* to your one year's time the ownership and use time of your deceased spouse. This is a genuine tax break.

Sale of Remainder Interest

A "remainder interest" is an actuarial fraction of ownership of property, based on the life expectancy of the life tenant. Its significance in principal residence situations relates to elderly owners (surviving spouses and retirees mostly) who need additional income, but who want to stay in their home until the end of life. The process is called: *actuarial partitioning*. The effect is that the property can be retitled in tenants-in-common fashion, where there is a life fraction and a remainder fraction. The remainder fraction can be sold like any other personal residence.

Remainder fractions are set forth in IRS actuarial tables, principally identified as **Table S**, based on **Table 90CM**. The "S" refers to the present worth of a single life remainder interest. The 90CM refers to the 1990 census (the "C") with its updated mortality tables (the "M") for that census. The latest IRS tables apply to property transfers and deaths after April 30, 1999. The next actuarial updates will take place on April 30, 2009. As you are probably already aware, the U.S. census is taken every 10 years. The tables are based on assumed rates of interest (time value of money) between 6% and 12% generally.

Each actuarial fraction is table computed to five decimal places. For example, a person aged 65 (at 9% per annum rate of interest) would have a remainder fraction of 0.41709. The corresponding life fraction would be 0.58291. The remainder fraction and life fraction must add to 1.00000 (0.41709 + 0.58291). The remainder fraction at age 75 would be 0.56591; at age 85 it would be 0.71823; at age 95 it would be 0.83592; and at age 105 it would be 0.90719. The present life expectancies go up to age 109. Obviously, the longer a person lives, the shorter is his life fraction and the greater is his remainder fraction in the home that he owns and occupies. Remainder fractions can be sold.

Assume, for example, that a 75-year-old person wants to sell his remainder interest in his home valued at $650,000. The selling price of his remainder fraction would be

$650,000 x 0.56591 = $367,841 sales price

Assume that the cost basis in the house was $185,000. How much capital gain would be realized on the sale of the remainder interest? Answer:

$367,841 – [$185,000 x 0.56591] = $367,841 – $104,693 basis

= $263,148 gain realized.

Assuming that all qualifications are met, how much of this gain is excludable? Answer: $250,000. Only the excess gain amounting to $13,148 is taxable. How come?

Enter now subsection 121(d)(8)(A): *Sales of Remainder Interests; In General*. The subparagraph (A) reads—

At the election of the taxpayer, this section [Sec. 121(a), (b)] shall not fail to apply to the sale or exchange of an interest in a principal residence by reason of such interest being a remainder interest in such residence . . .

The general idea prescribed is depicted in Figure 5.2.

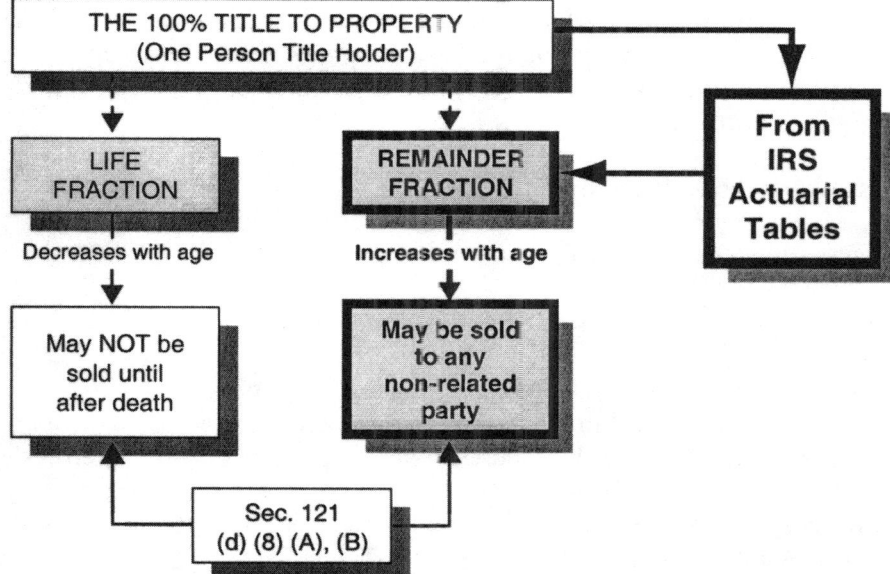

Fig. 5.2 - Fractioning of Ownership Interests in a Life Estate

In other words, the 75-year-old homeowner above could elect to sell his 56.59% remainder interest, get $367,841 for it, claim a $250,000 exclusion of gain, pay tax on $13,140, and *pay no tax* on $104,693 (which is his "return of capital"). This is a very attractive option for elderly homeowners who want to stay put.

What's the catch?

None really. There are two conditions, however. One condition is that the life tenant cannot sell his life fraction. This is because a life interest is treated as a consumption asset lasting until death of the occupant. This prohibition is spelled out in the last phrase of subparagraph (A), to wit—

This section shall not apply to any other interest in such residence which is sold or exchanged separately.

The term "any other interest," of course, is the life interest once the remainder interest is sold.

The second condition is a prohibition in subparagraph (B): ***Exception for Sales to Related Parties.*** The prohibition reads—

Subparagraph (A) shall not apply to any sale to, or exchange with, any person who bears a relationship to the taxpayer [who are family members, close business associates, or beneficiaries of grantor trusts].

In other words, the remainder fraction must be sold to nonrelated 3rd-party interests who expect to buy the life fraction *after* the life tenant dies. This delay can hinder the sale.

Tenant-Stockholder in Co-Op Housing

In heavily populated areas, some home ownerships are in the form of stock holdings in a cooperative housing/apartment corporation. The legal ownership structure is a corporate entity, rather than an individual person or persons. Stock ownership in the corporation is held by tenant-stockholders and nontenant stockholders (investors generally).

A "tenant-stockholder" is one who resides on the premises of which he is a fractional owner. He lives there as his principal residence. Although he may own some nontenant stock as an investment in the corporation, only that stock which represents his proportionate share of personal living space to the total stock issue qualifies as tenant stock.

To illustrate the significance of tenant stock, suppose a housing/apartment corporation had a total stock issue of 100,000 shares. Suppose each living unit is represented by 1,000 shares. Now, suppose a stockholder held 5,000 shares and lived in one of the units himself. He would have 1,000 tenant shares and 4,000 nontenant shares.

Suppose the above tenant-stockholder sold 3,000 of his shares and personally moved from the premises. What has he sold?

He sold 1,000 shares of tenant stock which qualifies as the sale or exchange of his principal residence. He would be entitled to the Section 121(b) exclusion amount, provided he met the more than two years' ownership and use test of Section 121(a).

In addition, he sold 2,000 shares of nontenant stock. Such sale does *not* qualify for Section 121 treatment. He pays tax on any capital gain; there is no exclusion of any kind. As you'll see subsequently, ownership of a residence can be fractioned.

Selling stock in a corporation ordinarily comes under tax rules for capital gains and losses. But, in the case of tenant-stockholders, there is a special situation rule. It is subsection 121(d)(4): ***Tenant-Stockholder in Cooperative Housing Corporation.***

The key parts of subsection (d)(4) read as follows:

If a taxpayer holds stock as a tenant-stockholder . . . in a cooperative housing corporation . . ., then—

(A) the holding requirements of subsection (a) shall be applied to the holding of such stock, and
*(B) the use requirement of subsection (a) shall be applied to **the house or apartment** which the taxpayer was **entitled to occupy** as such stockholder.* [Emphasis added.]

Particular care is required to establish the proportionate allocation of stock costs, basis adjustments, and improvements representing the actual living space of the tenant-stockholder. Once the tenant shares are properly cost identified and separated unto themselves, any gain on the sale of such shares can participate in the exclusion provisions of Section 121.

Equity Sharing Arrangements

A common financing arrangement these days is the sharing of ownership interest in a residence between occupants and non-occupants. This is particularly attractive for taxpayers (married or single) who are unable to arrange the financing of their home on their own. They need a sponsor (or angel) to put up the down-payment money, and provide contingency backing to the mortgage payments. The sponsors in these cases are usually parents, relatives, and friends. The sponsor does not occupy the residence in any manner. He/she/they are basically co-investors.

Such an arrangement is called *shared equity financing* or "equity sharing" for short. The term "equity" means ownership interest in property in excess of any mortgages and liens against it. It is the market value of the property at any time, less applicable legal encumbrances. Equity in and of itself is unrelated to Section

121. It is significant to Section 121 only in terms of ownership and use. It also has a bearing on the distribution of proceeds upon sale.

When a shared equity residence is sold, one of the first tax concerns is the title to the property at the time of its sale or exchange. The title (grant deed) must clearly spell out the fractional interest of each owner therein. For example, the occupant(s) may have a 65% ownership interest, and the nonoccupant(s) may have a 35% interest (or 50/50, or whatever). In other words, the grant deed would be in tenants-in-common form: meaning two or more separate owners.

A special rule addresses this subject. But it is not embodied in Section 121. It is set forth in Section 280A(d)(3), namely: ***Rental to Family Member, Etc., for Use as a Principal Residence***. Selected bits and pieces of this rule are as follows:

(A) [Occupancy] *shall apply . . . to a person who has an interest in the dwelling unit only if such* [property is rented at fair rental] *pursuant to a shared equity financing agreement.*

(B) *In* [such] *case, fair rental shall be determined as of the time the agreement is entered into and by taking into account the occupant's qualified ownership interest.*

(C) *The term "shared equity financing agreement" means an agreement under which 2 or more persons acquired qualified ownership interest in a dwelling unit, and . . .* [one of the persons] *is entitled to occupy the dwelling unit for use as a principal residence.*

When the residence is sold, the occupant/seller fractions all relevant items for computing his share of the capital gain, in accordance with the equity sharing agreement. For example, if the occupant's share were 65%, the selling price, selling expenses, tax basis of residence, and gain on sale would be 65% of the actual figures. The 65% fraction of gain **participates** in the maximum exclusion amount of Section 121(b), if the ownership and use test of Section 121(a) is otherwise met. Thus, the occupant gets his full allowable exclusion amount. This can be a boon to first-time home buyers (even second-time home buyers), who want to get money ahead for the down payment on their own 100% home.

Using the percentage assumed above, we depict the "graphics" of equity sharing in Figure 5.3. Note that, in concept, Figure 5.3 is analogous to Figure 5.2. The difference is that whereas Figure 5.2 is applicable primarily to elderly persons, Figure 5.3 is applicable primarily to younger persons.

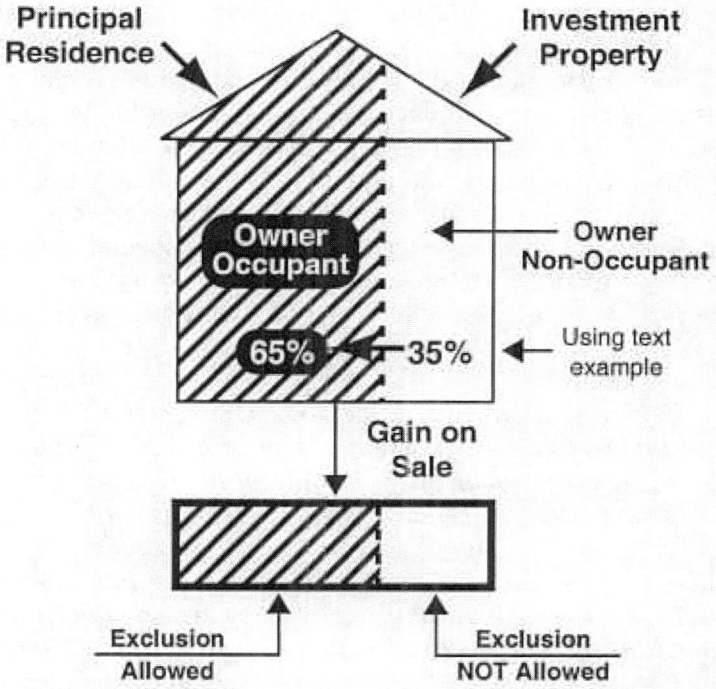

Fig. 5.3 - The Exclusion Feature When "Equity Sharing" a Residence

Reacquired Residence Resold

There are situations where a principal residence is sold, the allowable exclusion under Section 121 is claimed, and the seller takes back a note of indebtedness (a mortgage) secured by the property sold. This is what is called: *seller financing*, in whole or part. Subsequently, the buyer defaults on the mortgage and the seller reacquires his former residence. In the reacquisition process, the note is canceled. During the interim, the seller acquired another principal residence in an entirely unrelated transaction.

As an example, a taxpayer sells his residence and takes back a note secured by a Deed of Trust. Suppose the note is for $250,000 payable in monthly installments over 10 years. It turns out that this amount is all gain, which the seller properly excludes under Section 121. After paying, say, $35,000 on the note principal, the buyer defaults. The seller employs an attorney, forecloses on the buyer, and reacquires his former residence. The seller now has two residences: one his current residence and the other his reacquired residence on which he previously claimed the exclusion. Only one residence can qualify under Section 121.

What does he do with his reacquired residence? Does it disqualify the exclusion amount which he has already taken?

Reacquiring a seller-financed residence is a special situation, but not too uncommon. Since it is so, a special rule applies, namely: Section 1038(e)—*Certain Reacquisitions of Real Property; Principal Residences*. Its pertinent portions read:

> *If—*
> *(1) subsection (a)* [of Section 1038: NOT of Section 121] *applies to a reacquisition of real property . . . and*
> *(2) **within 1 year** after the date of the reacquisition of such property by the seller, such property is resold by him,*
>
> *then, . . . **for purposes of applying section 121**, the resale of such property shall be treated **as part of the transaction constituting the original sale** of such property.* [Emphasis added. This is called "tack-on" of ownership.]

Reference to subsection 1038(a) relates to the treatment that the reacquisition event is not a gain/loss recognition event on its own. The reacquisition is part of the former residence sale. That is, any money paid on the note principal that is forfeited by the buyer (i.e., the $35,000 above) is treated (after expenses of the reacquisition) as part of the original selling price. This means that the allowable exclusion amount under Section 121 has to be recomputed. For this, an amended return has to be filed and proper adjustments made. We illustrate the situation for you in Figure 5.4. As you can glean from this figure, there are some heart wrenching gain-on-sale recomputations to be made.

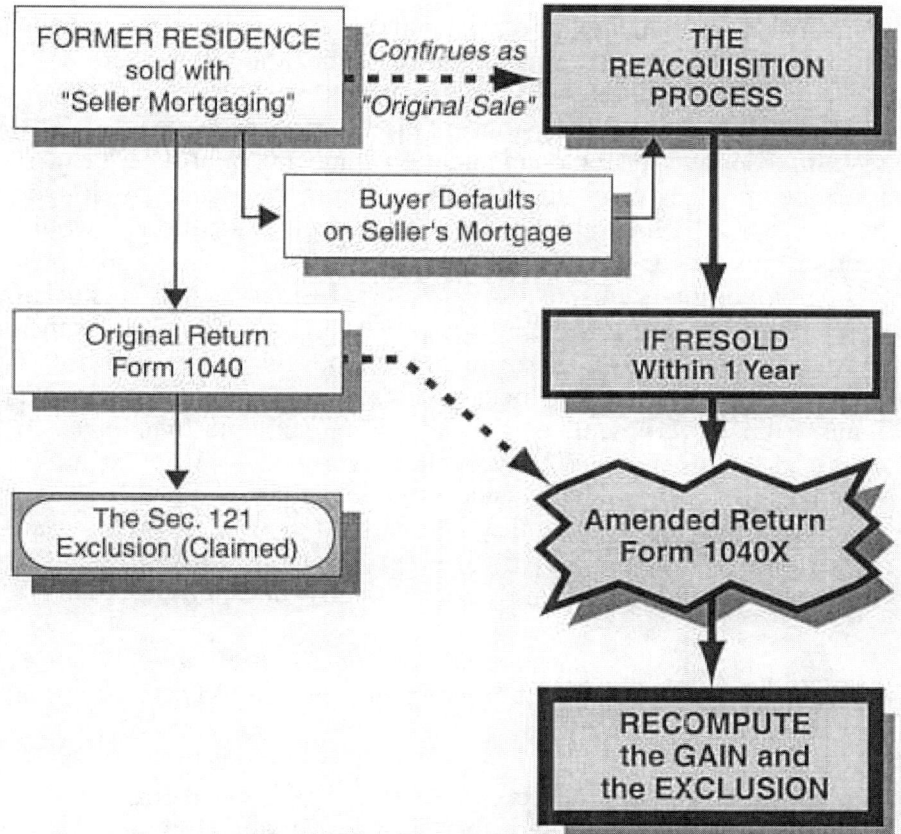

Fig. 5.4 - Sale of Reacquired Residence After Prior Exclusion Claimed

Involuntary Conversion "Sales"

There are situations in which one is compelled to give up his principal residence and seek another. No sale or exchange takes place involving the free choice or will of the owner. He disposes of his residence under compulsion and conditions over which he has no control. These dispositions are tax-termed *involuntary conversion* . . . against one's will.

Involuntary conversion results primarily from destructive forces and condemnation powers. Conversion by destruction covers all cases of physical damage caused by violent and external means. Examples are lightning, storm (tornado, hurricane), flood, earthquake, volcanic eruption, landslide, tidal wave, fire, and the like. Conversion by condemnation (or under the threat thereof) is the taking of property for public needs such as for freeway construction, airport expansion, public housing projects, etc. The resulting destruction or condemnation may not be 100%. But it must be of such magnitude as to render a residence no longer habitable. Or, if habitable, but not in its original location, it would require moving to a new location.

An involuntary disposition of one's residence may result in conversion into a replacement residence, or into money and other property. Whatever the form of conversion, there is possibility of gain. This is due to the excess of insurance proceeds, disaster loans from government, and other reimbursements over *basis* in the former residence. Whenever there is a gain — whether under compulsion or not — there is accountability for tax.

The required accountability is treatment as a "sale." This is so prescribed by Section 121(d)(5): ***Involuntary Conversions***. Its subparagraph (A) reads—

*For purposes of this section, the destruction, theft, seizure, requisition, or condemnation of property shall be treated as the **sale** of such property.*

The term "this section" refers to Section 121 in its entirety. That is, Section 121 applies only if there is a conversion gain.

The phrase "shall be treated as [a] sale" means that, after the amount of conversion gain is established, if any, the regular "up to" $250,000/$500,000 exclusion of gain benefits apply. Clearly, Congress did not intend that one be deprived of his exclusion benefits in those unfortunate circumstances where his principal residence is involuntarily converted. By treating the conversion as a "sale," one can wrap up his tax accounting at that time, and start over in a new residence of his choice.

Section 121(d)(5) also includes subparagraph (B): ***Application of Section 1033***, and subparagraph (C): ***Property Acquired After Involuntary Conversion***. Because of the uniqueness and complexity of these rules with respect to the determination of conversion gain, we will revisit Section 121(d)(5) in Chapter 11: Involuntary Conversion.

Exclusion Allowed in Bankruptcy

For years, under prior law provisions, the IRS has refused to allow the trustee of a bankruptcy estate to claim the (then) Section 121 benefits. The IRS argued that, under Section 1398: *Rules Relating to Title 11* [Bankruptcy] *Cases for Individuals*, title to a debtor's personal residence was automatically transferred to the bankruptcy estate, upon petitioning for bankruptcy protection by a debtor. This is the clear implication of Section 1398(a): *Cases to Which Section Applies*—

> *This section* [re bankruptcy procedures] *shall apply to any case under chapter 7 (relating to liquidation) or chapter 11 (relating to reorganization) of title 11 of the* [Bankruptcy Code] *in which the debtor is an individual.*

The IRS also argued that Section 1398(g): [Bankruptcy] *Estate Succeeds to Tax Attributes of Debtor*—

> provides a list of the debtor's tax attributes to which the bankruptcy estate succeeds in computing the estate's taxable income, which does not include the exclusion from bankruptcy; and that only an individual, and not a bankruptcy estate, could possess a principal residence.

And, for years, various courts have upheld this and similar IRS positions. This IRS position was trounced in 1998.

The very first court case to address the $250,000/$500,000 exclusion issue under Section 121 (as amended in May 1997) was that of *L. Popa*, BC-DC Ill., 98-1 USTC ¶ 50,276 [The "BC" is Bankruptcy Court; the "DC" is District Court; all DCs are followed by state of domicile of the court (Ill = Illinois); the "USTC" is U.S. Tax Cases; and the "¶" refers to the published case number in each year and volume indicated (98-1 = 1998, Vol. 1).] The abridged citation of the *Popa* court ruling reads (in part)—

> A debtor's residence constituted property of his bankruptcy estate, which was entitled to claim an exclusion up to $250,000 of gain [per debtor] upon the realty's sale pursuant to Code Sec. 121, as amended by the Taxpayer Relief Act of 1997 (P.L. 105-34). Resolving an issue of first impression under the current version of the statute, the court found that the estate was liable for the same tax, and entitled to the same exclusion, as the debtor

would be on the sale of the residence because it succeeded to the holding period and character of the property and was to be "treated as the debtor" for purpose of Code Sec. 1398.

The *Popa* court based its rationale on the provisions of Section 1398(f): *Treatment of Transfers Between Debtor and Estate.* The essence here is that a transfer of property from a debtor to his bankruptcy estate, and from the bankruptcy estate to its debtor, is NOT A DISPOSITION of title to property . . . in the ordinary business sense. Any such transfer is a *computational treatment* only. Such treatment is necessary for establishing the debtor's equity in his assets, for subsequent distribution to creditors.

Following the *Popa* court case (DC of Illinois), **six** other court cases have similarly ruled against the IRS. Said cases are:

1. *L.J. Godwin*, BC-DC Ohio, 99-1 USTC ¶ 50,287
2. *G.T. Kerr*, DC Wash., 99-1 USTC ¶ 50,310
3. *S.C. St. Francis*, BC-DC Ga., 99-1 USTC ¶ 50,495
4. *T.A Williams*, BC-DC Md., 99-2 USTC ¶ 50,738
5. *C.A. Slye*, BC-DC Md., 99-2 USTC ¶ 50,739
6. *J.D. Curran*, BC-DC Ga., 99-2 USTC ¶ 50,742

When the IRS gets beat over the head often enough by federal courts, it eventually succumbs to accepting the plain language of tax law. Accordingly, on August 10, 2000 the IRS notified its attorneys that Sections 121 and 1398 . . . *when read in their entirety, support the bankruptcy estate's claim to the exclusion.*

Benefits Denied Expatriates

When a tax law is so generous as Section 121, there is the likelihood that some taxpayer will abuse the law or take undue advantage of it. Such is the likelihood with regard to expatriates. An "expatriate" is a U.S. citizen or a long-term alien U.S. resident who voluntarily terminates his U.S. benefits and moves abroad permanently. The measuring time is 10 years or more abroad after giving up U.S. citizenship or U.S. residency.

The *presumption* is that one is terminating his U.S. citizenship or U.S. residency solely for tax avoidance purposes. The threshold for this presumption is $125,000 in *average net income tax* within five years of expatriation, **or** $2,000,000 in net worth the year before leaving the U.S. Upon attaining and surpassing these thresholds, and moving abroad permanently, the 24-word Section 121(e) comes into play.

Section 121(e) is titled: *Denial of Exclusion for Expatriates*. This subsection reads in its entirety—

> *This section shall not apply to any sale or exchange by an individual if the treatment provided by section 877(a)(1) applies to such individual.*

Ordinarily, expatriation is not a consideration by homesellers who qualify for the exclusion-of-gain benefits of Section 121. It is more favored by millionaire/billionaire citizens.

The referenced Section 877 is titled: *Expatriation to Avoid Tax*. Its subsection (a) is titled: *Treatment of Expatriates*. Its paragraph (1): *In General*, reads in part—

> *Every nonresident alien individual who, within the 10-year period immediately preceding the close of the taxable year, lost U.S. citizenship, unless such loss did not have for one of its principal purposes the avoidance of* [U.S. income, estate, or gift] *taxes . . . shall be taxable* [under U.S. laws] *for such taxable year . . .* [etc.]

The idea here is that there is no escaping U.S. tax laws for a period up to 10 years after giving up U.S. citizenship or U.S. residency. Once such status is terminated, a former citizen or alien resident is tax identified as a "nonresident alien individual." While in such status, all exclusion-of-gain benefits under Section 121 are denied. If a current or former principal residence is sold or exchanged, all gain is taxed. The statutory intent is to prohibit an expatriate from owning a home or other property in the U.S. from which he can conduct business, then escape taxation as a nonresident alien.

Subsection 877(a)(2): *Certain Individuals Treated as Having Tax Avoidance Purposes*, reflects the previously mentioned presumption thresholds of $125,000 net income or $2,000,000 net worth. These thresholds are indexed for inflation.

Against this presumption is a relief provision in subsection 877(c)(1): ***Tax Avoidance Not Presumed in Certain Cases***. The essence here is that subsection 877(a)(2)—

shall not apply to an individual if—
within the 1-year period beginning on the date of loss of U.S.
citizenship, such individual submits a ruling request for the
[IRS's] determination as to whether such loss has for one of its
principal purposes the avoidance of [U.S.] taxes.

In other words, an expatriate may be able to claim the Section 121 benefits if he submits to the IRS a ***Ruling Request: Tax Avoidance Not Principal Purpose of Expatriation***. Such a request would be a separate document from one's latest filed U.S. tax return. The request would have to follow **Notice 98-34** by providing the following information:

(i)   the date (or expected date) of expatriation;
(ii)   a full explanation of one's reason for expatriating;
(iii)   a list of all foreign countries where new residence is intended; and
(iv)   a comprehensive net worth statement.

There is a better option. Before expatriating, sell the U.S. principal residence, claim the exclusion (if qualified), file the tax return, and pay all current taxes due. If there are any prior tax issues outstanding, settle them. When the U.S. tax slate is totally clean, then expatriate. Under these circumstances, U.S. tax avoidance is unlikely to be construed as the primary motivation for termination of your citizenship or residency.

6

BASIS OF RESIDENCE SOLD

> **Your Current Residence May Have Been Acquired In One Of Several Ways. The Most Common Is By Direct Purchase, Including "Rollover Acquisition" And Self-Construction. To Derive EXCLUSION OF GAIN Benefits, Legal Ownership And Personal Living Must Prevail. Excess Acreage And Multifamily Units Do Not Count As Your Residence. At Time Of Sale, Your TAX BASIS Becomes An Important Reference For Establishing Capital Gain. "Basis" Includes Improvements To, And Subtractions From, Initial Acquisition Cost. Recovery Of Your Basis Capital Is Nontaxable, And Is Independent Of Exclusion Benefits.**

One cannot sell a residence he does not own. One might live in a residence for long periods of time and think of it as his own, but unless his name is on the title deed, he does not own it . . . or any part of it. If one does not own any portion of the property when it is sold, he cannot claim any of the Section 121 exclusion benefits. Section 121, recall, is titled: *Exclusion of Gain from Sale of Principal Residence*.

For refresher purposes and focus in this chapter, we cite again Section 121(a). It reads in full—

*Gross income shall not include **gain from the sale** or exchange of property if, during the 5-year period ending on the date of the sale or exchange, such property has been **owned and used*** *by the taxpayer as the taxpayer's principal residence for periods aggregating 2 years or more.* [Emphasis added.]

Note the two emphasized phrases above: "gain from the sale" and "owned and used." One has to determine his *gain* (capital gain) before any exclusion can be claimed. One has to be an *owner* (or part owner) before he is eligible for any exclusion.

To determine the amount of gain when you sell your residence, you must have a tax basis in that residence. The term "basis" is the amount of capital (money) that you cumulatively invested in the property when sold. Your basis money comes back to you as "return of capital." Any return of capital is not subject to tax. It is therefore **not part** of any exclusion amount that you may otherwise be allowed. It is your *excess over basis* — the gain — to which the exclusion applies.

In the sequence of events leading up to your claiming the exclusion, we want to familiarize you with the fundamentals of property acquisition, what constitutes your principal residence, and how you determine and track your tax basis in that residence. Suppose, for example, that as a single person your residence sold for $350,000. You have a $100,000 basis in that residence which you can prove. With your $250,000 exclusion of gain benefit, you'd pay no tax. If you couldn't prove the $100,000 basis, you'd pay tax on said amount. This is what this chapter is all about: showing you how to establish your tax basis in a residence, and establishing the extent of your legal ownership at the time of its acquisition. There are several methods of acquiring title to property. The most common being by purchase, either directly, via an exchange, or by self-construction (using a contractor).

Methods of Acquisition

One cannot sell a residence until he/she acquires one. There are several methods of acquisition, the most common being by direct purchase. That is, one uses his savings (or "borrows" from close family members) to make the down payment. He uses his occupation and source of employment as the means for making the mortgage payments. (The mortgage is "secured" by the residence itself.) With the cash down and mortgage contract, he buys the residence outright. For most homeowners this is the most frequent method of acquisition.

Many residences these days have been acquired through rollover-of-gain replacements under prior law Section 1034. That section was titled: *Rollover of Gain on Sale of Principal Residence*. As long as the rollover residence was acquired within two years of sale old — as most were — the replacement is treated as a purchase. Title matters are not so much a concern in rollovers as is one's tax basis therein.

Another form of purchase is by a like-kind exchange. That is, one has acquired other residential property that he has rented to others for some time. Then, via a Section 1031 tax-deferred exchange, a primary residence is acquired. The amount of deferred gain that results reduces the basis in the property so acquired. Various appraisal, escrow, and cash "boot" fees must be paid.

Another form of purchase is self-construction. One sets out to build his own house, acquiring first a parcel of land on which to do so. He then buys or barters for the necessary materials, and buys or barters for the necessary labor (other than his own). The bartering aspects are a little tricky because seldom is there any documentation on the bartered materials and services. Along the way, one has to put up cash for various permits, fees, inspections, and utilities. Using a licensed contractor is recommended.

Hence, acquisition by purchase consists of four variant forms: (1) direct purchase, (2) rollover (now less frequent), (3) exchange (now more frequent), and (4) self-construction.

In all these variants, money and money's worth, called "consideration," changes hands. Thus, full and adequate consideration is paid, after which title is conveyed.

There is a form of acquisition for which full consideration is not paid. It is by *gift*. Instead of money or money's worth, the consideration is love and affection (as between members of a family), or gratitude and appreciation (as between friends and associates), or kindness and benevolence (as between the "haves" and the needy). Gift of a first residence is more common than is generally believed.

The party (or parties) gifting a residence is called the "donor"; the party (or parties) receiving it is called the "donee." A bona fide gift presupposes three conditions, namely:

1. relinquishment of dominion and control over the property by the donor (as the former owner),
2. affirmation of "acceptance" by the donee, and
3. transfer of title accompanied by physical possession.

When all three of these conditions are present, the residence belongs to the donee just as though he/she/they had purchased it outright. The tax catch is a "transfer of basis" from the donor.

Still another form of acquisition is by *inheritance*. That is, one acquires his residence from a decedent, usually a parent or other blood relative. The transfer is by an instrument called a "will." Consideration is the fact that upon death of the decedent, the full market value of the residence is included in the decedent's gross estate and death-taxed accordingly. Once so taxed, it passes to a designated heir or legatee as though it were purchased outright.

Must Be "Principal Residence"

It is not uncommon for a taxpayer to own two or more personal residences at the same time. One may have a home in the city, and a vacation home in the mountains or at the seashore. Or, one may have a home in each of two cities where he works part-time each year at different jobs. The number of residences is not the concern. Only one residence, however, can be designated as the taxpayer's primary/principal residence: first in importance.

The test of a principal residence is the number of days' occupancy each year. Suppose one had three residences: A, B, and C. Residence A is occupied 110 days of the year; residence B is occupied 190 days; and residence C is occupied 65 days. Residence B would be the principal residence. Why? Because "for the year," A and C would comprise 175 days (110 + 65) versus 190 for B.

Days of occupancy is the test because Section 121(a) contains the clause: *used by the taxpayer*. The verb "use" means: to habituate, to put into action or service, to avail oneself of, to employ, to utilize, to enjoy, to come back to frequently.

Legal title to the property may be placed in the names of one or more persons, separately, jointly, or severally. It does not matter whether a residence is separately owned, jointly owned (such as joint tenancy), or severally owned (such as tenants-in-common). Each person named in the title owns his or her share of that property. Upon sale, each such person can claim his prorata share of the gain, for Section 121 purposes.

There is no requirement that a taxpayer actually occupy his residence at the time of its sale. If vacant or rented temporarily at that time, and such vacancy or rental is necessitated by the exigencies of the real estate market, and arises from the taxpayer's use of the residence as his principal residence, he will not be denied the benefits of exclusion of gain when it is sold.

This is the rationale behind the 2-out-of-5-year rule, depicted back in Figure 1.1 (on page 1-6). All that is required (generally) is two or more years' residence use out of any 5-year period of property ownership. There are two variants to this general rule. One, the two years of use become five years for like-kind exchanges. Two, the 5-year period for a qualifying sale can be extended to 10 years for members of uniformed services.

Surrounding Acreage Limited

A personal residence is where one lives. This includes his family and their recreation. Most fixed residences are built on land. Consequently, a certain amount of land is necessary for personal living and enjoyment.

For example, personal living land includes a driveway and carport or garage space. It includes walkways, lawn and shrubbery, and other decorative landscaping. It may also include recreation space, such as patio, barbecue, swimming pool, shuffle board, tennis court, and a limited amount of open space.

But if one buys a home on 40 acres of land, he does not need the entire 40 acres for personal living. The "excess acreage" surrounding the land is *an investment*. It is not personal living land. Sale of this excess land does not qualify for Section 121 benefits.

Just what is, and what is not, excess land, if any, can only be determined by the fact situations of each case. In most residential living areas (urban, suburban, rural), there are minimum zoning laws. In such cases, local ordinances specify the amount of land deemed essential for personal living. Where residential property is acquired with minimum zoning parcels, the federal tax structure accepts this as part and parcel of one's primary residence.

Now if one buys a minimum zoned residence, and in addition buys one or two adjacent parcels of land, he has made two purchases. He has purchased a residence and a nonresidence. Even if he buys both in the same "package deal," he has made two purchases. The residence portion qualifies for Section 121, whereas the nonresidence portion does not qualify. In this case, the buyer is well advised to arrange for two separate escrows. Who knows, some day he may want to sell the nonresidence (nonpersonal) land separately from his residence.

Similarly, if one buys a large undivided parcel of land with a farmhouse, ranchhouse, or estatehouse on it — say 40 acres again — he has made two purchases. Because the land is undivided, ordinarily there would be only one escrow. In this case, the buyer might want to instruct the escrow agent to prepare the closing statement in two parts. One part should be designated as personal residence. It should have attached to it a photocopy of the local zoning ordinance. The second part of the settlement statement could be the nonpersonal land surrounding the residence. A map plot should be attached to the second part of the escrow. Figure 6.1 is presented to help illustrate the principles above. There has to be some boundary beyond which land has other uses.

We must point out that there is a Section 121 distinction between excess acreage and adjacent vacant land. The distinction is addressed in Regulation § 1.121-1(b)(3): *Vacant land*. The term "vacant land" is that land which is adjacent to the land containing the dwelling unit and is used as a part thereof. If such land is not sold simultaneously with the residence, it may still qualify as such . . . IF. That is, if the adjacent land is sold . . . *within 2 years before or 2 years after* . . . the sale of the residence. However sold, the residence and vacant land constitute a **single unit** for purposes of the $250,000/$500,000 exclusion of gain.

Term "Basis" Defined

With the allowability of such a large exclusion amount in Section 121 ($250,000/$500,000), the IRS will be very fastidious about what constitutes one's principal residence. This makes it all the more important that you know precisely the extent of your tax basis . . . for return of capital.

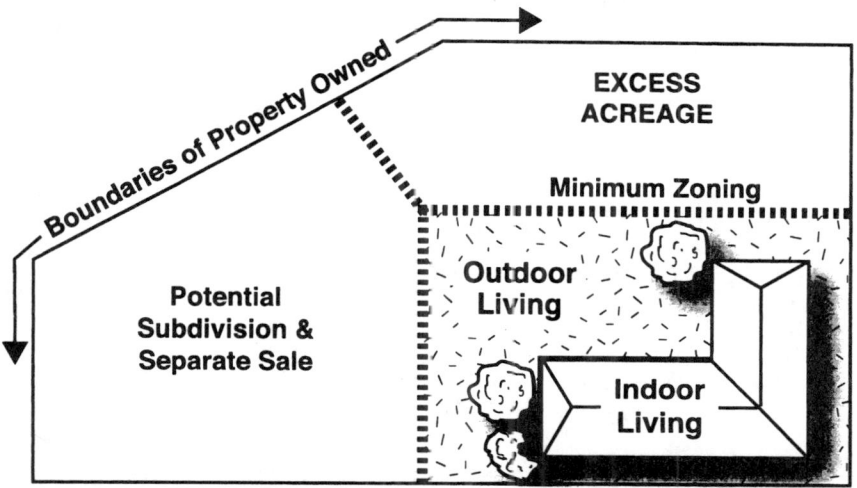

Fig. 6.1 - "Residence" Limited to Personal Living Space

The term "basis" is a tax accounting concept which describes the amount of capital invested in property, up to the point of its sale. It is a cumulative term covering all costs, improvements, and adjustments to cost, from date of acquisition to day before date of sale. It is the basis for determining gain or loss from such sale. It is that amount which goes in Column (e): *Cost or other basis*, on Schedule D of your Form 1040.

If you buy a residence with your own funds, make no improvements, experience no casualties, and have no local assessments against it, your basis is simply your acquisition cost. But this is a rarity. Usually, acquisition cost, or other acquisition basis, is merely the starting point. There are various subsequent adjustments to make.

Although, technically, you could sell your residence every two "plus" years and enjoy the exclusion-of-gain benefits, usually there are a number of years between acquisition and sale. During the interim, many homeowners make changes to their residence. They add built-ins; they make improvements; they change the landscaping; they do some remodeling; they install a new roof. Rarely do they take the time to keep their basis records up to date.

When no records, the IRS asserts a "zero" basis. When the time comes to sell, poor basis records translate directly into higher taxes than necessary . . . even with the Section 121 exclusion amount.

So that you'll understand why "tax basis" is so important when selling your home, let us present the computational sequence of events for arriving at "gain on sale."

Step 1 — Selling price of home

Step 2 — Expense of sale

Step 3 — **Subtract** Step 2 from Step 1

Step 4 — BASIS OF HOME SOLD

Step 5 — **Subtract** Step 4 from Step 3
(This is your **Gain on sale**)

Obviously, the higher the basis of the home that you sell, the lower the gain (for a given selling price) . . . and the lower the taxes (whenever). Therefore, you want to include everything that you legitimately can in your tax basis.

Basis When Purchased

The basis of a residence which is purchased is its cost. However, because of the mish-mash of escrow procedures, the initial cost of property to a buyer is more than just the purchase price alone. To the purchase price there are added other items of cost that are frequently overlooked. Such costs are—

1. Buying costs
2. Mortgage costs
3. Title costs
4. Transfer costs
5. Appraisal costs
6. Closing costs

All of these are "add on" costs to the purchase price agreed to between buyer and seller. These are called capital costs because they cannot be recovered until the property is sold. Hence, they are "capitalized" and become part of the investment in your home.

Buying costs are all those which precede an accepted offer to a candidate seller. Examples of such costs are referral fees, tax counseling, exploratory expenses, advertisements, legal fees, preparation of sales contract, and so on. Most persons do not keep track of these costs, and so they are rarely documented. However, if one makes a deposit on a residence, and later forfeits it for some reason, such an outlay is usually documented. A forfeited deposit is indeed a buying cost which is an add-on to the initial basis of whatever home is ultimately purchased.

Mortgage costs are those associated with satisfying the lender that the buyer is credit-worthy and employment-capable of paying off the mortgage loan(s). Title costs are those associated with title search, perfection, and recordation. Transfer costs are those associated with local government services, transfer privileges, stamp taxes, improvement assessments, and special liens. Appraisal costs are those for inspections and valuations. Closing costs are those necessary for completing the transaction between buyer and seller.

Because these add-on costs are not uniformly standard, the possible variants in each category are itemized in Figure 6.2.

BUYING COSTS	MORTGAGE COSTS
● House-hunting travel	● Loan application fee
● Deposit forfeitures	● Inspection / appraisal fees
● Finders fee / referrals	● Credit checkout
● Tax counseling	● Assumption / refinance fee
● Preparation of contract	● Loan discount fee
TITLE COSTS	TRANSFER COSTS
● Title search abstract	● City transfer tax
● Title insurance	● County transfer tax
● Attorney fees	● Local assessments
● Document preparation	● Special district fees
● Recording fees	● Removal of liens

CLOSING COSTS	
● Covenant abstracts	● Pest inspection
● Notary fees	● Mandated repairs
● Delinquent taxes	● Closing fees

Fig. 6.2 - Capitalized Costs When Purchasing a Home

Every home buyer is given a *Settlement Statement* by the escrow agent or attorney involved. This statement details the actual costs (other than buying costs) in Figure 6.2 applicable to one's own acquisition. This statement is the most important "starting document" for establishing the cost (or acquisition) basis in your current residence.

Personal Items Discounted

The settlement statement also includes other items of cost which are not chargeable to your capital investment. There are three categories of such costs, namely: (a) items which are deductible on your tax return in the year of purchase; (b) operating expenses which are not deductible ever; and (c) personal items which are lumped in with the deal. All of these must be separated out; they are not part of the investment in your home.

Those closing expenses which are tax deductible in the year of purchase (and *not* capitalized) are—

1. loan origination fees,
2. prorata interest on mortgages, and
3. prorata property taxes.

Loan origination fees are treated as prepaid mortgage interest, when computed as a direct percentage of the loan principal. The prorations of taxes and interest commence on the day of purchase and are extended on the escrow statement to the next regularly scheduled payment date. These expenses are deductible as taxes and interest on Schedule A (Form 1040).

Those closing items which are not tax deductible ever are—

1. mortgage insurance,
2. hazard insurance,
3. impound reserves,
4. personal debts, and
5. temporary rent.

Mortgage insurance is nothing more than life insurance on the buyer, whereby the mortgagor (lender) is the named beneficiary.

Upon death of the buyer, the mortgage is paid off. Even though required by the mortgagor, life insurance on a buyer is not a cost of investment, nor is it income tax deductible.

Similarly, hazard insurance (fire, flood, earthquake, vandalism, theft) is neither an investment cost nor a tax deduction. Impound reserves are advance payments required by the mortgagor to cover liens against your property for which he is not responsible. Personal debts in a settlement statement are usually those which some creditors insist on payment before giving you a favorable credit rating. An unfavorable rating can hold up your sale.

Temporary rental of one's intended residence, before title transfer, is purely a personal expense. Because of other inconveniences in your personal living, a seller may allow you to move into his property before escrow is closed. For this courtesy, he is entitled to charge you rent. In no way does this rental charge influence your capital investment in the property. Your rental payments are no different from renting a dwelling elsewhere.

Personal property items included in a settlement statement are *not* part of the real property that you are purchasing. Such items as furniture, furnishings, and fixtures often are purchased as a package with one's residence. These are items that can be readily removed by hand or with hand tools (washer/dryer, for example). These are not integral parts of the residence structure. Therefore, special awareness is required to identify these personal property items in order to deduct their cost from the settlement statement, for tax basis purposes.

Basis When Exchange-Acquired

As touched on a few pages back, there are two forms of exchange-acquired residences. One form, essentially obsolete, is the former Section 1034 rollover of gain from one personal residence to another such residence. The more currently used form is a Section 1031 like-kind exchange. The term "like-kind" refers to the conveyance of productive (business) or investment (rental) use property in exchange for similar property acquired. If the acquired property is of the type suitable for residential rental use, it must be held as such for at least one full year. After this minimum period of time, that which was acquired as a rental residence can be self-converted to the owner's principal residence . . . by personally occupying it.

In both the 1034 and 1031 exchanges, one common misperception prevails. Both forms are marketed as tax-free exchanges. They are NOT tax free; they are **tax-deferred**!

That which is tax deferred is the amount of realized capital gain that is held in suspense (as it were) until the property is ultimately sold (outright). In the meantime, how is the deferred gain basis-accounted-for? The quick answer is that the deferred gain *subtracts from* the prior-to-exchange cost basis of the property conveyed. This reduced basis is then transferred to the exchange-acquired property as its **basis transfer**. We depict this feature for you in Figure 6.3. Note that a Down Exchange invokes taxable gain, whereas an Up Exchange **adds** to the basis transfer.

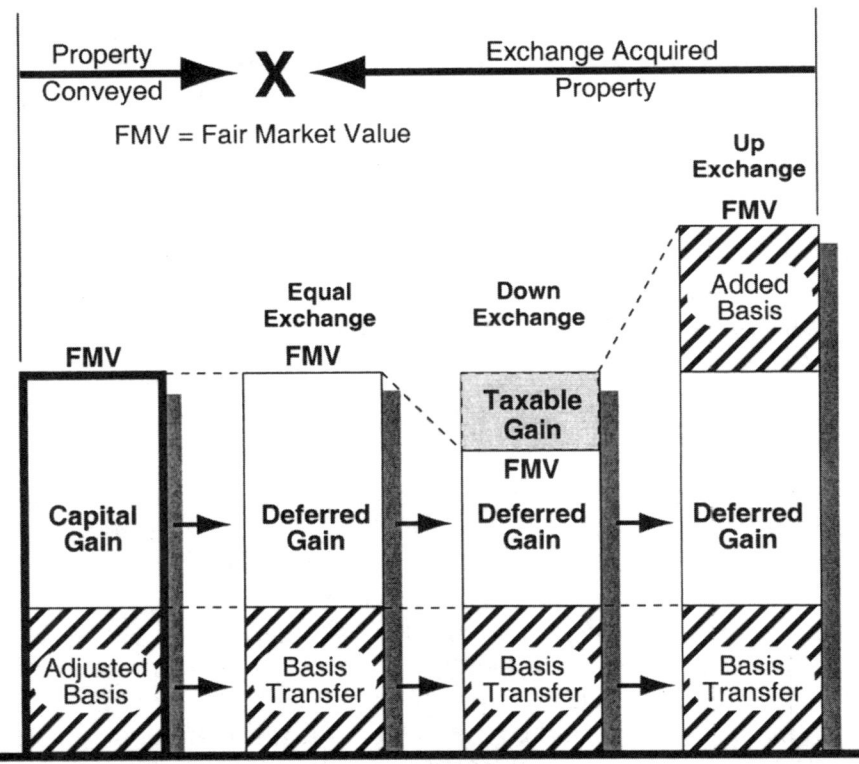

Fig. 6.3 - Fundamental Features of Any Tax Tax Qualified Exchange

For example, suppose a parcel of section 1031 property were purchased for $200,000 (including all related costs). Further assume that the property were exchanged for a parcel FMVed at $500,000. Were it not a tax-deferred exchange, the $300,000 capital gain (500,000 – 200,000) would be taxed. Instead, the basis in the property acquired is reduced from its $500,000 FMV to $200,000. [The term "FMV" is noted in Figure 6.3 as: Fair Market Value.]

In addition to the transfer basis, other costs will be involved. These will consist of exchange expenses, broker fees, "facilitator" fees (for expert exchange counseling), cash paid or received, "boot" (other than cash) conveyed or received (to achieve equality of the two FMVs), increased debt assumption (if any), and ordinary title and closing costs. the result is a new start basis as depicted in Figure 6.4.

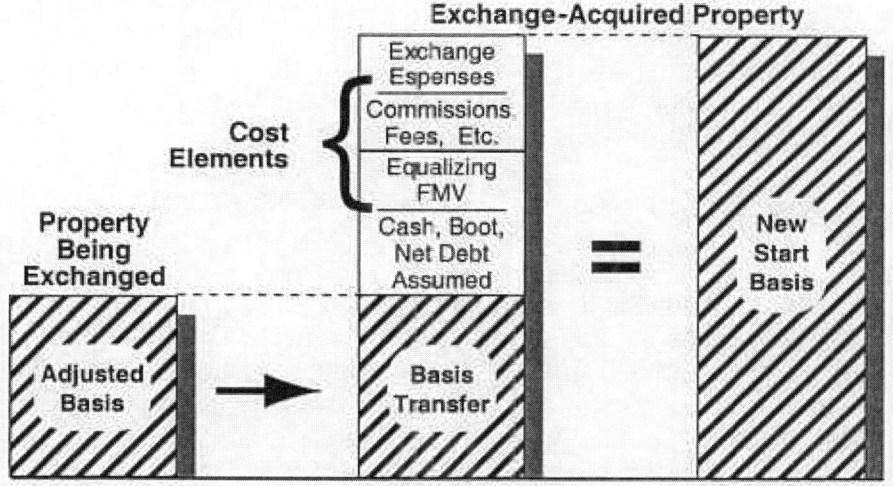

Fig. 6.4 - The "Cost" Elements in Basis of Exchange - Acquired Property

Basis When Gifted

When property valued at more than $12,000 (in 2006) is gifted to a donee, a federal gift tax return is required. This is **Form 709**: *U.S. Gift Tax Return*. (The $12,000 is an *annual* exclusion amount.) Form 709 contains such information as—

A. donor's adjusted basis in the property,
B. date of gift (evidenced by a Gift Deed),
C. fair market value on date of gift (evidenced by a professional appraisal), and
D. amount of gift tax allocable (even if exempted).

There is a special rule for determining basis in property acquired by gift. It is embodied in IRC Section 1015: ***Basis of Property Acquired by Gifts and Transfers in Trust***. Though complicated, its gist is that basis in the hands of the donee is—

1. the donor's adjusted basis

OR

2. the fair market value

whichever is *lower*. The "whichever lower" is then increased by an "appreciation fraction" for the amount of gift tax computed. Usually, but not always, the donor's adjusted basis is lower.

As a general rule, the *donee's basis* becomes:

$$\text{Donor's basis} + \left[\text{Computed gift tax} \times \frac{\text{Net appreciation}}{\text{Fair market value}}\right]$$

"Net appreciation" is the amount by which the fair market value of the gift exceeds the donor's adjusted basis immediately before the gift. The "computed gift tax" is that which appears on Form 709 for the calendar year of the gift, after adjustments for prior-year gifts (if any). Cumulative prior gifts increase the rate of tax. The gift tax rates are graduated from 20% to 45%.

Suppose, for example, that a father gave his daughter a residence worth $182,000. He paid $65,000 for the property, as adjusted. Assuming the father made no other gifts, what is the daughter's basis in her residence?

Using Form 709, the computed gift tax is $45,200. This figure derives from the gift tax table for a total taxable gift of $170,000 (that is: $182,000 less the $12,000 annual exclusion). Note use of the word "computed" gift tax. The amount of tax actually paid may well be zero. This is because, in addition to the annual exclusion, there is allowed a *lifetime* exclusion up to $1,000,000 (Section 2505: *Unified Credit Against Gift Tax*).

Putting numbers in the expression above, the daughter's basis would be—

$$65,000 + \left[45,200 \ \times \ \frac{(182,000 - 65,000)}{182,000} \right]$$

$$= 65,000 + \left[45,200 \ \times \ \frac{117}{182} \right] \quad \text{where } \frac{117}{182} = 0.6429$$

$$= 65,000 + 29,060 = \mathbf{94,060} \quad (45,200 \times 0.6429 = 29,060)$$

There are problems with this gift-basis computation. The donor, being a sincere and generous person, does not think to provide the donee a copy of his gift tax return with attachments (basis computations, fair market appraisal, and gift deed). The donee, being grateful and appreciative, does not want to embarrass the donor by requesting such personal financial information. Furthermore, at time of gifting, neither party thinks ahead to the time when the residence may be sold By such time, the donor may have misplaced his copy of the gift tax or may have died.

The message above should be self-evident. That is, the donee must have a copy of the donor's gift tax return (Form 709) with all of its attachments and computations. If this is not obtained at the time of the gift, the donee must specifically ask the donor for it, before the gifted residence is sold.

Basis When Inherited

The basis of a residence acquired by bequest or inheritance from a decedent is its fair market value on the date of the decedent's death. If so elected by the executor, an "alternate valuation date" of six months after date of death may be used (Section 1014).

In case of real property left by a decedent, many states require some form of inheritance tax declaration. An appendage to this declaration is an *Inventory and Appraisement*. On this is recorded an official valuation of the residence by an appointed referee.

Once this valuation is professionally established, it is unlikely to be changed by the IRS (when there are no irregularities).

Inheritance taxes are based on the value of property in the inventory and appraisement. Ordinarily, these taxes are paid out of the liquid assets of the decedent's estate. If liquid assets are insufficient, then some of the assets have to be sold to pay the taxes. If the residence to be inherited is a candidate for such "estate sale," the heir or legatee designated to receive the property has the option of paying "his" proportionate share of the taxes in lieu of the sale. In this case, payment of the proportionate share of the decedent's death taxes is added to the basis of the residence inherited. Doing so is advisable only when it makes sound economic sense, devoid of family emotional issues.

When property is acquired from a decedent (**other than joint tenancy**), there is a substantial time lag between the inherited rights of ownership and actual physical dominion and control. This time lag can be on the order of nine months or more. Yet, the legal right of ownership commences upon the decedent's death.

Invariably, there are many personal property items accompanying a residence upon death. Such items are personal clothing, artifacts, furnishings, furniture, appurtenances, and other paraphernalia. If any of these items is valued in the inventory and appraisement for death tax purposes, care must be taken to separate such values from the appraised value of the residence itself.

The term "death tax" is a federal designation whereas the term "inheritance tax" is a state designation. Where applicable, the federal death tax established on Form 706: *U.S. Estate (and Generation-Skipping) Transfer Tax Return*. This is a straight-out tax for the privilege of transferring property to others gratuitously. Because of the federal exemption amounts ($1,000,000 to $3,000,000 depending on year of death), a Form 706 is not always required. If such is the case, a professional appraisal of the inherited residence must be expressly obtained. Otherwise, the FMV of the inherited residence is designated as Item 1 on Schedule A – *Real Estate* of Form 706. Either a separate appraisal or a Schedule A (706) is a "must" for acquisition basis purposes when real property is inherited.

In the event that probate (proving of title transfer) is required, an *Order Directing Final Distribution* is issued by the probate court. This order, assigning the inheritee title to the residence, has the same effect as a title deed in an ordinary purchase. To give public notice of the acquisition, the court order should be recorded in official records of the county where the property is located. If no probate is required, the executor for the decedent's estate must retitle the inherited residence similarly.

In the case of joint tenancy (with right of survivorship), no probate is required. The surviving joint tenant acquires clear title by "operation of state law." In this case, the surviving joint tenant needs to pay for a professional appraisal of the property (fair market value) at the time of the decedent's death.

Improvements Add to Basis

Upon acquisition of one's residence — by purchase, exchange, gift, or inheritance — the next course of events, usually, is making improvements thereto. Improvements are those cost outlays which increase the capital investment in the property. Consequently, improvements *add* to the basis of property.

For a personal residence, there is a definite tax distinction between improvements and maintenance. Improvements are those expenditures which are "fixed to" the structure of the residence, and increase its value beyond that at the time of its acquisition. Maintenance, on the other hand, is that expenditure which restores the property to its value when acquired. Improvements *enhance* the existing structure and equipment, whereas maintenance repairs and restores. Improvements are basis recognized; repairs and maintenance are not.

There are subtleties to the basis distinction between improvements and maintenance. A few examples may help to clarify these subtleties.

Suppose one paints a room in his home. Is that an improvement or maintenance?

It depends. If the walls previously were unpainted or were papered, then painting would be an improvement. The surfaces have been changed: improved. If nothing else, there could be aesthetic improvement that could enhance the value when sold. But if the walls previously were painted, then repainting them (regardless of change in color) would be maintenance.

If one repaints two rooms in a six-room house, what is that? It is maintenance. But if one repaints all six rooms in their entirety, that is an improvement. The rationale is that one has upgraded the entire internal structure, and by so doing has extended its useful life. Whether it does so or not is another matter.

Suppose, now, one repaints his entire house, inside and out. And suppose he has done this three times while living there prior to sale. Has he made one improvement or three improvements? One improvement: the very last complete repainting job. A homeowner cannot repeat an improvement and have it count more than once. Only the last one adds value.

Just one more example. Suppose the water heater goes out (or any other built-in appliance) and it is replaced. If it is replaced with exactly the same model, construction, and capacity as the old one, it is maintenance. If it is replaced with a different model, different construction, and larger capacity, an improvement has been made. The larger capacity alone is a new benefit.

In the majority of situations, it is fairly obvious as to what is an improvement and what is not. A listing of the many forms of home improvements is presented in Figure 6.5. The listing is illustrative only; it is not exhaustive. The intent of Figure 6.5 is to stimulate the segregation of expenditures into those which are tax recognized for basis purposes.

Virtually every home improvement that one makes can be documented by a receipt from the seller or service person involved. Any single improvement costing $1,000 or more should be documented with a job description, installation contract, and/or loan application. For improvements less than $1,000, cash-register receipts or other personal notations and records, suitably dated, are acceptable documentation. All such receipts and documents are tax-important when the home is sold. It is tragic how careless most homeowners are on the recordkeeping of their improvements.

One final note on improvements. A homeowner's personal labor does not count! If you buy the materials and parts and do the installation yourself, only the materials and parts count. If you pay someone else to do the work (who is not a member of your household), then the cost of that labor is an improvement. The value of your own labor is presumably translated into greater capital gain, when your home is eventually sold.

INTERIOR SURFACES	BUILT-IN APPLIANCES
● Carpets & drapes ● Paneling & wallpaper ● Complete repainting ● Wall mirrors ● Planter boxes / cabinets	● Stove, oven, bar ● Washer, dryer, dishwasher ● Heating & A/C system ● Water heater / softener ● Garbage disposal / compactor
STRUCTURAL REMODELING	EXTERIOR ATTACHMENTS
● Floors / basements ● Walls, doors, windows ● Bathroom(s) & kitchen ● Termite renovations ● Adding on rooms	● Insulation / storm windows ● New roof or porch ● Sun shades / solar panels ● Finishing basement / garage ● Cable & TV antenna
RECREATIONAL FEATURES	FOUNDATION LANDSCAPING
● Patio : slab or deck ● Barbeque & benches ● Playhouse / playrooms ● Swimming pool & shower ● Pet runs & kennels	● Trees & lampposts ● Lawn & shrubbery ● Sprinkler system ● Fencing & gates ● Walkways / driveways

Fig. 6.5 - Categories of Capital Improvements to Residence

Adjustments to Basis

For tax accounting purposes, the total basis in your residence consists of three elements, namely: acquisition, improvements, and adjustments. The term "adjustments" involves factors of ownership and investment *other than* acquisition and improvements. There are "plus" adjustments and there are "minus" adjustments.

For example, if you refinance your home to obtain money for other investments or for paying off personal debts, the refinance costs (*not* the usable money obtained) become a plus adjustment.

Similarly, if title to your residence is clouded by legal attack, or by judgment liens, the cost of clearing and protecting title is a plus adjustment. Other plus adjustments include assessments by local governments for community improvements and capital expenditures (such as streets, lighting, parking areas, cemetery districts, sewerage systems and so on).

Now, suppose that your residence suffers fire, flood, earthquake, or other casualty damage and that your insurance covers all replacement costs. And suppose that you do the work yourself. There is a minus adjustment to basis. For example, if you spend 70% of the insurance reimbursement and pocket 30% for yourself, the 30% is *return of capital*. Basiswise, this reduces the capital investment in your residence.

A major *minus* adjustment occurs when acquiring a residence via a Section 1031 or Section 1034 exchange. The tax deferment concept rests computationally upon the FMV (fair market value) of the exchanged-conveyed property. The FMV is treated as its "sales price" for computation of its realized capital gain. As discussed previously and presented in Figure 6.3, all gain realized is deferred. Thereupon, the deferred amount becomes a sub-traction from, or minus adjustment to, the FMV.

There are other minus adjustments as well. For example, you might sell off part of your residence, such as a corner of land or some detachable structure. Or, you might put your residence up for sale, get a deposit, and the sale falls through. If so, you get to keep the deposit. These and similar situations are called "partial sales." Any money derived from a partial sale is return of capital; it becomes a *minus* adjustment.

The whole purpose of adjustments to basis is to keep a running account of the actual capital put into, or taken out of, your residence. If you do not do this diligently, there is good possibility of paying more capital gain tax than is necessary.

Basis: Mixed-Use Residence

The term "mixed use" means that your residence has been, or is being, used also for business purposes. The business may be conducted in-home or out-of-home in a separate structure on your residence land. Any business use of residential property, whether in home or out, is subject to a tax deduction allowance called: *Depreciation* (Code Section 167). The IRS publishes tables of depreciation allowances for all kinds of business-use property.

In the case of residential property, if the business use is for rental purposes, the depreciable life is 27.5 years. If used for production, sales, or service-type activities, the depreciable life is

39 years. Whether 27.5 or 39 years, the method of depreciation is straight line, all the way. No accelerated depreciation on residential property is allowed.

The portion of your residence used for business must be fractioned off and a business-use basis established. (The fractioning concept involved is depicted in Figure 6.6). Assume, for example, that the business use fraction (whether in home or out of home) is 18.6% or 0.186. Also assume that the acquisition-adjusted basis in your residence is $390,000. In this case, your business use basis would be:

$390,000 x 0.186 = $72,540

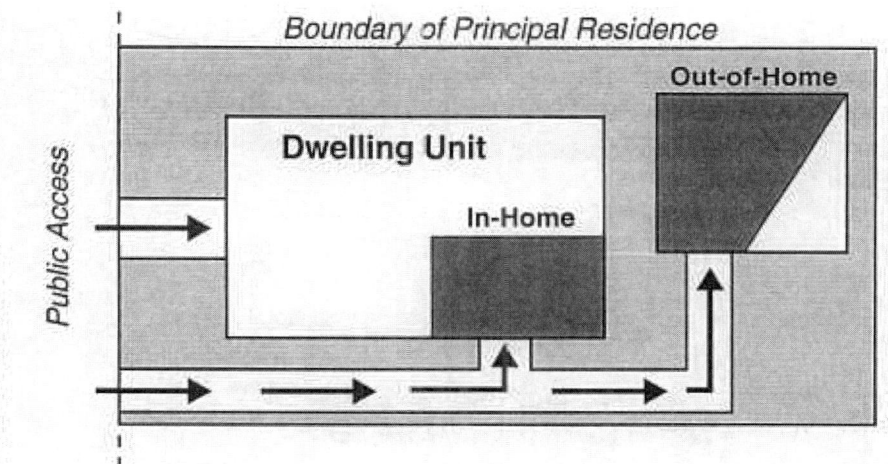

Fig. 6.6 - Fractioning the Business Use Portion of a Residence

If rental use, the depreciation (tax deduction) would be—

$72,540 ÷ 27.5 yrs = $2,638 per year.

If productive use, the annual depreciation allowance would be—

$72,540 ÷ 39 yrs = $1,860 per year.

The total depreciation allowed is the annual amount times the number of years used for business.

For example, if the depreciation deduction allowed was $3,000 per year, for 6 years, the cumulative total would be $18,000

($3,000/yr x 6 yrs). When your $390,000 residence is sold, its "adjusted basis" (assuming no other adjustments than depreciation) would be $372,000 (390,000 – 18,000). Thus, obviously, any business-use depreciation taken becomes a minus adjustment to your residence basis.

When depreciable property is sold, there is normally what is called: *depreciation recovery.* That is, since the depreciation was treated as a deduction against ordinary income, its "recovery" is treated as reverse ordinary income. How this plays out in Section 121 sales depends on other factors. We'll cover such factors in Chapter 10: Prorata Business Use.

Meanwhile, we summarize the basis rules below:

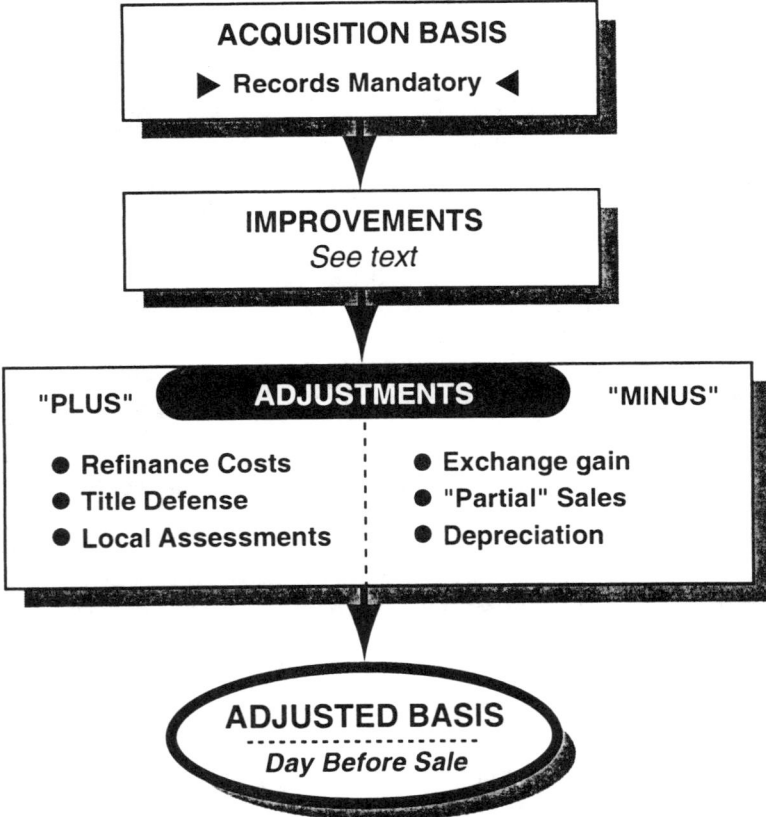

Fig. 6.7 - Summary of Basis Rules: Current Residence

7

SALES PRICE REPORTINGS

A "Real Estate Reporting Person" Is A Title Company, Attorney, Or Broker Who Prepares An Itemized Statement Of Your Account, When Your Residence Is Sold. A Duty Imposed On Him Is To Report The GROSS PROCEEDS (Selling Price) To The IRS On FORM 1099-S. A Copy Is Furnished To You, Along With Other Closing Papers ("Tons" Of Them). The "Sale," However, Does Not Close Until The Grant Deed To The New Owner (Which You Signed) Is Recorded In Official Records Where The Property Is Located. You Want A Copy Of The Recorded Deed, And A Copy Of The Cashier's Check To You, For Tax Record Purposes.

For many years, the IRS has been pressuring Congress for direct authority over middlemen (brokers) between sellers and buyers of capital assets. The initial such authority was granted via the Tax Reform Act of 1976. A then-new IR Code section was added, namely: Section 6045 — *Returns of Brokers*. The intended "returns" are *information returns*. Each is a tax information return along the lines of a Form W-2: Wage and Tax Statement. Instead of "wages," it is a **Gross Proceeds** statement showing the Tax IDs of broker and customer (the transferor/seller).

Section 6045 defines broker and customer as—

The term "broker" includes . . . any person who (for a consideration) regularly acts as a middleman with respect to property or services.

The term "customer" means any person for whom the broker has transacted any business.

Statements of gross proceeds paid, etc., were to be made on official forms prescribed by the IRS, with a copy going to each payee (customer). The idea was to tax the gross proceeds as wages, unless the payee self-reported the transaction on his own return.

The Tax Reform Act of 1986 extended the broker reporting requirements to real estate transactions. This was accomplished by adding a new subsection to Section 6045, namely: subsection (**e**) — ***Return Required in the Case of Real Estate Transactions***. Additional amendments to Section 6045(e) were made, pursuant to the Taxpayer Relief Act of 1997. The "relief" was supposedly accomplished by increasing the burden on brokers, thereby relieving some of the burden from taxpayers and home sellers. Still, one has to keep an eye on his real estate broker.

Not only do we want to cover in this chapter the specifics of Section 6045(e), we must also tell you of the information return form used, namely: **Form 1099-S**. If there are multiple co-owners of a residence who are not husband and wife, instructing the sale closing agent as to the exact ownership percentage of each co-owner is extremely important. Also, we will tell you about the general information found on a title deed which — now more than ever — becomes vital tax information for the IRS. Throughout this chapter, we want you to keep in mind one key point. Under the provisions of Section 121 (the exclusion of gain allowance), every home sale is now a closed separate tax event of its own. Being aware of this point, you want to assure yourself that your broker reports to the IRS correctly what he is supposed to . . . and nothing more. Otherwise, you'll spend years fending off the IRS's computer tyranny — called "e-harassing" — that can be unleashed against you. So, be forewarned.

Introduction to Section 6045(e)

Code Section 6045(e) applies to all real estate transactions closing after August 5, 1997. It applies to ALL broker transactions whether residential or nonresidential buildings, or whether raw land, farm land, or resource land.

The required reporting to the IRS is made electronically or on paper . . . **at time of sale**. It is not made at the end of the year, unless the sale itself occurs at year end. Nor is the reporting — on Form 1099-S — mailed separately to the homeseller in January or February, as is customary for all other 1099 forms and W-2s. When there is an IRS penalty on the line — potentially up to $100,000 each year [Code Sec. 7203] — brokers are going to report every residential sale at time of sale, regardless of any inconvenience to the seller.

Section 6045(e), as it stands after the amendments which take Section 121 into account, consists of about 500 words. It is arranged into five paragraphs which are titled as:

(1) In General —
(2) Real Estate Reporting Person —
(3) Prohibition of Separate Charge for Filing Return —
(4) Additional Information Required —
(5) Exceptions for Sales or Exchanges of Certain Principal Residences — [those less than $250,000].

Paragraph (1) is short . . . and quite demanding. It reads as—

*In the case of **a** real estate transaction, the real estate reporting person **shall file a return** under subsection (a)* [reporting the gross proceeds] *and a statement under subsection (b)* [copy furnished to each customer] *with respect to such transaction.* [Emphasis added.]

Note the emphasized phrase: "shall file a return." What is not stated in subsection (e), nor elsewhere in Section 6045, is that there is a $50 penalty for failing to file a return with respect to each separate real estate transaction. There is also a $50 penalty for failing to file a correct return; another $50 penalty for failing to correct an incorrect return; and another $50 penalty for failing to file a "complete" return with all of the information required by the IRS. If there is any *willful failure* involved, the reporting person's penalty jumps to $25,000 [Section 7204].

The paragraph (1) reference to subsection (a) of Section 6045 goes back to the general rule for all broker reportings, whether or not real estate transactions are involved. Subsection (a) reads in principal part as—

> *Every person doing business as a broker shall . . . make a return, . . . showing the name and address of each customer, with such details regarding* **gross proceeds** *and such* **other information** *as the* [IRS] *may by forms or regulations require.* [Emphasis added.]

Note particularly that it is the *gross proceeds* that are reported to the IRS. This is the gross selling price of a principal residence (or any other real estate property). There are no offsets for selling expenses, broker commissions, cost basis of residence sold, and other cost information. "Why only gross proceeds?" you may ask.

Answer: The IRS treats the gross proceeds as the taxation equivalent of gross wages and salaries, similar to the reportings on a W-2 form. If the payee (home seller) fails to correspondingly report the gross proceeds on his next regular tax return, he is electronically tagged by the IRS with a "gross proceeds tax." This tax, with its penalty and interest add-ons will definitely get your attention. The gross proceeds in a real estate sale are usually much greater than the gross wages and salaries paid to a home owner.

Statement Furnished to You

Paragraph (1) of subsection (e) also references subsection (b) of Section 6045. Subsection (b) is titled: **Statements to be Furnished to Customers**. The gist of this subsection is—

> *Every person required to make a return under subsection (a) shall furnish to each customer whose name is required to be set forth in such return a* **written statement** *showing—*

all information that is electronically reported to the IRS by the real estate closing broker. The electronic reporting of tax information is a tax mining bonanza for the IRS.

What is the written statement?

Answer: It is a specific IRS form designated as **Form 1099-S**. (The "S" signifies "Sale" of real estate.) The official title of this form is: ***Proceeds from Real Estate Transactions***.   The "furnishing" aspect consists of—

Copy A — for IRS
Copy B — for Transferor (seller)
Copy C — for Filer (reporting broker)

Copies A and C are electronically filed and stored, whereas Copy B is paper furnished to the seller whose name first appears on the title deed of the property being sold.

The tax information on Copy B of Form 1099-S consists of:

Box 1.   Date of closing (month, day, year)
Box 2.   Gross proceeds $_____
         [Gross proceeds is the full selling price unreduced by selling expenses, sales commissions, and tax basis.]
Box 3.   Address or legal description (of property sold)
Box 4.   Transferor received or will receive property or services as part of the consideration (if checked)
         ▶ ☐
Box 5.   Buyer's part of real estate tax $_____

We present in Figure 7.1 an abbreviated version of IRS Form 1099-S. The official paper form is about 3¼" by 7" in size.

FORM 1099-S	FILER'S Name & Address	Year 20___	Proceeds From Real Estate Transactions	
FILER'S Fed. ID No.	TRANSFEROR'S Soc. Sec. No.	Date of Closing	Gross $ Proceeds	Copy A IRS
TRANSFEROR'S Name & Address		Address or legal description of property sold		Copy B Seller
Account No. ____		Check if consideration is other than cash ▶☐		Copy C Filer

Fig. 7.1 - Highly Edited & Abbreviated Version of Form 1099-S

Note that, for instructional purposes here, three boxes are bold emphasized. The three are: (1) Transferor's Soc. Sec. No., (2) Date of Closing, and (3) Gross Proceeds. These are primarily only what the IRS wants to see. The term "Filer" is used to identify the "real estate reporting person." The term "Transferor" is used instead of "seller" because it signifies the legal transfer of title from the owner/seller to the buyer/owner.

Preprinted instructions on the face of Copy B say—

This is important tax information and is being furnished to the Internal Revenue Service. If you are required to file a return, a negligence penalty or other sanction may be imposed on you if this item is required to be reported and the IRS determines that it has not been reported [by you].

What this instruction is telling you is that, somewhere on your own tax return (for the year of sale), you have to exact-match the gross proceeds amount. We'll explain how to do so in Chapter 8: Claiming Your Exclusion.

Way before Form 1099-S is prepared, there are many activities to be performed by you, and many duties to be performed by your broker. A bird's-eye foretaste is presented in Figure 7.2

As a homeseller/taxpayer, you should feel more comfortable with the broker reporting the sale, followed by your reporting it on your own tax return. You can compute your capital gain, and show specifically the amount of exclusion you are allowed. Should you be audited one day, you'll have something in writing on your return to explain that the tax free money you have was not ill gotten. You earned it; you reported it; it was properly excludable.

Title Passing Is "Sale"

A sale occurs when legal title to property passes from a former owner to a new owner; that is, when title passes from seller to buyer (from "transferor" to "transferee"). This legal passing occurs upon "closing of escrow" via a real estate title company or a real estate attorney. The title company or title attorney is a third-party interest who verifies that a bona fide transfer has occurred, and that it was legally recorded in official records.

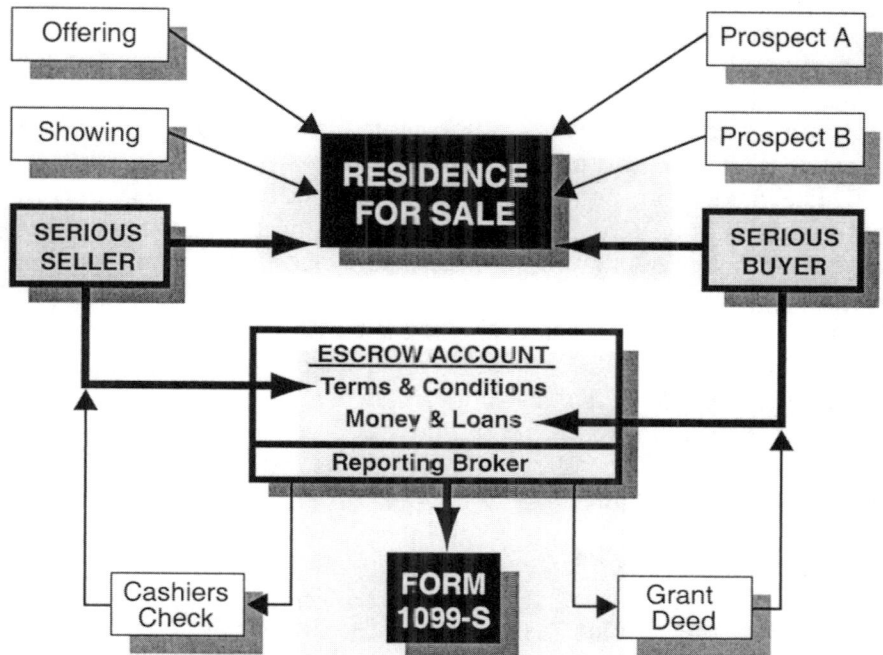

Fig. 7.2 - Escrow Duties for Real Estate Closing Transactions

Title passes only after the signatures of both seller and buyer appear on the escrow settlement papers. It is not uncommon for either seller or buyer to sign the closing papers a few days, or even a few weeks, before the other party signs. These are matters of practical convenience. Nevertheless, until the second signature appears, title is in limbo. The property still belongs to the seller, even though he himself may have signed it off.

The term "second signature' is collective. If there is a husband and wife, or other co-owner seller, the two (or more) co-owners constitute one signature. Similarly, if there is a husband and wife, or other co-owner buyer, the two (or more) co-owners constitute one signature. Thus, all signatures of seller(s) and of buyer(s) must be complete and officially recorded before title passes.

To illustrate the crucial importance of *title passing*, here's a true story. Husband and wife sold their home and signed all papers. Husband and wife buyers also signed all papers, including the check for their down payment. All of this was consummated after close of business hours, midweek. It was agreed that the title transfer would be recorded "first thing" the next morning. Upon departing the escrow office, the buyers asked the sellers for the keys to the empty house so that they could plan placement of furniture and selection of colors for furnishings. The sellers consented and handed over the keys.

The next morning, the house had burned down. The buyers immediately intervened and stopped recording of the title transfer. After the fire investigation, it was determined that the buyers were at fault. They had turned on several wall heaters in the empty/cold house, and inadvertently left one of their own coats over one of the wall heaters. Of course, there were law suits. But the end legal pronouncement was that the house had not been sold. It was still the sellers' house when it burned down. The buyers lost only their down payment. The sellers lost their house, though they retained ownership of the land.

Sale Procedures Confusing

Selling one's home is accompanied by much emotion and commotion. There are anticipations, expectations, and disappointments. Offers and counter-offers whisk back and forth. Many financial arrangements are proposed. Compromises are made. Many pieces of paper are signed . . . and re-signed. Invariably, foul-ups and misunderstandings arise, and more documents have to be signed.

Selling real estate is not like selling a piece of furniture. To be legal, the sale must be a written contract, and the title transfer therewith ultimately has to be recorded in official records in the county where the property is located. The procedures can be confusing and misleading as to when title actually passes. The burned-down house in the example above makes our point.

The mere signing of a sales contract by both parties does not, of itself, constitute a sale for tax reporting purposes. Nor does the offer and acceptance of earnest money deposit constitute a sale. Neither does the completion of the down payment. A sales contract is an itemization of mutually agreed-to conditions that must be satisfied in full, before the seller relinquishes his title rights to the property. Relinquishment does not take place until a title deed is officially recorded.

The transfer of title to real estate is legally signified by a *deed*. This instrument may be called a grant deed, trust deed, title deed, quitclaim deed, gift deed, or other nomenclature involving the word "deed." The transfer**or/grantor** of the deed is the seller: he who conveys title. The transfer**ee/grantee** of the deed is the buyer: he who accepts title.

After all terms of the sales contract are met and all financial arrangements made, a closing (or settlement) statement is prepared by the escrow officer or attorney overseeing the transaction. This includes preparation of a deed showing transfer of legal title.

A simplified format of a title deed is presented in Figure 7.3. Note that it contains the names of the seller(s) and buyer(s). Note that only the signature of the seller appears. This is because the seller is the party conveying title (giving it up). He must sign the deed, under oath, before a notary public.

Note also in Figure 7.3 that two dates appear. In the upper right-hand corner is the date of recording in the official records of the county where the property is located. In the lower left-hand corner is the date of execution before a notary public (wherever the seller may be at the time). Do not be confused by these two dates. The date of recording (upper right) is controlling. Said date includes the time of recording . . . by hour and minute.

By all means, **insist** that the title company, escrow officer, attorney, or broker handling the transaction provide you with a *recorded copy* of the title deed that you signed off on. You want to retain said copy among your records when you report the sale on your tax return. Should the IRS question who owned the property at time of sale (whether as single, unmarried, married, or in co-ownership with others), the title deed is your document of proof. If your name is not on the transferring deed, and you claim any exclusion of gain, you'll get real experience trying to clarify things.

A common problem occurs these days when two or more adult persons live in a single home. One person may own it; the other (or others) may share all expenses therewith: mortgage payments, property taxes, improvements, etc. Tax issues arise when each payer wants to claim his/her itemized deductions on Schedule A (Form 1040) and his/her sale-year exclusion-of-gain prorata on Schedule D. The longer the arrangement goes on, the more likely will exclusion-sharing controversies develop.

Upon Recording Mail to:	Instrument No. _____
	Book _____ Page _____
_____	Date Recorded _____
Donald C. Buyer	
Jane D. Buyer	*OFFICIAL RECORDS*
(Address)	County of _____

GRANT DEED

For valuable consideration, receipt of which is hereby acknowledged

JOHN A. SELLER and MARY B. SELLER,
husband and wife

HEREBY GRANT TO -

DONALD C. BUYER and JANE D. BUYER,
husband and wife, as joint tenants with right
of survivorship

ALL THAT REAL PROPERTY situated in the City of _____,
County of _____ , State of _____ ,
described as follows to wit:

*Full legal description of
property transferred*

IN WITNESS WHEREOF this instrument is executed this

_____ day of _____ , 20_____

Verification & Seal of Notary Public

_____ /s/ _____
John A. Seller
_____ /s/ _____
Mary B. Seller

Fig. 7.3 - Generalized Grant Deed for Transferring Property Title

Clarify Co-Owner Percentages

If you are a single or unmarried person (widowed or divorced), and the home you sell is in your name only, you are the 100% owner thereof. Your name only is on the grant deed transferring title to your buyer. If true, there should be no ownership sharing or reporting problem.

If you are married, and married at time of sale, the usual presumption is that the residence is 50/50 co-owned by you and your spouse. This presumption holds unless there has been a prior tenants-in-common understanding as to a non-50/50 arrangement. If such exists, you are well advised to clarify the specific ownership percentage of each spouse *before* the sale closes. It could be, for example, the husband owns 62.15% and wife owns 37.85% (62.15% + 37.85% = 100%). It could be that after the sale closes, each spouse intends to file a separate return.

If you are one of *three* co-owners of a residence, for example, and none of the three is married, you and your co-owners must embark on a pre-sale clarification effort. You must establish the exact percentage or fraction of ownership of each person, on any terms to which you all agree. One way of doing so is to resurrect each owner's capital contribution to the residence: down payment, payments on mortgage principal, payments for improvements, etc. Prepare a bona fide tabulation of each owner's contributions, total them, then compute each's fraction of the total. Do it right by having each co-owner verify and approve the results. The results might be (for example):

Co-Owner A — 23.769% or 0.23769 fraction

Co-Owner B — 35.127% or 0.35127 fraction

Co-Owner C — <u>41.104%</u> or <u>0.41104</u> fraction

100.00%   1.00000

Once the ownership interests are settled, prepare a to-be-notarized document. Label it: **Request for Issuance of Three Separate Forms 1099-S**. List each owner's name, Tax ID, and ownership percentage or fraction. All three sign the document in the presence of a notary public. Then submit the document to the real estate reporting person before the sale closes.

Otherwise, here's what could happen. Suppose the home sold for $650,000. If your name is the first one on the transferring title, and you don't give the closing agent specific instructions to the contrary, one Form 1099-S will be filed with the IRS in your name only. It will show the entire gross proceeds of $650,000 going somewhere into your pockets. Even if you claimed the full $250,000 single-person exclusion, you'd be charged with a capital gain tax on $400,000. If you are willing to pay the other two co-owners' taxes, the IRS doesn't care.

By instructing and insisting that the real estate reporting person prepare and file three separate Forms 1099-S, here's what each of you would report separately on your returns:

Co-Owner A — $650,000 x 0.23769 = $154,500
Proceeds $154,500 less $250,000 exclusion
= Zero taxable

Co-Owner B — $650,000 x 0.35127 = $228,325
Proceeds $228,325 less $250,000 exclusion
= Zero taxable

Co-Owner C — $650,000 x 0.41104 = $267,175
Proceeds $267,175 less $250,000 exclusion
= $17,175 taxable

As you'll see in Chapter 8: Claiming Your Exclusion, this one tip alone (if applicable) will save you months and years of IRS computer mismatching harassment.

Culling Those Papers

If you've ever sold a residence before, you'll know what we mean. When the sale finally closes, you are left with tons and tons of papers. There are listing contracts, advertising flyers, offers to buy, counter offers, disclosure statements, credit reports, mortgage balances, building inspections, licenses and permits, comparable sales statistics, termite inspections, warranty contracts, title search reports, preliminary closing statements, revised statements, final statements, on and on — you get the idea. Fully 95% of these papers have no ongoing value after the sale closes.

What you must do is to cull through all those papers and select out the ones that are important for your tax records. As a guide route in this regard, we present Figure 7.4. Start the moment you receive the cashier's-type check paying you the net cash proceeds out of the sale. Be fully aware that the amount shown on your cashier's check will bear no resemblance to the amount reported on Form 1099-S.

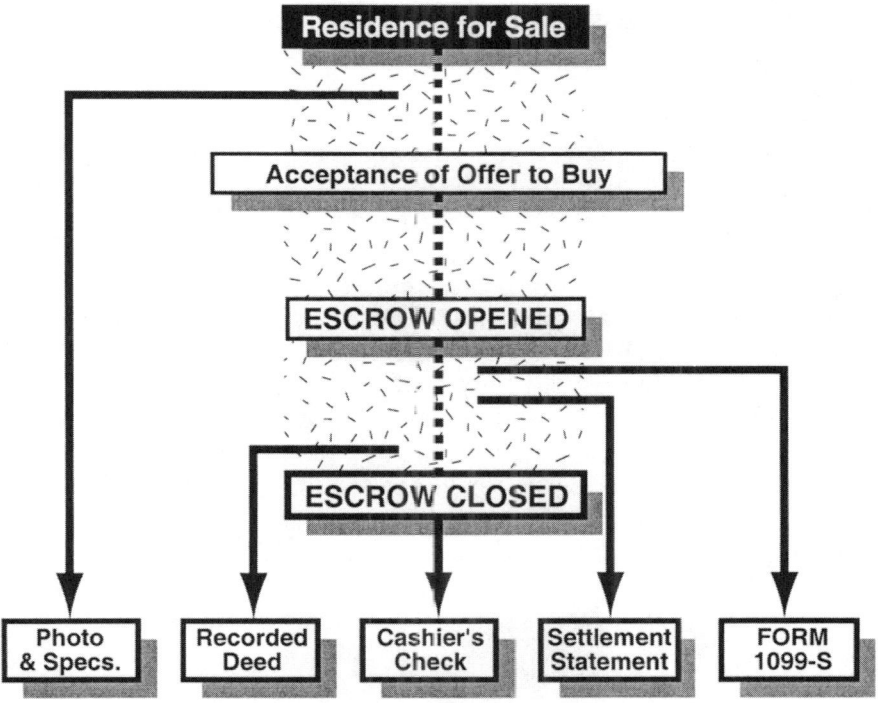

Fig. 7.4 - Culling "Tons" of Paper for Bits of Tax Gold

The first thing you do — yes, the very first — is **photocopy** that cashier's check for your tax records. The closing broker will report "gross" proceeds to the IRS. Your photocopy of the closing check establishes your "net cash" proceeds. There's quite a difference in the two dollar amounts. Deposit the check in a bank (or other financial institution) in a separate transaction of its own. Then photocopy the deposit statement.

Next, search through your pile of papers and select out the *Final Settlement Statement*. This is a cash balancing summary of all monies in and out of the escrow account in your name. You don't want the preliminary, or the revised; you want the final. Sometimes the word "final" appears on it; sometimes not. Sometimes the closing agent's signature appears on it; sometimes not. If you are not sure which settlement statement you have, contact the title company, escrow agent, or closing attorney and insist that you be provided with a final such statement. You have already paid for it.

While at it, insist on a photocopy of the *recorded* grant deed transferring title of your residence to the buyer. We've already cited the importance of this.

Look through that pile of papers again and select out the print ad or flyer that offered your home for sale to the general public. Most such flyers display a photo of your former home, with a listing of its attributes (number of rooms, type of structure, etc.). Keep the flyer as part of your tax records. It will come in handy if a tax dispute arises over what was actually sold.

And, finally, of all remaining papers, search for and select out Copy B of Form 1099-S. It's there someplace. You were charged for it on the settlement statement. If you can't find it, you'd better ask for it — now! Don't wait for tax filing time when panic sets in.

Once you have the five items above (as per Figure 7.4), place them with your tax records for your year of sale return. All other unculled papers can be bundled up and set aside. When all warranties have expired, throw them away. Under Section 121, each sale is a closed event; therefore, close it!

8

CLAIMING YOUR EXCLUSION(S)

> **Make Your Exclusion Claim On Schedule D (Form 1040) By Entering The Selling Price Of Your Home In Its Column (d), Your COST OR OTHER BASIS In Column (e), And GAIN (No Loss) In Column (f). The Column (e) Includes Acquisition Cost (Or The Equivalent), Improvements, And Selling Expenses. Simultaneously, On A Separate Line, Enter Your Allowable EXCLUSION Amount: $250,000 or $500,000 Or Prorata Thereof. Enter In Column (f) In < > Symbols Indicating Subtraction From The Gain. If The Result Is Zero Or Less, There Is No Tax To Pay; If More Than Zero, Favorable Capital Gain Tax Applies.**

Section 121(b) allows up to $250,000 exclusion of gain for each individual homeowner/seller. The exclusion amount jumps to $500,000 for married individuals filing a joint return. These are truly unprecedented tax-free amounts in these days of meticulous tax accounting. We can expect — and rightly so — that the IRS will be very particular about allowing such high exclusions on poorly prepared tax returns and claims.

The starting point for staking your claim is **Schedule D (Form 1040):** *Capital Gains and Losses*. This form is the mainstay for reporting all sale and exchange transactions involving capital assets: stock, land, mutual funds, commodity contracts, and other items (including your home). It is a summary sheet of all capital transactions throughout the year. Pertinent instructions relating to Schedule D read—

If you sold or exchanged your main home, do not report it on your tax return unless your gain exceeds your exclusion amount . . . [and] *you meet the* [statutory] *tests.*

Because of the underlying premise of this book — which is the **saving** of your tax-free exclusions — we will depart from the official instructions and have you report *all* home sales.

Accordingly, we want to familiarize you with the computational steps you need to pursue, in order to claim your exclusion. The presumption in this chapter is that you've sold your home at a *gain*: not at a loss. You can only claim the Section 121 exclusion if you have a gain. Unfortunately, loss on home sales can occur in distressed markets and disaster areas.

Furthermore, you can claim the exclusion only after you have the **Closing Escrow Statement**: *Seller's copy* in your possession. We have a lot to tell you about this closing/settlement statement. It is a "third party" document which the IRS accepts as prima facie evidence of the dollar amounts that transpired. Whereas Form 1099-S exhibits only the gross selling price (gross proceeds), the escrow settlement statement provides many lines — 15 to 25 or so — of entry dollar amounts. You have to pore over these entries and select only those needed for establishing your gain.

Exclusion Not Automatic

The high exclusion amount can lead to fundamental misconceptions. The impression is likely that unless you make more than $250,000 in gain from your sale, no reporting of the sale is required. Such is NOT TRUE! You should be realistic enough to know that the IRS is not going to hand you automatically a plum-sized exclusion on a silver platter. You are going to have to do some computational work, and keep adequate records for a minimum of three to five years **after** the sale.

Your personal residence is a *capital asset*. As such, at time of sale, it is subject to capital gain or capital loss. To determine whether it is a gain or a loss, you need to report the transaction on your return for the year of the sale. If you do not do so, the presumption could be that your tax basis is zero, and that you have forfeited any exclusion you might otherwise be allowed. Once this presumption is asserted by the IRS, your gross proceeds are all taxable . . . as ordinary income: not capital gain.

An exclusion is not the same as an exemption. To claim the exclusion benefit, you must first report the gross proceeds received, and subtract your selling expenses and basis. Then apply — as applicable — your exclusion. The excess gain over the exclusion, if any, is taxable. If there is no excess gain, there is no tax. End of report. End of tax accounting for that sale.

An exemption works differently. If statutorily exempt, whatever amount it may be is not reported.

Nowhere in Section 121 are the words "exempt" or "exemption" used. Here and there, with respect to certain applicable rules, the words "except" or "exception" appear. An exception is not the same as an exemption. An exception is the override of a general rule, when caused by exceptional circumstances. Said circumstances have to be clearly identified in the applicable tax law.

In contrast, Section 121(a) is officially titled: *Exclusion*. The very opening clause in this subsection says—

Gross income shall not include gain from the sale . . . of . . .

And subsection (b)(1): *Limitations*, says—

The amount of gain excluded from gross income . . . shall not exceed $250,000.

The plain language of these words is that a home seller has to establish the amount of his gain first, then apply the exclusion. The gain cannot be established without reporting the gross proceeds from the sale. Nothing in Sections 121(a) or 121(b) says or implies that the gross proceeds themselves are excluded. The exclusion applies to the "gain from the sale": NOT to its gross proceeds.

The "Exact Matching" Trap

In prior Chapter 7 (Sales Price Reportings), we discussed the broker reporting requirements when a principal residence is sold. The IRS form that the closing broker (title company or attorney) uses is Form 1099-S: *Proceeds from Real Estate Transactions*. Why do you suppose the IRS wants this particular form used?

Answer: It sets its automatic computer trap for you. It tags your Tax ID account for the taxable year of the sale. It (the IRS) sits back and waits until your tax return for the year of sale is filed. If its computer does not find an amount on your return that exactly matches — to the dollar — the gross proceeds reported to it via an electronic version of Form 1099-S, you'll be sent a computer demand to pay additional tax . . . plus penalty . . . plus interest. The demand will arrive approximately 18 to 24 months after your return is filed. If your gross sale proceeds were $385,000, for example, the demand for tax payment could be $100,000 or more.

The demand would be headed:

We changed your Account. You Owe Additional Tax

. . . or words to this effect. Attached would be a payment voucher for the full additional amount due. You are given 10 days to pay, or to make arrangements for payment. If you disagree with paying, you are directed to call an 800 number. Pray and hope that you can get through. If your prayers are answered and you are able to speak to a human being, explain your situation and inquire what steps you can take to correct the IRS's *erroneous billing*. It **is** erroneous and is intended to be! The billing is based on the gross proceeds from the sale: **not** on what the IRS thinks your gain would be after your selling expenses, tax basis, and exclusion.

Why not save yourself the erroneous billing hassle, and self-report your residence sale timely and properly? Compute your gain, claim your exclusion, then wrap up the records on that sale . . . and go on to other matters. Put the exclusion amount aside in a long-term savings account. Save your exclusion computation and tax documents, to counter possible hostile accusations.

In Figure 8.1, we portray in schematic form the computer matching process that goes on, when you self-report your residence sale. Knowing that the arrangement shown does take place, make sure that the amount you show as "sales price" (on Schedule D) exact-matches that shown as "gross proceeds" on Form 1099-S. If the 1099-S amount is an error, you can correct matters on your Schedule D as a selling expense adjustment.

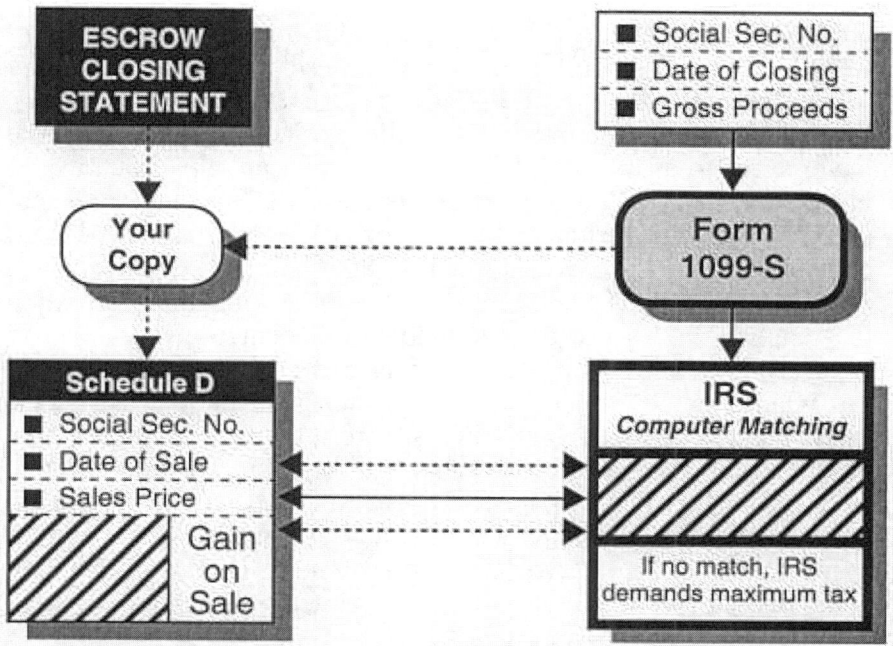

Fig. 8.1 - The Process for "Exact-Matching" Your Residence Sale

Escrow Closing Statement

In case you are not already familiar with the term "escrow," in everyday language it means:

Money, property, bond, or deed put into the custody of a third party and not delivered to grantee until all agreed conditions are fulfilled.

— Webster's II New College Dictionary

What is "put into escrow" is the sale contract agreed to by yourself and your buyer, the grant deed to your property, mortgage and debt information, and warranties and instructions by you. The buyer puts into escrow cash money, mortgage money, a trust deed (if any) and warranties and his instructions.

As you'll note in Figure 8.1, the first item indicated is *Escrow Closing Statement*. This is your starting point when getting prepared to exact-match the dollar amount on your copy of Form 1099-S. The first dollar entry on the escrow statement is the selling price (for you) or the purchase price (for your buyer). Make sure that the escrow-entered selling price is what you and the buyer agree to as the correct amount. This means that you have to make sure that you get in your hands the "final" closing statement prepared for your residence that has been sold. Separate the draft copies for destruction, when you have the final.

For instructional and recall purposes, the kind of information that appears on an escrow settlement statement is generalized in Figure 8.2. Below the selling price, there are batches of other information which we categorize as mortgage debt, trust deeds, sales commissions, prorata items (prorata between seller and buyer), escrow costs, closing costs, and unpaid consumer debt of seller (if any). There is no IRS form for a settlement statement. State laws differ and settlement practices between different escrow agencies also differ. However, most statements consist of about 50 entry lines, of which about 30 are preprinted entries and about 20 are blank lines for other entries.

Should the selling price on your escrow statement differ from that on Form 1099-S broker reported to the IRS, use the 1099-S amount as your matching target. Do not attempt to contact the IRS or the escrow agency to correct it. Trying to do so would be such a hassle. You can adjust for any difference on your own. Note the amount of difference. If the 1099-S is higher than the escrow selling price, **add** the difference to your selling expense. If the 1099-S is lower than the escrow selling price, **subtract** the difference from your selling expense. Because selling expenses are *subtracted* from the selling price, any adjustments you make are automatically self-compensating.

For example, suppose the escrow statement shows the price at $650,000 but Form 1099-S reports it as $615,000. The difference is $35,000 less than the escrow listing. If the selling expenses were $50,000, the results would be:

	Escrow	Diff.	1099-S
Selling price	650,000	<35,000>	615,000
Selling expense	<50,000>	30,000	<15,000>
Net result	600,000		600,000

ESCROW STATEMENT	☐ Preliminary ☐ Final	☐ Buyer ☐ Seller

Title Company (or Attorney)	Location of Property	
• • •	• •	

Escrow Officer	Escrow Number	Date

Item	Debit	Credit
Purchase Price/Selling Price		
Mortgage Accounting		
• Old mortgage(s)		
• New mortgage(s)		
• Prepayment points		
• New loan fee		
• Mortgage broker fee		
Title Accounting		
• Title insurance		
• Preparation of deed(s)		
• Escrow fee		
• Reconveyances		
• Recordings		
Prorata Accounting		
• Property taxes		
• Mortgage interest		
• Hazard insurance		
• Rent		
• Utilities		
Closing Accounting		
• Sale commission(s)		
• Termite inspection		
• Code requirements		
• Home warranty		
• Transfer taxes		
Other Items		
•		
•		
•		
•		
•		
Balance Due ☐ Buyer ☐ Seller		
Totals: Must Balance	**XYZXYZ**	**XYZXYZ**

Fig. 8.2 - Generalized Contents of Escrow Closing Statement

Overview of Schedule D

Your escrow closing statement is prepared by someone other than yourself. That "someone" has no specific interest in your tax return, though, of course, he wishes you well. From such point on, you have to prepare your own Schedule D to compute your gain and claim your exclusion. Therefore, we should tell you something about the form.

As stated previously, Schedule D (Form 1040) is titled: *Capital Gains and Losses*. Based on those title words alone, there is no hint that it accommodates the sale of your home. The separate instructions accompanying Schedule D address, in about 200 words, the two homesale exclusions of $250,000 (single) and $500,000 (joint). These instructions conclude by saying that—

If your gain exceeds your exclusion amount, see [IRS] *Publication 523* [Sale of Your Home] *for more details.*

Schedule D (Form 1040) is arranged into three parts, namely:

Part I   — Short-Term Capital Gains and Losses: Assets Held One Year or Less

Part II   — Long-Term Capital Gains and Losses: Assets Held More Than One Year

Part III   — Summary: Combine Parts I and II
   • Potentially, four separate worksheets may apply: (i) qualified dividends, (ii) Schedule D tax, (iii) Section 1050 gain, and (iv) 28% rate gain.

Most home sales claiming either of the two exclusions are reportable in Part II: Long Term. This is because, except for the special rules that we discussed in Chapters 4 and 5, the preponderance of exclusion claims derive from homes owned and used more than two years before sale.

Part II (as well as Part I also) is arranged into six columns with the following headings:

Col. (a) *Description of property* [sold]

Col. (b) *Date acquired (mo., day, yr.)*
Col. (c) *Date sold (mo., day yr.)*
Col. (d) *Sales price (See instructions)*
Col. (e) *Cost or other basis (See instructions)*
Col. (f) ***Gain or (Loss)***. *Subtract (e) from (d)*

We'll tell you now that **column (e)** is where all of your tax attention should be focused. The IRS via the broker reporting Form 1099-S has you "locked in" at column (d). Your only recourse for recovering your capital investment and selling expenses, and claiming your exclusion, is via strict attention to accounting details. If the IRS ever challenges your column (f) gain amount, or queries you (via a tax demand) for not reporting the sale at all, your only salvation is the documentation you have for reconstructing the proper entry in column (e). We emphasize that column (e) on Schedule D (Form 1040) can make or break your homesale exclusion-of-gain case.

Editorial Note: Do not confuse Schedule D (Form 1040) with the Schedule Ds for Forms 1041 (trusts), 1065 (partnerships) or 1120 (corporations). All of these schedules look somewhat alike, but **only** the Form 1040 version accommodates principal residence sales.

Ambiguity from Instructions

The instructions in IRS Publication 523: *Sale of Your Home*, direct you to combine your exclusion amount along with other items in column (e): *Cost or other basis*. Doing so muddies column (e) in such a way that you cannot instantly determine from Schedule D what your allowable exclusion is. This particularly occurs where the allowable exclusion is less than the maximum exclusion possible. The instructions also tell you that column (f): *Gain or <loss>*, cannot be a loss for a personal residence. The column must be either a gain or a zero.

Let us cite two simple examples of what we are getting at: Case A and Case B. Assume that the sales price of your home [Col. (d)] is $635,000. Further assume that your adjusted tax basis in that home is $285,000 and that your selling expenses are $50,000. In Case A, you are single; in Case B you are married. In all other respects, the home sale qualifies for the Section 121 exclusions of $250,000 and $500,000.

For Case A, the column (e) entry amount would be—

$285,000 (basis) + $50,000 (expenses) + $250,000 (exclusion, single) = $585,000

Consequently, the amount in column (f): Gain or <loss> would be $50,000 *gain* ($635,000 [Col. (d)] less $585,000 [Col. (e)]).
For Case B, the column (e) entry amount would be—

$285,000 (basis) + $50,000 (expenses) + $500,000 (exclusion, joint) = $835,000

For Case B, what would be the proper entry in column (f)?
The instruction there says—

Subtract (e) from (d)

If you follow this instruction, you would enter a loss of <$200,000> in column (f) [$635,000 Col. (d) minus $835,000 Col. (e)]. But Publication 523 tells you that a loss entry is a "No-No". Therefore, you must enter "zero" in column (f).

Editorial Note: The < > symbols indicate a negative amount.

Suppose you put the $500,000 joint exclusion amount into a savings account, as we urge. Some years later "out of the blue" you are questioned by the IRS about paying no tax on that $500,000. Now . . . What do you do? How can you show on an official tax form what your correct tax-free exclusion amount was?
The answer is: You can't. You have to unravel the components in column (e) and "back compute" your allowable joint exclusion with column (f) being zero. The back computation goes this way:

Zero = $635,000 − [$285,000 (basis) + $50,000 (expenses) + X]

The X turns out to be $300,000 (635,000 − 335,000). This is your allowable joint exclusion amount: NOT the $500,000 maximum exclusion that you combined in column (e).

How do we propose isolating on Schedule D (Form 1040) the correct tax-free exclusion amount? This is where we depart from the official instructions.

Make TWO Simultaneous Entries

Columns (a) through (f) are spread out horizontally across Schedule D, and delineated by separate lines for making the columnar entries. For **each** of Case A and Case B above, we urge making two simultaneous line entries. The entries in columns (a) and (f) would read:

Col. (a): Description	Col. (f): Gain	
"Sale of Residence A"	$300,000	
"Sec. 121(b)(**1**) Exclusion"	<250,000>	
	$ 50,000	gain
"Sale of Residence B"	$300,000	
"Sec. 121(b)(**2**) Exclusion"	<300,000>	
	-0-	zero

We present the treatment above in Figure 8.3. Assuming that there are no other required entries on Schedule D than the sale of your residence, our results in Figure 8.3 are identical to what the official instructions expect. The only difference is that we have separated for quick identity purposes, the allowable tax-free exclusion amounts. The exclusion identified as "Sec. 121(b)(**1**)" is for a single filer, whereas that identified as "Sec. 121(b)(**2**)" is for a joint filer. Note the sub-parenthesis distinction.

For every qualifying exclusion cf homesale gain that you claim, we insist that you keep a permanent copy of the relevant Schedule D for each such sale. We further insist that you make two simultaneous entries as listed above and as depicted in Figure 8.3. Why do we so insist?

Suppose that after five qualified — and lucrative — home sales, your Exclusion Savings Account had grown to $1,553,690. That's one million 553 thousand, and 690 dollars. You have paid not one cent of tax on this amount. It's all tax legitimate. But without our insistence on measures above, how do you prove to a skeptical IRS agent sniffing for unreported taxable income where that $1,553,690 for an ordinary taxpayer came from?

Schedule D (Form 1040)	CAPITAL GAINS AND LOSSES				
Part II	Long Term : More Than One Year				
Col. (a) Description	(b) Date Bought	(c) Date Sold	Col. (d) Sales Price	Col. (e) Cost or Other Basis	Col. (f) Gain or <Loss>
					↓
Residence "A"	5/99	7/03	635,000	335,000	300,000
Sec. 121 (b)(1)	EXCLUSION ————————————————→				<250,000>
					↓
Residence "B"	5/99	7/03	635,000	335,000	300,000
Sec. 121 (b)(2)	EXCLUSION ————————————————→				<300,000>
					↓
					⋮
Other indirect forms, distributions, and carryovers					⋮
					↓
Part II Subtotal ▶					

Fig. 8.3 - Two Simultaneous Entries for Each Qualified Residence Sale

Here's how.

You pull from your permanent records five Schedules D, each corresponding to an exclusion-qualified homesale. You photocopy the five schedules (for submission to the IRS) and highlight the segregated exclusion amounts on each. On a separate document, you tabulate the exclusion amounts and the corresponding account-accrued (tax exempt) interest for each. The grand total results should come pretty close to your exclusion account savings balance. The point is: **SAVE** your exclusion-year documents!

Pulling numbers strictly "out of the air," your totalizing document might look something like this:

Homesale	Allowable Exclusion	Accrued Interest
Sch. D (#1)	$ 215,760	$ 17,260
Sch. D (#2)	403,210	32,250
Sch. D (#3)	162,350	12,970
Sch. D (#4)	285,170	22,810
Sch. D (#5)	372,130	29,780
	1,438,620	$115,070
	115,070	
Grand Total	$1,553,690	

And for each homesale Schedule D, you have a corresponding Escrow Closing Statement, a Form 1099-S, and backup support for the gain entry in column (e): *Cost or other basis* (**without** the exclusion). This way you are loaded for bear. The IRS will be flabbergasted at your disciplined recordkeeping. You are now free to move on to your next exclusion-of-gain home sale.

Selling Expenses: Escrow

In Chapter 6 (Basis of Residence Sold), we discussed those items that constitute your capital investment in each principal residence that you put up for sale. Your investment — called "adjusted basis" with improvements, etc. — is the starting point and primary component that goes into column (e): *Cost or other basis*, on Schedule D. There is also another significant column (e) component: Selling expenses. Both your basis capital and selling expenses come back to you as *Return of Capital*. Said amount is not taxed. Somewhere along the way, you've already paid tax on it. After-tax money is not taxed a second time.

Selling expenses are those incurred to effect the sale of your residence, without physically improving the property itself. Generally, most of these expenses are shown on the seller's copy of the closing escrow as debits against the seller. Sometimes they are labeled: "Paid from seller's funds." All bona fide selling expenses are deductible against the selling price. We summarize these for you in Figure 8.4.

• **Sales Commissions**
  - selling agent
  - listing agent
 	
• **Title Costs**
  - mortgage "points"
  - mortgage broker fee
  - title insurance
  - new grant deed
  - new trust deed
  - escrow fee
  - reconveyance fee
  - document fees
  - recording fee
  - county transfer tax
  - city transfer tax
	• **Closing Costs**
	  - code inspection
	  - code updates
	  - termite inspection
	  - termite repairs
	  - home warranty
	  - credits to buyer
	  - notary fees
	  - express delivery
	
	• **Outside Escrow**
	  - property appraisals
	  - fixing-up expenses
	  - deposit forfeitures
	  - advertising costs

Fig. 8.4 - Example Selling Expenses Subtracted from Selling Price

The most common selling expenses are sales commissions, seller's points, prepayment penalties, statutory repairs, warranty costs, title clearance, and nominal closing fees.

The sales commission is usually a specified percentage of the selling price. The percentage is negotiable but is of the order of 6%. Whatever it is, as agreed between seller and sales agent, it is set forth in the listing contract, the sales contract, and the settlement statement. This is a pure selling expense and is fully deductible by the seller as one element of his cost or other basis.

Seller's points and prepayment penalties are opposite sides of the same mortgage barrel. If the seller induces the buyer to assume the existing mortgage, he (the seller) pays "points" to the mortgagor. If the buyer gets a new mortgage elsewhere, and credits the seller, who in turn pays off the existing mortgage, the seller pays a "penalty" to the mortgagor. Points and/or penalties typically range from 1 to 3% of the mortgage principal outstanding on date of sale. These, too, are fully deductible selling expenses.

Statutory repairs and warranty costs are those required by state and local law when transferring residential property to a new owner. These mandated expenditures include termite rework, rewiring, replumbing, fire retardation, reroofing, and so on, to meet updated building codes and inspections. Warranty costs are those required by ordinances to insure the working condition of appliances, lighting fixtures, burglar alarms, plumbing facilities, and heating and cooling systems. Federal housing standards are directed towards a one-year warranty on all working parts of a personal residence. All such regulatory costs are fully deductible by the seller.

Title clearance and closing fees often are shared between seller and buyer. The particular arrangement depends on customary practice in the area, and personal trade-offs between the two parties. Only those expressly debited to the seller's side of the escrow statement are deductible by the seller.

There are other expenses to selling a home which do not show up on the escrow settlement statement. Most of these, such as cleaning, hauling trash, and "fixing up" the property, are not selling expenses. You should have done these things all along. Still, some non-escrow costs do qualify as selling expenses.

Sometimes a seller may change his mind and decide not to sell after all. He might do this after the listing contract is signed or after the sales contract is signed. Either way, he has breached a contract. The injured party may insist on some compensatory award, including attorney fees. Any such awards and fees are legitimate selling expenses. But they are not deductible until the property is actually sold. So, we call them "pre-selling" expenses.

Summary of Methodology

The reporting of a home sale on Schedule D (Form 1040) is an anomaly. It is an anomaly in the sense that said schedule was expressly designed to accommodate all business and investment-type capital assets where gain or loss is tax recognized. Selling a home is the only reportable asset thereon where a capital loss is not recognized. Should such a misfortune occur, the event is treated as a *personal loss* (not business or investment) and, therefore, a "loss/loss" or "No/No". Furthermore, a home is the only asset where a flat-out exclusion of gain is allowed (up to certain limits). And, still further, a home sale is the only transaction where official instructions say—

Do not report . . . unless your gain exceeds your exclusion amount . . . [and you meet certain tests].

We have previously explained why you should report, even though you may not be required to do so.

There is a certain computational methodology that you should have in your backup records on every homesale. Whether you report or not, as we depict in Figure 8.3, there are seven sequential steps involved. They are—

Step 1 — Selling price of home $ _____
- from "Gross proceeds" on 1099-S
- corresponds to "Sales price" at Col. (d) on Sch. D

Step 2 — Expense of sale   < _____ >
- for items in Fig. 8.4
- from Closing escrow statement
- plus reconciliation adjustment (1099-S vs. escrow) where necessary

Step 3 — Adjusted sales price   _____
[subtract step 2 from step 1]
- net sales proceeds to you

Step 4 — Basis of home sold   < _____ >
- return of capital: nontaxable
- from your records à la Ch. 6

Step 5 — ***Gain on Sale***   _____
[subtract step 4 from step 3]
- enter at Col. (f) on Sch. D as per Fig. 8.3
- subtract step 5 from step 1 to arrive at Col. (e) on Sch. D

Step 6 — Applicable exclusion   < _____ >
- as per Fig. 8.3
- enter at Col. (f) with "< >"

to indicate subtraction, as per
Fig. 8.3

Step 7 — ***Gain in Excess of Exclusion***   _____
[subtract step 6 from step 5]
• if gain, will appear in Col. (f)
summary at bottom of Sch. D
• if no gain, Col. (f) summary
unaffected

The end purpose of a home sale being reported on Schedule D is to establish its gain (if any) in excess of the allowable exclusion. Knowing what the allowable exclusion is requires substantial attention and care by each homeseller. While we present in Figure 8.5 practical guidelines on claiming the applicable exclusion amount, it is always advisable to review the statutory provisions covered in Chapters 1 through 5 . . . where appropriate.

To claim an amount of exclusion to which you are not entitled can result in the entire gross proceeds on Form 1099-S being taxed in full. It would be so taxed, if you had no records such as outlined above. The IRS's computer would "see" your Schedule D as—

Part I   — Short-Term Capital Gains
Col. (a) — Sale of residence
Col. (d) — Gross proceeds
Col. (e) — Zero (no records)
Col. (f) — Gain from sale
            Same as Col. (d)

In such case, ordinary (noncapital) tax rates would apply. The computer billing and demand for such tax is purposely designed to get your attention and traumatize you.

Only Excess Gain is Taxable

If, after applying the correct Section 121 exclusion, there is reportable gain, it is taxed. It is taxed at favorable capital gains rates which are generally lower than ordinary tax rates. You get three shots at favorable tax treatment when you use Schedule D.

Section 121	EXCLUSION OF GAIN FROM SALE OF PRINCIPAL RESIDENCE
General Limitations	1. One sale every 2 years 2. Allowable amount of exclusion not to exceed actual gain realized 3. No recognition for any unused portion of maximum allowable.

Subsec.	AMOUNT and APPLICATION
121 (b) (1)	$250,000 Max - single filer
121 (b) (2)	$500,000 Max - joint filers
121 (c) (2)	Prorata of maximum. Sale due to change of employment, health, etc.
121 (d) (1)	Either spouse meets ownership and use test
121 (d) (2)	Property of deceased spouse
121 (d) (3)	Property owned by former spouse
121 (d) (4)	Tenant in co-op housing corp.
121 (d) (5)	Involuntary conversions
121 (d) (6)	No exclusion for depreciation recapture
121 (d) (7)	Out-of-residence care
121 (d) (8)	Sale of remainder interests

Fig. 8.5 - Short Table of Home Sale Exclusion Amounts

You get your first shot at favorable treatment when you combine your homesale gain with all other capital gains and losses. The combining includes both the short-term (one year or less) and long-term (more than one year) gain or loss results. The overall combination of gains and losses is entered in Part III of Schedule D: *Summary*. There are two preprinted courses of action there: (i) if there is a net gain, and (ii) if there is a net loss. Hence, the combining of your homesale gain with all other gain or loss items may dilute the tax effect on your home.

For example, suppose that after the maximum allowable exclusion, the excess gain on your home sale was $165,000. Suppose that, in the same taxable year, you sold a variety of other capital assets which, unto themselves, produced a net loss of <$176,000>. When combining this amount of capital loss with the $165,000 capital gain on your home, you wind up paying no tax

[<176,000> + 165,000 = <11,000>] on your home sale. If the net loss from other assets was <$76,000> instead of <$176,000>, the taxable portion of the homesale would be $89,000 [165,000 + <76,000>]. Obviously, when selling a home with a reportable gain, it pays to rid your asset holdings of those which produce a capital loss. This, again, is your first shot at getting favorable tax treatment. By absorbing capital losses, you reduce taxable gain.

You also have a *second* shot at favorable treatment. This comes when you combine your homesale gain with other asset gains to produce a net long-term gain. In such case, you are directed (as applicable) to either a *Capital Gain Tax Worksheet* (19 lines) or a *Schedule D Tax Worksheet* (37 lines).

Why so many tax computational steps on Schedule D?

Because not all gains from capital assets are treated the same. Certain adjustments are made and as many as four different tax rates apply: 5%, 15%, 25%, and 28%. (The 25% and 28% rates are rare.) For "get to the point" purposes, only a rate of 15% applies to homesale capital gains. This is certainly favorable when compared to ordinary tax rates of 25% to 35% or so.

It is beyond our discussion to present all of the tax ramifications of Schedule D. All that we are attempting to do here is to indicate how your home sale and its allowable exclusion of gain fits in to the montage of other transactions that are reported on Schedule D (Form 1040).

Installment Sale Option

Whereas Schedule D tends to entry-favor cash sales, there are times when an installment sale is preferred. An installment sale allows you to stretch out your capital gains tax to subsequent-to-sale years. The supplemental form for doing so is Form 6252: *Installment Sale Income*. The bottom line on Form 6252 directs you to Schedule D. This is your third shot at favorable tax treatment, when selling your home. Why pay the tax promptly if you can spread it over several years without penalty?

An installment sale allows you to become a mortgage holder on the residence that you sell. Instead of accepting all cash in the year of sale, you can stipulate payments over 5, 10, 15, or more years. The tax law on point is Section 453: *Installment Method*. The principle behind this method is the determination of a *Gross profit percentage*: GPP.

$$GPP = \frac{\text{Gross Profit}}{\text{Contract Price}}$$

The GPP is a fixed percentage that applies to all payments on principal received throughout the life of the installment contract. IRS Form 6252: ***Installment Sale Income***, steps you through the GPP process (via 26 steps).

The "gross profit" is your gain in excess of your applicable exclusion (designated as Step 7 on page 8-17). A special line on Form 6252 just before establishing gross profit says—

If the property described above was your main house, enter the amount of your excluded gain.

This officially noticed "exclusion line" supports our earlier urging (in Figure 8.3) that there be a separate line entry on Schedule D that displays the amount of excluded gain.

The "contract price" is the total amount of principal that you are to receive over the life of the installment contract. Often, this is sales price itself, if you are the 100% mortgage holder. Otherwise, if the buyer assumes your existing mortgage, the sales contract price is reduced by said amount. Additionally, if the existing mortgage which the buyer assumes exceeds the tax basis in your home (which can happen when you borrow indiscriminately against your buildup of equity), the sales contract price is further reduced. Follow the instructions at each line on Form 6252, and you'll arrive at the correct contract price.

Also follow the instructions in Part II of Form 6252 to arrive at the amount of capital gain that you report on Schedule D for each installment year. Because we think installment sales are important in your retirement years, we'll come back to Form 6252 in Chapter 12: Nest Egg Commentary.

9

IMPACT OF DIVORCE

After The Final Decree, Former Spouses Have Up To 6 Years To Retitle Their Marital Residence (Or Any Other Property) Without Its Being Treated As A Sale. If Valued At $250,000 Or Less, Transferring All Ownership To One Spouse Makes Sense, Especially If Minor Children Are Involved. Otherwise, JOINT OWNERSHIP Should Be Retained, But NOT As "Husband And Wife." The Co-Ownership Form May Be 50/50 Or Non-50/50. Under Section 121(d)(3), Special Rules Apply: (A) Tack-On Of "Ownership" By The Stay-In Spouse, And (B) Tack-On Of "Use" By The Move-Out Spouse. Also Applicable Are The Interspousal Gifting Rules of Section 1041.

Nearly 50% of all first-time marriages end in divorce. A much lower percentage of second-time marriages likewise end. As a consequence, the sale of divorce residences is commonplace in the social and economic fabric of this nation. So much so that the tax accounting aspects thereof cannot be overlooked and "special ruled" away. Each divorce situation has to be examined in terms of its own facts and circumstances.

Under prior law (rollover of gain and the over-55 exclusion), a serious injustice was created for one spouse or the other and, in some cases, for both spouses. Under the rollover rules, the residence had to be occupied at the time of its sale. If one spouse moved out, whether voluntarily or court-ordered, that spouse was deprived of the rollover benefits. If both spouses lived in the residence at time of sale, and one got a replacement residence and the other did not, the spouse with no replacement residence paid full tax. The situation worsened if one spouse remarried and the other did not. If one spouse was under age 55 and the other spouse over age 55, and the exclusion of gain was exercised by the over-55 spouse, the under-55 spouse was subsequently deprived of the exclusion.   No matter how the divorce residence sale was structured there were always inequities under prior law.

Current law (exclusion of gain regardless of rollover or age) is a marked improvement over prior law. Each spouse is treated as an individual taxpayer of his or her own. The 2-years-out-of-5 ownership and use rule gives the moving-out spouse a break. If he/she occupied the marital residence for the minimum length of time, and the home is sold no more than three years after moving out, the move-out spouse can still claim his/her exclusion. Section 121 definitely levels the playing field between divorcing spouses at time of residence sale.

In this chapter, therefore, we want to review the ramifications of divorce that reflect on the ownership and use of the residence at time of sale. We want you to be cognizant of differences between divorce date, the sale date, and the year-ending date of your tax return. We'll discuss transfers between spouses, quitclaim deeds, 50/50 co-ownership, and non-50/50 co-ownership at time of sale. We'll present numerical examples of how non-50/50 ownership percentages can be established (or negotiated). If the residence sale is court ordered, there will be difficult ownership allocation and accounting problems unless the ownership percentages can be firmed before sale. As a safe haven for after-sale reportings to the IRS, insistence on two separate Forms 1099-S is a MUST.

Date of "Final" Important

The important date in a divorce situation is the date that a judge signs the final decree. The judicial signature is that of a Superior Court Judge or a Domestic Affairs Arbitrator, depending on local practice. Divorce is not a federal jurisdictional matter. Hence, all procedures, including the signature of finality, come under state jurisdictions. What we mean by "final" is termination of the marriage only: not termination of property settlement issues. Property settlement can go on for several years thereafter.

The final piece of paper that attests to a divorce is a Decree of Divorce (Final), Dissolution of Marriage (Judgment), or a Decree of Legal Separation. Any one is a legal document that should be among every affected spouse's important papers. It is surprising the number of spouses who do not have in their possession a copy of their divorce decree. Many do not know the actual (legal) date of their divorce. They are totally unaware of the tax importance of such a document. They just want to get the whole affair behind them and disregard its potential tax impact.

Most important to the tax accounting of the spouses involved is a *certified copy* of the final decree. The signed original is always kept by the court having jurisdiction. Attorneys seldom think of the tax accounting importance of a certified copy of the decree they processed. Therefore, it is up to the divorced parties to know enough, and be alert enough, to specifically request a certified copy of the final decree. To do so, each party separately has to go to the clerk's office of the Court House where the case was heard. The payment of a modest certification fee is required.

A certified copy of the decree has much the same effect as a deed transferring title to property. It pinpoints the legal date of severance of the taxpayer unit: husband and wife. Tax consequences may differ depending on whether the residence is sold prior to, concurrent with, or subsequent to the date the decree is entered into court records.

The date of the final also establishes the tax year for dissolving the joint returns and filing separate tax returns. Marital status is determined at the *close* of the taxable year. That is, midnight on December 31. Consequently, if the final decree is dated December 31 (during court business hours), each party is "single," for tax purposes, for the entire year!

The tax law authorization on this point is found in Section 7703: **Determination of Marital Status**. Section 7703(a) reads—

*(1) the determination of whether an individual is married shall be made as of the **close of his taxable year** . . .; and*

*(2) an individual legally separated from his spouse under a decree of divorce or of separate maintenance **shall not be considered as married**.* [Emphasis added.]

Hence, once the marriage is legally terminated, there is no opportunity to file a joint return claiming the $500,000 exclusion of gain upon sale of the marital residence.

End-of-the-year divorces are always critical, taxwise. Although attorneys may submit the final papers for signature early in December, many judges, bailiffs, and clerks are totally unmoved by the tax ramifications of divorcing spouses. In such cases it is often necessary for the tax-conscious spouse to visit the court and personally expedite the certified copy.

Property Settlement Terms

Where ownership of a marital residence is involved, disposing of that residence generally becomes the *key bone of contention* of the property settlement. Most divorcing spouses can agree on "his" and "her" portions of personal items, insurance, checking accounts, autos, furniture, land, business assets, and other forms of property. But where the personal residence is concerned, there is emotional scheming and dickering.

Any hangup over the marital residence can be softened to some extent, via property settlement terms which are clear and specific. But rarely do attorneys for either side portray clarity and specificity. Invariably, child support and alimony payments are commingled with property settlement matters. The way around such commingling is a clear reference in the divorce decree to Section 1041 of the Internal Revenue Code. This section is titled: **Transfers of Property Between Spouses or Incident to Divorce**. By "clear reference," we mean a statement along the lines that—

> The parties understand that for federal tax purposes, Section 1041 shall apply to all property transferred between them, as the consequence of their termination of marriage.

Such wording, we believe, makes the tax treatment intent clear. This should permit adequate time to work out other concerns, before all property matters are settled.

If minor children are involved, the custodial parent usually seeks to retain the residence for continuation of his/her personal living. If this be the case, the custodial parent — if the residence is quitclaim deeded to that parent — should be particularly tax wary.

He/she who acquires clear title to the residence, incident to the divorce, is subject to all tax accounting when the residence is sold.

Where children are not involved, oftentimes the parties agree to sell the marital residence. If they so agree, it should be made clear when the sale shall take place: before, concurrent with, or after the final decree of divorce. The property settlement terms also should make clear the fractional interest of each spouse in the residence, if it is not 50/50.

If sale is to be made after the divorce, the title deed should be changed to reflect nonspousal ownership. Although the names on the deed can be the same, any reference thereon to "husband and wife" certainly should be deleted. Title in joint tenancy or tenants-in-common is appropriate. (Joint tenancy implies right of survivorship whereas tenants-in-common does not.) The title changes should be imposed and made part of the final decree.

Sometimes, financial difficulties between spouses mandate that the residence be sold before the divorce. This almost invariably results in painful tax accounting by *both* parties. The sale is necessitated by the need to liquidate all spousal debts before the final decree is issued.

Attorney Fees and Debt Liens

When an attorney senses, or acquires direct knowledge of, financial impasses between divorcing spouses, one of his first acts is to record a lien against the residence for his own fee. He does this as part of the initial filings in the divorce proceedings. This way he gets priority payment.

In addition, he also seeks disclosure of all other debts (by both parties) as part of his duties as an "officer of the court." He publishes a legal Notice to Creditors, and in some cases contacts them directly. This is a signal to the creditors for them, too, to record liens against the residence. There is nothing conspiratorial about this. Responsible citizens are supposed to pay their debts.

If the residence is sold in order to pay off the marital debts, the misimpression is that these debts are part of the selling expenses and therefore deductible against the gain on sale. Such is definitely *not* the case. Attorney fees and personal debts are not part of the property costs.

Attorney fees in divorce cases are not deductible for sale-of-residence accounting. They are not deductible by either party: husband or wife. This is so regardless of who initiated the divorce or who contested the property settlement. However, the cost of actually changing the title deed would be a property cost item.

Attorney fees in divorce and separation are considered to be matrimonial expenses and, therefore, are personal. Similarly, paid-off personal debts such as charge accounts, credit cards, auto repairs, clothing shops, and furniture stores are neither capital expenditures for the residence nor its selling expenses.

The only exceptions to the above are mechanics' liens (for repairs and improvements to the residence), appraisal fees (for market valuation), and regulatory inspections (termite, roof, fire, etc.). These are all properly chargeable to basis of residence sold.

Transfer Between Spouses

Where minor children are involved, it often happens that the marital residence is transferred to the spouse who is the custodian of the children. Said transfer could arise from the "equitable swapping" of all marital assets. It could arise from the "horse trading" of all debts incurred by one spouse, for his or her ownership interest in the residence. It could arise from a "negotiated agreement" for the relinquishment of marital rights and obligations. Or, the transfer could arise from a "buy out" of the equity interest of one spouse by the acquiring spouse. Whatever the reason for the arrangement, one spouse winds up with ownership of the residence in its entirety. Co-ownership is no longer a factor.

Involved in this interspousal transfer is a *quitclaim deed*. That is, one spouse quitclaims his/her interest in the residence to the other. A quitclaim deed is a legal document giving the transferee (acquiring) spouse full dominion and control over the residence. Sample wording of a typical impending divorce quitclaim deed is presented in Figure 9.1. It could be prepared by the spouses themselves (without an attorney), so long as it is officially recorded in the county where the property is located. Preprinted quitclaim deeds (for your state of residence) are generally available from office supply stores where common legal documents are sold.

QUIT CLAIM DEED

KNOW ALL MEN BY THESE PRESENTS, that JOHN J. JONES*, husband, and resident of the County of _____, State of _____, for and in consideration of the dissolution of our marriage, and in connection with the equitable distribution of all of our marital assets, receipt of which is hereby acknowledged, and the the release from all mortgage debt on the property herein described, do, by these presents RELEASE and FOREVER QUIT CLAIM unto MARGARET ANNA (MORRISON) JONES*, wife, and to her successors and assigns, all right, title, and interest in, and to that certain parcel of land, together with its buildings and appurtenances, located at 1234 Blue Lagoon Drive*, City of _____, County of _____ , State of _____, described as follows to wit:

> **Full legal description of property transferred**

IN WITNESS WHEREOF this instrument is executed this _____ day of _____ , 20____ .

> **Verification and Seal of Notary Public**

_____
JOHN J. JONES

All names are fictitious

Fig. 9.1 - Sample Divorce Wording on Quitclaim Deed

Because the quitclaim transfer is between spouses, it is *not* treated as a sale. It is treated as a gift. *Gifts between spouses are nontaxable.* Therefore, no gain or loss is (tax) recognized on the transfer . . . and no Form 1099-S is required. Because so, the property's tax basis remains unaltered. It becomes a "basis carryover" to the recipient spouse.

As already mentioned, the specific tax law on point is Section 1041: *Transfer of Property Between Spouses or Incident to Divorce*. Note in this title two distinct situations: (1) Transfer *between* spouses, and (2) Transfer *incident to* divorce. The general rule therewith is subsection 1041(a), which reads—

No gain or loss shall be recognized on the transfer of property from an individual to (or in trust for the benefit of)—

(1) a spouse, or

(2) a former spouse, but only if the transfer is incident to the divorce.

As per subsection 1041(c), the term "incident to divorce" means—

If such transfer—

(1) occurs within 1 year after the date on which the marriage ceases, or

(2) is related to the cessation of marriage.

The term "related to the cessation of marriage" is addressed in Regulation § 1.1041-1T(b)(Q/A-7). It means **within six years** *after* the divorce is final. This is quite adequate time for the spouses to work out their property settlement differences. So long as one spouse or the other retains the residence, there is no sale. But a problem arises. As time moves on, the tax basis records (amount of capital invested) become garbled and indistinct. Often, they are lost or trashed.

Basis to Transferee Spouse

The transferee spouse is the one who acquires full title to a residence, incident to divorce. As a consequence, the transferee spouse has the full burden for basis accounting when the residence is someday sold. When a subsequent-to-divorce sale takes place, Form 1099-S and Schedule D will be required. Then, the stickler issue will be: "basis of residence sold." By the time a sale does take place, the basis records will have been emotionally bungled.

This issue is addressed specifically in Section 1041(b), to wit—

In the case of any transfer described in subsection (a)—

*(1) the property **shall be treated** as acquired by the transferee **by gift**, and*

*(2) the basis of the transferee in the property shall be the **adjusted basis of the transferor**.* [Emphasis added.]

To put the above in perspective, let us illustrate with some basis numbers. Do keep in mind that "basis" represents capital investment which is recoverable, without being taxed.

Assume that spouses had been married for 10 years, and had sold two previous residences for which the prior law rollovers were claimed. They are in their third residence at the time of divorce. Their present house is worth $685,000. However, its adjusted basis, including the two prior deferred gains, is $185,000. Thus, there is a potential gain on sale of $500,000 ($685,000 value less $185,000 basis).

The $185,000 is the adjusted basis as husband and wife. For tax purposes, husband and wife are treated as a single economic unit. Upon divorce, the transferee spouse becomes also a single economic unit. Therefore, there is *no change in basis*. The transferee spouse takes on (retains) the same basis as the husband and wife unit.

Suppose the transferee spouse "bought out" the transferor spouse's 50% interest in the $500,000 equity gain. That is, the transferee spouse paid the transferor spouse $250,000 by refinancing the property. Does the transferee spouse get an addition to basis of $250,000?

The answer: No. The $250,000 was an interspousal gift.

Does the transferor spouse pay tax on the $250,000 received?

The answer: No. The $250,000 was an interspousal gift.

In other words, any "buy out" between spouses has absolutely no effect on the basis of the residence retained, when "incident to divorce." This suggests that any buy out arrangement should be undertaken with downstream tax consequences in mind.

This concept of *retention of basis* by the transferee spouse is one of those silent tax traps. It snaps closed when the house is subsequently sold. If there is tax to pay, the transferee spouse pays it! He/she cannot go back to the (former) transferor spouse to share in the tax accounting liability. Since the transferee spouse gets all of the gain, he/she pays all of the tax. In the above example, the tax would be on $250,000 ($500,000 gain less $250,000 exclusion). Had the residence not been transferred to one spouse, but had been sold by two co-owning former spouses, each could have been entitled to a separate $250,000. The result would be no tax to pay.

When Not to Quitclaim

Quitclaiming one's former residence to a transferee spouse is often a practical way to settle many of the property issues of divorce. This is particularly true if the market value of the residence is less than $250,000. But, as we've seen in the example above, if the selling price exceeds $250,000, the transferee spouse, more likely than not, will have tax to pay. It is too late then to share the tax pain with the former spouse.

If the market value of the marital residence is less than $250,000, it is better to delay any quitclaiming intentions until you see what the real estate market does. You have up to six years after the divorce to do the quitclaiming. This 6-year rule appears in IRS Regulation § 1.1041-1T(b)(A-7) as—

*A transfer of property is treated as related to the cessation of the marriage if the transfer is **pursuant to a divorce or separation instrument**, . . . and the transfer occurs **not more than 6 years** after the date on which the marriage ceases. A divorce or separation instrument includes a modification or amendment to such decree or instrument. Any transfer occurring more than 6 years after the cessation of the marriage is presumed to be not related to the cessation of the marriage.* [Emphasis added.]

Six years is quite adequate time after a divorce to work out property settlement issues between former spouses. If the value of the property within this time frame is likely to exceed $250,000 — and certainly if over $350,000 — quitclaiming may not be the wisest tax choice. It is better to have the property retitled in co-ownership form (OTHER THAN as husband and wife) and wait things out a while. In the meantime, one spouse can stay in the residence until a later decision is made regarding its ultimate sale or buy out by the occupying spouse.

In Figure 9.2 we try to summarize the role of Section 1041 transfers as they relate to the single filer $250,000 exclusion-of-gain amount in Section 121. As you'll see in a moment, a "new twist" in the application of Section 1041 is added in Section 121. The focus in Figure 9.2 is on the *marital residence*. But it also could apply to secondary residential property for the spouse required to move out of the marital residence.

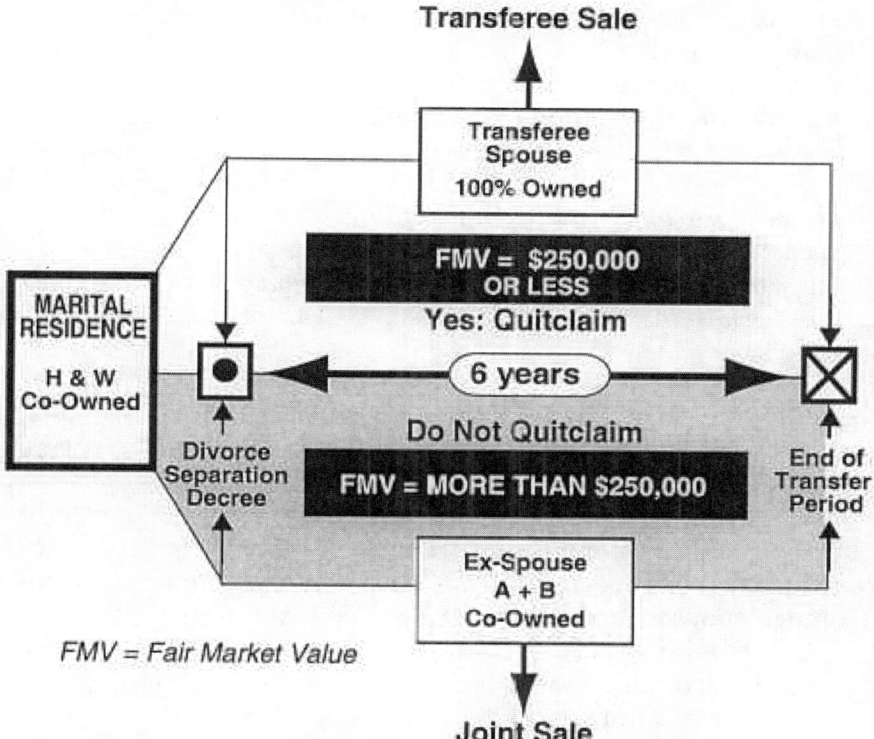

Fig. 9.2 - When & When Not to Quitclaim Your Marital Residence

Spousal Ownership "Tack-On"

Let's take a divorce situation where there are *two* residential properties involved. One property is the marital residence. The other property is a rental residence, a second home, or an inherited residence. To make the example more instructive, suppose one spouse owns both residences: the marital and the nonmarital. Can the nonmarital residence be transferred (quitclaimed) to a spouse or former spouse within the meaning of Section 1041? Yes, it can.

The particular rule on point is Section 121(d)(3): ***Property Owned by Spouse or Former Spouse.*** Here, the term "spouse" refers to the period of time before any decree of divorce is in effect, or before any legal separation decree is in effect. The spouses are still legally married. They may already be separated, either voluntarily or by restraining order. The term "former spouse" refers to the spousal status after the divorce (or legal separation) is final.

Subparagraph (A) under Section 121(d)(3) is titled: **Property Transferred to Individual from Spouse or Former Spouse**. It reads—

> In the case of an individual holding property transferred to such individual in a transaction described in **section 1041(a)**, the period such individual owns such property **shall include** the period the transferor owned the property. [Emphasis added.]

The reference to Section 1041(a) pertains to interspousal gifts "incident to divorce" (as per our earlier citations). The focus here is transfer of ownership.

The "shall include" refers to the period that the transferor spouse owned the property, irrespective of whether both spouses owned it together or not. This opens up the opportunity for divorcing spouses to transfer *any* residential property between themselves, without tax reporting it as a sale. The property transferred need not be the principal residence of the marriage. It could be rental property, inherited property, recently acquired property, or newly constructed property. The *ownership* aspects from one property to the other **tack on** to each other. So, too — by implication — would the use aspects of the transferee tack on. The presumption follows that the transferee spouse occupies and uses the transferred property as his/her principal residence.

Section 121(d)(3)(A) is an extremely liberal rule when transferring residential properties incident to divorce. Apparently, Congress intends that spouses work out their personal residence affairs in such a way that *both* — though separately — can claim the maximum exclusion allowance at time of sale. Our version of what Congress probably had in mind is portrayed in Figure 9.3. Until some pertinent contrary revenue ruling or court ruling is published, we believe that our Figure 9.3 represents the "plain language" interpretation intended. If the past is any indication of the future, any judicial "spin" on the plain language often takes many years of debate and dispute. Without specific guidance to the contrary, the plain language of tax law is acceptable.

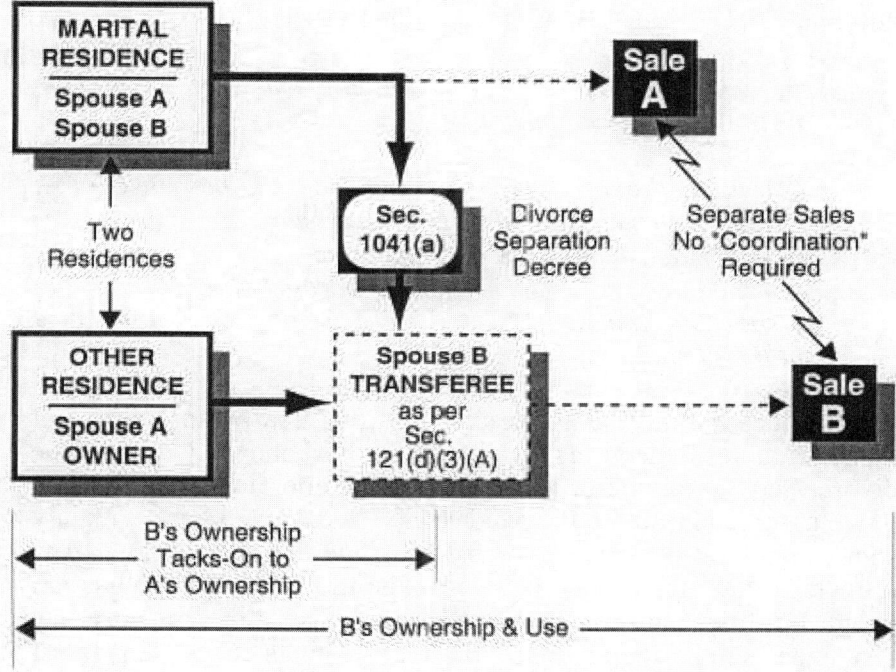

Fig. 9.3 - Principle of Ownership "Tack-On" Under Sec. 121(d)(3)(A)

Move-Out Spouse's Use Period

In contrast to the above, subparagraph (B) of Section 121(d)(3) focuses on the move-out spouse who has not quitclaimed title to the residence to the stay-in spouse. The difference here is a compulsory move-out by the divorce/separation decree. The title to subparagraph (B) reads: ***Property Used by Former Spouse Pursuant to Divorce Decree, Etc.*** Its text reads:

*Solely for the purposes of this section, an individual **shall be treated as using** property as such individual's principal residence during any period of ownership while such individual's spouse or former spouse is granted use of the* *property under a divorce or separation instrument (as defined in Section 71(b)(2)).* [Emphasis added.]

Reference to "this section" means Section 121 in its entirety. Reference to Section 71(b)(2) is the citation that—

*(2)   **Divorce or Separation Instrument**. The term "divorce or separation instrument" means—*

(A) a decree of divorce or separate maintenance or a written instrument incident to such a decree,
(B) a written separation agreement, or
(C) a decree (not described in subparagraph (A)) requiring a spouse to make payments for the support or maintenance of the other spouse.

The idea behind the above two citations is a presumption that the marital residence was co-owned by husband and wife. The divorce/separation decree must require that one of the two spouses move completely out of the residence. This is necessary to legally signify physical termination of the marriage under state law. Any property separation can come later. The move-out spouse has not given up his share of ownership, just his ability to use the residence as his principal place of abode. This is not tax harmful if the residence is sold within a reasonable period of time.

Federal tax law recognizes the situation as an involuntary conversion of one's use rights to his own property. As an expression of this recognition, Section 121(d)(3)(B) enables the move-out spouse to tack on to his/her actual use time the continued use time of the former spouse. This puts both former spouses on an equal footing with regard to the "two years or more" ownership and use requirements of Section 121(a). This enables *each* of the two former spouses to claim the maximum allowable $250,000 exclusion of gain when the residence is finally sold. As we portray in Figure 9.4, subparagraph (B) of Section 121(d)(3) is an overdue correction to the injustice that prevailed under prior law.

Our depiction in Figure 9.4 is not without legal challenge should a marital residence be sold more than three years after the move-out spouse moves out. As yet, there is no judicial resolution of conflict between the 3-year "vacancy rule" of Section 121 and the 6-year "incident to divorce rule" of Section 1041. Resolution depends on the comparison of facts and circumstances.

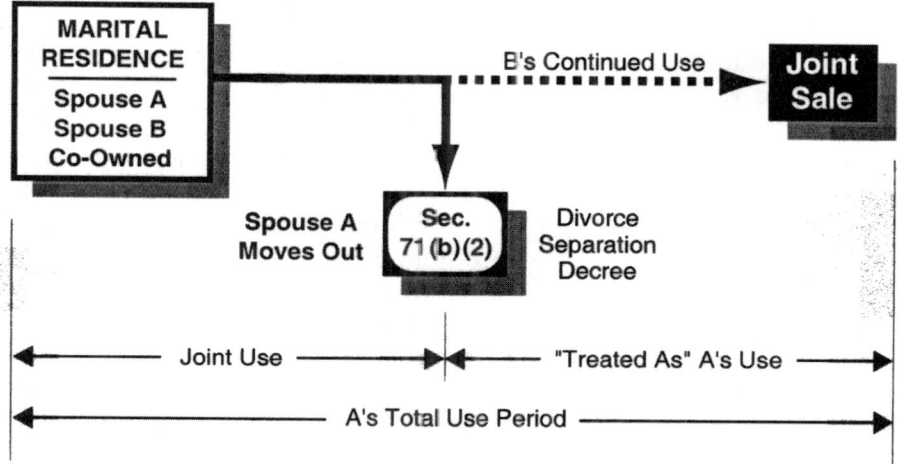

Fig. 9.4 - Principle of Move-Out Spouse's Use Under Sec. 121(d)(3)(B)

The 50/50 Presumption

In sale of divorce residence situations, the presumption is that ownership interests are 50/50. This has nothing to do with state laws on property settlement. It is strictly a federal tax presumption for division-of-property purposes. In 1982 Congress repealed all gift taxation between spouses. Spouses can now engage in unlimited commingling and gifting of assets between each other, without having to account to the IRS for each asset transfer. Divorce was not the underlying reason for the change. Rather, it was the impracticality of interspousal gift tax administration..

For those who want a tax law citation on point, it is Section 2523: *Gift to Spouse*. Subsection 2523(a) thereof reads in full—

Where a donor who is a citizen or resident transfers during the calendar year by gift an interest in property to a donee who at the time of the gift is the donor's spouse, there shall be allowed as a deduction in computing taxable gifts for the year an amount with respect to such interest equal to its value.

In simple language, Section 2523(a) says that *any interest* in property gifted to a spouse is allowed as a deduction when computing taxable gifts. Ordinarily, any gift over $11,000 is taxable. But, in the case of spouses, any amount gifted is deductible. Hence, no gift tax accounting applies.

Thus, the presumption is that where spouses have property in *any* cotenancy form, it is owned 50/50 by each. This is presumed so, even if one spouse contributed 100% to the property acquisition. Such is the premise of Section 1041(b) whereby *any transfer of property* between spouses, be it of ownership, use, or otherwise, is treated as a gift. Without good records, serious inequities can arise from this presumption.

As an example, consider the case where one spouse, say the wife, was previously married. She acquired the residence from her previous spouse by quitclaim. Although the house was worth $250,000, her carryover basis is $50,000. She remarries and puts the name of her new husband on the title deed. For this, he agrees to make all mortgage payments. Some two years and $10,000 in mortgage and other payments later, divorce ensues. The house is sold for $350,000. What happens in this case?

Since the residence was in cotenancy form at time of the divorce sale, 50% is presumed to belong to the husband. He gets $175,000 cash (less 50% of the selling expenses) out of the deal. He also gets 50% of the wife's $50,000 basis, which constitutes $25,000 as "return of capital" to him. In this case, as per Section 121(b)(1), all cash received after expenses (approximately $162,500) is tax excludable. Yet, the husband put only $10,000 into the residence.

Is the 50/50 presumption fair?

In the example above, it is not fair. But it is the presumptive position taken by the IRS when spouses file separate Schedules D following a divorce. If contested, the presumption prevails unless the injured spouse can convincingly trace her greater-than-50% ownership interest.

Non-50/50 Fractional Interests

To show how complicated things can get, suppose two divorcing spouses, who agree to sell their marital residence, had signed a prenuptial (or other written) agreement when they married. They had agreed that the marital residence they would buy would be owned in direct proportion to the identifiable *capital contribution* of each. They were both working at the time and had separate (though unequal) sources of income.

The separate accounting agreement was not a matter of distrust of each other. It was merely an act of prudence arising from the "horror stories" of their working-couple friends who had gone through divorce. The idea was that, at any time, separate fractional ownership interests in their residence could be established.

What constitutes a capital contribution? It is actual money (capital) put into the residence by each spouse. It *excludes* personal labor, payments of mortgage interest, and ordinary maintenance and repairs. The cumulative accounting starts on date of purchase and ends on date of sale. Let us illustrate.

Assume that the marital residence was purchased for $300,000 and that a 20% down payment ($60,000) was required. Of this, Spouse A contributed $36,000 and Spouse B contributed $24,000. Thus, their initial ownership interests were

Spouse A: $\dfrac{36,000}{60,000}$ = 60%

Spouse B: $\dfrac{24,000}{60,000}$ = 40%

100%

Each spouse was required to sign the mortgage papers on the $240,000 balance, with the result that each was co-liable. However, they could contribute equally or unequally to the mortgage payments. But only payments on principal count as capital.

Assume that during marriage up to the date of sale, each spouse could separately identify the following contributions of capital:

Mortgage principal—

Spouse A: 13,000
Spouse B: 12,000

25,000

Capital improvements—

Spouse A:	8,640
Spouse B:	5,960

14,600

What is each spouse's adjusted fractional interest on date of sale?

The total capital contributed (down payment plus mortgage payments on principal plus improvements) is $60,000 plus $25,000 plus $14,600 for a total of $99,600. Based on this amount, each spouse's adjusted fractional interest would be—

$$\text{Spouse A:} \quad \frac{36,000 + 13,000 + 8,640}{99,600} = \frac{57,640}{99,600} = 57.87\%$$

$$\text{Spouse B:} \quad \frac{24,000 + 12,000 + 5,960}{99,600} = \frac{41,960}{99,600} = 42.13\%$$

100.00%

It takes effort to generate the spousal allocations exemplified above. But, if at all achievable, the intention to do so should be incorporated into the divorce decree. At the same time, the "real estate reporting person" should be instructed to show the proper allocation (fractional share of selling price) on each of **two separate** Forms 1099-S: one for Spouse A; one for Spouse B.

In short, our position is that, unless a divorce residence is to be quitclaimed outright to one spouse (it being $250,000 or less in value), it should be retained in co-ownership form. Thereupon, the decree should require that it be sold within three years of the cessation of the marriage. Under such an arrangement both former spouses could enjoy allocably the tax-free benefits of Section 121.

10

PRORATA BUSINESS USE

When Portions Of Residential Property Are Used For Business Purposes, Different Rules Apply When The Property Is Sold. This Is Because Business Activities Enjoy A DEPRECIATION Deduction Which Has To Be "Recaptured" At Time Of Sale. None Of The Recapture Amounts Participate In The Section 121 Exclusionary Benefits. Different Recapture Rules Apply Depending On Whether The Business Is WITHIN Your Principal Residence Or NOT WITHIN IT. When "Mixed Use" Property Is Sold, You Treat The Matter As TWO Separate Sales: A Residential Portion And A Non-Residential Portion. For This, A New IRS Form Is Required.

One is entitled to use his residential property for business purposes, if he so desires. Doing so, of itself, does not disqualify it as a personal residence. However, when the property is sold, the business use portion *does not participate* in the exclusion benefits of Section 121 with respect to any gain. This means that special attention must be given to proper allocations between personal use and business use of residential property at all times.

There are four general categories of business use of one's property. These are:

1. Office in home
2. Subdivision of land
3. Rental income
4. Side farming

Different tax allocation situations arise from each category of use.

"Office in home" pertains to the use of one or more rooms (including shop, studio, and storage space) for one's primary business. This applies to such persons as outside salesmen, consultants, artists, accountants, and others who are considered to be independent proprietors. No office/shop/studio space is provided by an employer. They report their business income and expenses on Schedule C (1040): ***Profit or Loss from Business***. The term "expenses" includes an allowance for *depreciation* of the office-in-home structure.

Subdivision of land occurs when a homeowner parcels his adjacent excess acreage, and offers it for sale. Depending on local zoning ordinances and amount of adjacent land, the parcels may be improved or unimproved. Land itself does not depreciate, though some improvements thereto may. Gain and expenses of sale are reported on Schedule D (1040): ***Capital Gains and Losses***.

Rental income from the use of one's residence is the offering of a portion of it to others for use as a residence. The rented portion may be one or more rooms, separate living quarters, or one or more separate rental units. Renting to business tenants is also included. The rental income and expenses are reported on Schedule E (1040): ***Supplemental Income Schedule***. Here, again, the term "expenses" includes an allowance for *depreciation.*

Side farming consists of breeding animals (e.g., alpacas, horses, parrots), vineyard growing, grafting nursery stock, raising berries, fruit, nuts, etc. Farm income and expenses are reported on Schedule F (1040): ***Profit or Loss from Farming***. Included as "expenses" are *depreciation* allowances for farm buildings, breeder animals, fruit trees, and equipment.

In all these business activities, the business-use portion of residential property must be carefully — diligently — prorated. Hence, the term "prorata" in the title of this chapter.

Allowance for Depreciation

The term "depreciation," as you may already know, is a tax-recognized allowance (deduction) for any real or tangible property used for business purposes. The basic law on this is Section 167(a): ***Depreciation; General Rule***. This general rule reads in full—

There shall be allowed as a depreciation deduction a reasonable allowance for the exhaustion, wear and tear (including a reasonable allowance for obsolescence)—

(1) of property used in a trade or business, or

(2) of property held for the production of income.

A companion law to Section 167(a) is 168(a): ***Accelerated Cost Recovery System; General Rule***. This also reads in full as—

Except as otherwise provided in this section, the depreciation deduction provided by Section 167(a) for any tangible property shall be determined by using—

(1) the applicable depreciation method [accelerated, straight line],

(2) the applicable recovery period [in years], *and*

(3) the applicable convention [mid-month, mid-quarter, half year].

Section 167 consists of approximately 3,000 statutory words, whereas Section 168 consists of nearly 18,000 such words. When adding regulations, rulings, and explanations of the variants of Sections 167 and 168, nearly 800,000 — yes, 800 *thousand* — words of tax text are involved. From this vast "tax text," all you really need to know is that, for purposes herein, the allowability of depreciation applies only to the **business use** portion of property. It does not apply to any personal-use portion of a principal residence. Consequently, you should expect some additional rules under Section 121 when a mixed-use residence is sold.

Depreciation after May 6, 1997

To make sure that you do not miss the nonexclusivity of certain gain when selling the business portion of your residential property, a special rule applies. Said rule is Section 121(d)(6): ***Recognition of Gain Attributable to Depreciation***. These title words alone put you clearly on notice. The "recognition of gain" bit is another way of saying that any depreciation deduction allowed is *recaptured* (in some manner). There are two forms of this recapture, namely: (1) as ordinary capital gain (with no Section 121(a) exclusion), and (2) as ordinary income (to the extent of certain depreciation deductions presale allowed).

The phrase *Attributable to Depreciation* is your cue that it is the business use portion of your residence that is targeted for "recognition of gain." Only property which is used in a trade or business, or in the production of income, can claim a depreciation deduction. When such property is sold, there is a recognition-of-gain element with respect to the Section 121(a) exclusion.

More specifically, the gain recognition rule of subsection 121(d)(6) reads as—

> *Subsection (a)* [re exclusion of gain] ***shall not apply*** *to so much of the gain from the sale of any property as does not exceed the portion of the depreciation adjustments . . .* ***attributable to periods after*** *May 6, 1997 in respect of such property.* [Emphasis added.]

The Section 121 exclusion-of-gain benefits were first applicable to all sales of principal residences occurring after May 6, 1997. The extent of any depreciation properly allowable after that date is treated as *nonexclusionary gain*. As mentioned above, certain "depreciation recapture" rules apply.

Regulation § 1.121-1(d)(2): ***Depreciation taken after May 6, 1997; Example***, illustrates the simplest form of recapture. This official example reads (in key part)—

> On July 1, 2003, Taxpayer A moves into a house that he owns and had rented since July 1, 2001. He took depreciation deductions totaling $14,000 for the period that he rented the property. After using the residence as his principal residence for 2 full years, A sells the property on August 1, 2005. A's gain realized from the sale is $80,000. [There are no other tax complications.] Only $66,000 ($80,000 gain realized – $14,000 depreciation deductions) may be excluded under Section 121. A must recognize $14,000 of the gain [under the ordinary rule for capital gains when nonprincipal residence real property is sold.]

We call this example the *within* recapture rule. That is, the business-use portion of the property was within the structural shell of the taxpayer's dwelling unit. There is also a *not within* recapture rule which is more complicated and which we explain below. Meanwhile, we depict in Figure 10.1 the distinction between within and not within business usage of residential property.

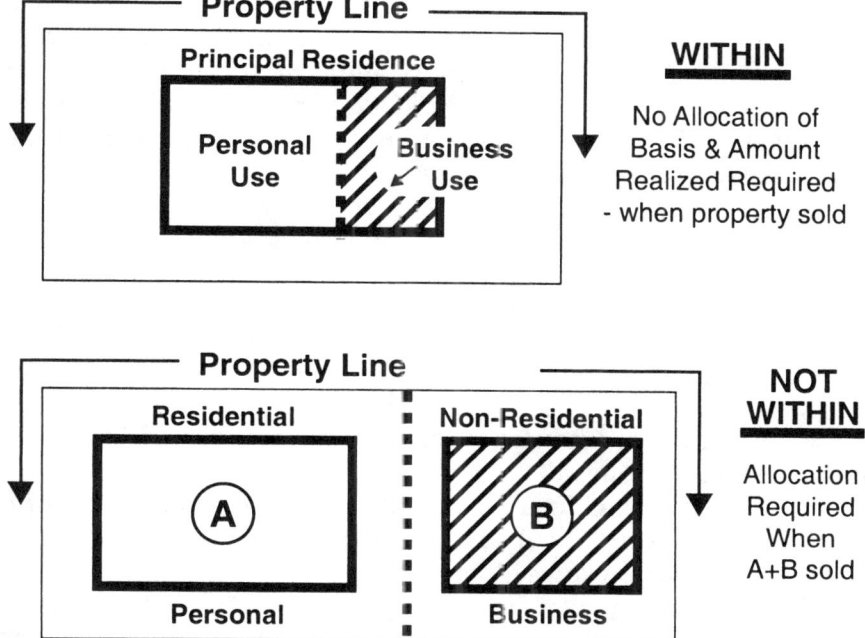

Fig. 10.1 - The "Within" & "Not Within" Business Use of Residential Property

The "Not Within" Allocation Rule

When business-use property is not within the structural confines of your dwelling unit, Regulation § 1.121-1(**e**) comes in. Its caption is: *Property used in part as a principal residence.* As used in this caption, the term "property" includes both the residential and non-residential uses of the common parcel that you acquired. The "used in part" clearly implies that part of your property may be used for non-residential (business) purposes. But where does the "not within" aspect come forth?

Answer: It lies in paragraph (1) of said regulation which is captioned: *Allocation required.* Although we'll cite three of the four sentences of this 110-word regulation, you'll not find the term "not within" directly stated. It appears in the parenthesized clause:

(separate from the dwelling unit). The "separate from" surely means "not within." While this is obvious when we point it out to you, it is not so obvious when you read the regulatory text itself.

The first three sentences of Regulation § 1.121-1(e)(1) read—

> *Section 121 will not apply to the gain allocable to any portion (separate from the dwelling unit) of property sold or exchanged with respect to which a taxpayer does not satisfy the [2 out of 5 year] use requirement. Thus, if a portion of the property was used for residential purposes and a portion of the property (separate from the dwelling unit) was used for non-residential [business] purposes, only the gain allocable to the residential portion is excludable under Section 121. No allocation is required if both the residential and non-residential portions of the property are within the same dwelling unit.*

What's the real substance of this regulation? What is it fundamentally getting at?

Answer: Since its focus is on Section 121: ***Exclusion of Gain***, etc., no gain can be calculated until the property is actually sold. When sold, what are you selling?

You are selling two different-use portions of your property: personal and business. The personal (residential)-use portion has different tax characteristics from the business (non-residential)-use portion. Hence, the regulation says that allocation/separation of the two different use portions is required. The result is like making two sales at the same time. Sale A may be X percent of the total sales price, whereas Sale B may be Y percent. The two allocable portions X and Y must total 100%.

Handling "Two Sales"

When you sell residential property consisting of some "not within" business-use activity, it's like making two separate sales. True, it is one sale (a "package") insofar as the real estate broker (reporting person) is concerned, but it is **two** tax accountings insofar as the IRS is concerned. Two different domains of tax rules are involved. We advise, therefore, that you emphatically instruct your broker to prepare the escrow settlement statement as two prorata sales: a residence portion and a business portion.

Why do we tell you this?

Because the residence portion of the sale goes on Schedule D (as you should be well aware of by now, from Chapter 8). The business portion of the sale goes on an entirely different form, namely: **Form 4797**: *Sales of Business Property*. We'll explain more about this form shortly below.

As an example of what lies in store for you, suppose you sold your home and separate business-use portion for $365,000. Assume that your business-use portion was 20%. Its selling price would be $365,000 x 20% or $73,000. Your residence portion would have a prorata sale price of $292,000 ($365,000 x 80%).

Can't you imagine the computer-matching *miscommunication* that you'd be subject to by the IRS when it receives your Schedule D with $292,000 reported, when your broker reports $365,000 on Form 1099-S?

In situations like this, the IRS assumes that the $292,000 on your Schedule D was, somehow, inadvertently unreported by your broker. So, it will accept your Schedule D. But, IN ADDITION, it will assume that you made a separate sale of other property for $365,000. It will then computer tax you on two amounts: $292,000 + 365,000 = $657,000.

You can avoid this unpleasantry by insisting that your broker issue **two** Forms 1099-S: one for the residence portion and one for the business portion. To emphasize this point, we present Figure 10.2. The message is that, at time of sale of your "mixed use" property, you have engaged in two separate tax accounting activities. Obviously, proper precautions must be taken.

Overview of Form 4797

Especially note in Figure 10.2 that the business-use portion of your allocated/separated sale is reported on **Form 4797**. As stated earlier, this particular form is titled: *Sales of Business Property*. Its format and calculational procedures are quite different from those on Schedule D: *Capital Gains and Losses*. Hence, we show both of these forms in Figure 10.2

The purpose of Form 4797 is to separate the business portion gain into two tax components: (1) capital gain, and (2) ordinary income. The capital gain amount is directed onto Schedule D where it combines with other non-Section 121 gains and losses. The ordinary income amount is directed onto Form 1040: *Individual Income Tax Return*, for combining with other sources of income and loss. This ordinary income amount (on Form 1040) is the recapture of the business-use depreciation deductions that we alluded to earlier.

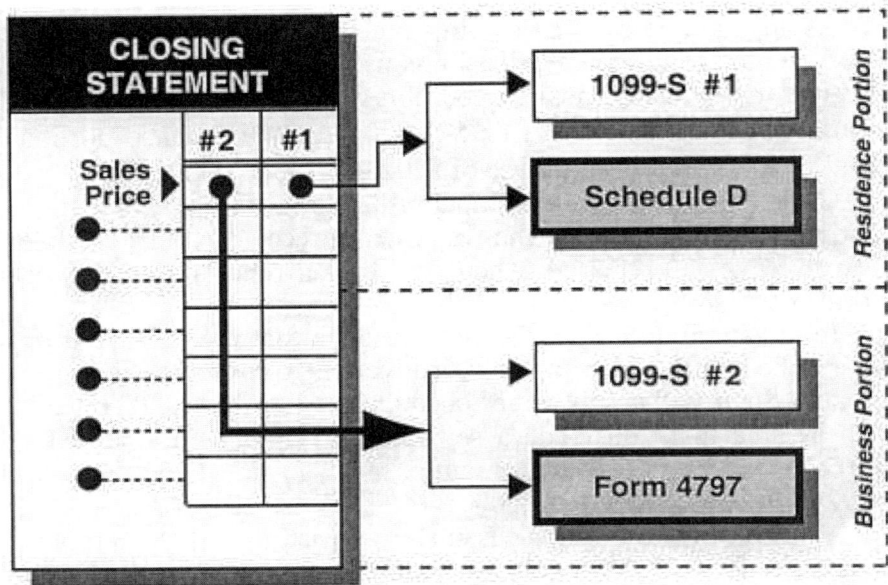

Fig. 10.2 - The "Two Sales" of Mixed Use Residential Property

To attain its purpose, Form 4797 is arranged into three parts, I and II on the front, and part III on the back. Each part can accommodate four sales simultaneously in the event that the "package" consists of different types of depreciable items. The small-print headnote on Form 4797 instruction says—

Enter the gross proceeds from sales or exchanges reported to you on Form(s) 1099-B or 1099-S (or substitute statement) that you are including [in Parts I, II, and III].

This is your cue that you are expected to have a separate 1099-S for the business-use portion of your property sale. Initially, you report the business-use portion of the sale on Part III (we'll explain why in a moment). Before so, however, Part I contains valuable instructive information. Part I is titled: *Sales or Exchanges of Property Used in a Trade or Business . . . Held More than 1 Year*. It consists of seven columns, namely:

(a) *Description of property*
(b) *Date acquired*
(c) *Date sold*
(d) *Gross sales price*
(e) **Depreciation allowed or allowable since acquisition**
(f) *Cost or other basis, plus improvements* [before sale] *and expense of sale*
(g) **Gain or <loss>**. *Subtract (f) from the sum of (d) and (e)*.

Upon reading these columnar headings you become aware that the terminology on Form 4797 differs from that on Schedule D. The principal difference is column (e): *Depreciation allowed or allowable since acquisition*. The term "allowed or allowable" means that if you overclaimed the proper amount, you recapture that amount. If you underclaimed the proper amount, you recapture the proper amount. For sales of residential property, the term "since acquisition" means after May 6, 1997.

Part II of Form 4797 is captioned: **Ordinary Gains and Losses**. Part III is captioned: **Gain from Disposition of** [Certain Business] **Property**. The bracketed term "certain business" refers to those businesses identified by Sections 1245, 1250, 1252, 1254, and 1255. Note that the term "losses" does not appear whatsoever in the Part III caption.

The idea is to do the Part III gain *first* (it has similar columns to Part I) because it adds many (about 17) computational lines for sorting out different types of depreciation for recapture. The summary (bottom line) to Part III designates which portion of the total gain is capital gain and which portion is ordinary income. Then the capital gain portion goes to Part I and the ordinary income portion goes to Part II. The functional aspects in this regard are depicted in Figure 10.3. If you want or need more information than this, you must get a copy of the official Form 4797 **and** its seven pages of 3-columnar instructions.

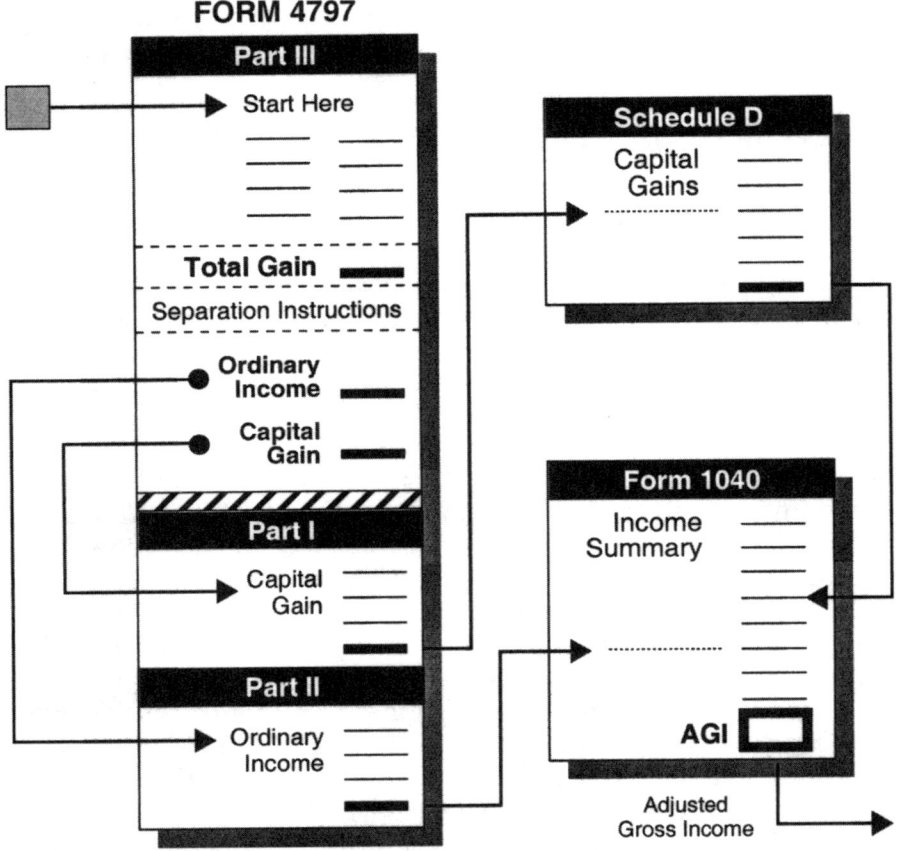

FORM 4797

Fig. 10.3 - The Separation of Depreciation Recapture Events on Form 4797

Method of Allocation

Regulation § 1.121-1(e)(3): *Method of allocation*, states that—

For purposes of determining the amount of **gain** *applicable to the residential and non-residential* [business use] *portion of the property, the taxpayer must allocate the* **basis** *and the* **amount realized** *between the residential and non-residential portions of the property using the* **same method** *of allocation that the*

*taxpayer used to determine depreciation adjustments . . .
[where] applicable.* [Emphasis added.]

Do keep in mind that this allocation requirement applies specifically to those business activities that are separate and apart from (that is, those which are **not within**) your dwelling unit. The reference to "basis" and "amount realized" (for gain) are items which appear on Schedule D **and** on Form 4797. How you compute these items depends on how well you kept your own records with respect to allocation and depreciation matters. You'll have to do your own take on this, but we'll give you some pointers.

Depending on the nature of business activities that you conduct on your residential property, we suggest you pursue three general allocation concepts. These three concepts involve—

1. **Land** — does not depreciate,
2. **Buildings** — only straight line depreciation, and
3. **Equipment** — usually, accelerated depreciation.

Editorial Note: The term "equipment" is a catchall for any depreciable item not treated as a habitable-type building.

For each of these categories, you need to establish a **Business Use Fraction: B.U.F.** That is, you determine what portion of the land, what portion of the buildings (on the land), and what portion of equipment (either on the land or in the buildings) is used for business purposes. The measuring index for these fractions is either *area* or *time*. If it is land, acreage is used (1 acre = 43,560 sq. ft.). If it is one or more buildings, square footage is used. If it is equipment, hours per year are used (1 year = 8,760 hrs). In some business-use situations, you could have three separate B.U.F.s. However, in terms of the amount of income generated, one category of business usage generally dominates the others.

Whatever measuring index you use, you must apply that index to both the business use of your property and its personal residential use. The mechanics for doing so appear as follows—

$$\text{B.U.F.} = \frac{\text{Business use}}{\text{Business use} + \text{Personal use}} = \text{some fraction less than } 100\%$$

The resulting B.U.F. is applied to the initial acquisition basis of your property (business plus personal), AND to its gross sales price. Because of so many different depreciation rules (which are beyond our discussion here), the business portion of your initial acquisition basis will change over business-use time. At this point, we need to exemplify what we are getting at.

A "Not Within" Example

Suppose you bought a 3-acre parcel of residential property with two separate habitable buildings fixed thereon. You occupy one of the buildings as the principal residence for yourself and family. You rent the other building for whatever best business use (highest rental income) you can derive from it. Further, suppose that the amount of usable space by the business tenant is 3,800 square feet (including driveways, parking space, and garage). Similarly, your residential use portion is 4,200 square feet. The rest of your property (2.816 acres) is vacant land. What is your B.U.F. for allocation of basis and sales price purposes?

$$\text{Answer: Your B.U.F.} = \frac{3,800 \text{ sq. ft}}{3,800 + 4,200} = \frac{3,800}{8,000} = 47.5\%$$

This fraction applies "across the board" to your *initial* acquisition basis and to your gross sales price. "Across the board" includes the 2.816 acres of vacant land. [43,560 sq. ft. per Ac – 8,000 sq. ft. usage ÷ 43,560 = 0.816 acres. To this, add 2 acres.] Unless you sell the vacant land separately, it is all part of the same acquisition and sales package.

A visualization of this example is presented in Figure 10.4. Note that we also show a dotted line area which we designate as *Equipment*. The term "equipment," when used broadly, is construed to include any property item that is movable. It is movable if it is not fixed permanently to the land, or not fixed to a building which itself is fixed permanently to the land. Because it is movable, equipment is not normally part and parcel of a real estate purchase and sale. It can be bought separately and can be sold separately . . . . or it can be junked separately.

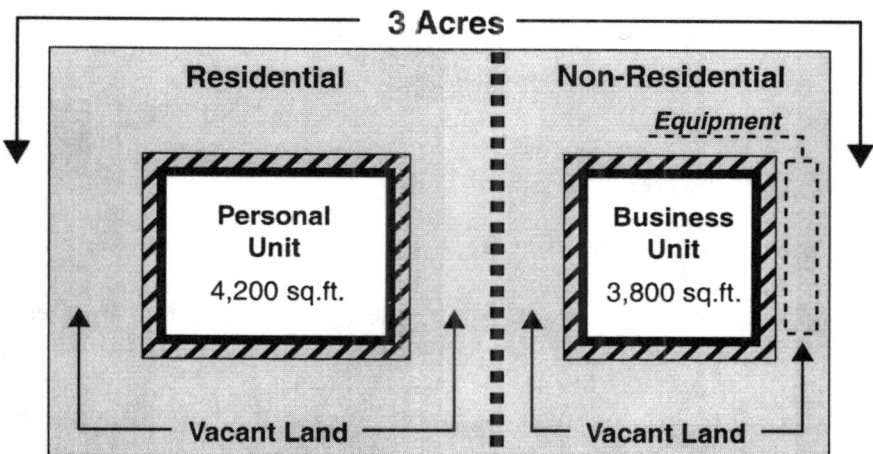

Fig. 10.4 - A "Not Within" Allocation Example of Residential Property

Now, suppose the land and buildings in Figure 10.4 (without equipment) were purchased for $365,000 and sold for $985,000. Using the B.U.F. of 47.5% above, what are the allocations to the basis and gross sales price? [*Caution*: Basis can vary. So, be sure to use the "adjusted basis" for the total property at time of sale.]

Initially, the respective bases (for calculating gain) are:

Business Portion: $365,000 x 0.475 = $173,375

Residential Portion: 365,000 x $\frac{0.525}{1.000}$ = $\frac{191,625}{\$365,000}$

Correspondingly, the gross sales price is allocated as—

Business portion: $985,000 x 0.475 = $467,875

Residential portion: 985,000 x 0.525 = 517,125

Recall that Regulation § 1.121-1(e)(3): *Method of allocation*, cited above, says—

the taxpayer must allocate the basis [as adjusted for depreciation] ***and the amount realized*** *between the residential and non-residential portions of the property.*

Have we done this? No, we haven't. We have allocated the gross sales price which is necessary for determining the amount realized. We haven't determined the amount realized because we haven't gotten into *basis adjustment* matters. It is one's **adjusted basis** in property sold, when subtracted from its gross sales price, that establishes the amount realized.

Adjusted Basis & Amount Realized

In the simplest terms possible, one's adjusted basis in property (whether land, buildings, or equipment) is its initial acquisition cost (or the equivalent thereof) *plus* or *minus* certain adjustments. Plus adjustments are improvements to property, fixed additions thereto, or defense of title regarding its ownership. Minus adjustments are detachments from the property, casualties thereto (after insurance reimbursements), and — for business usage only — depreciation allowances. Except in rare cases, your adjusted basis at time of sale will differ from that at time of acquisition.

Once your adjusted basis is established, the amount realized is simply gross sales price LESS adjusted basis. The amount realized on a Section 121-related property sale must be a gain. Hence, the amount realized and total gain are one and the same. Putting these matters another way, we have—

Step 1 — Gross sales price
Step 2 — Cost or other basis plus expense of sale
Step 3 — Depreciation allowed or allowable
Step 4 — Adjusted basis: subtract Step 3 from Step 2
Step 5 — Amount realized (total gain): subtract Step 4 from Step 1 ["total" = recapture gain + exclusionary gain]

This 5-step sequence is the exact sequence of entry events to Part III of Form 4797. (Recall Figure 10.3.) Thereafter, depreciation recapture computational events apply. The recapture events (as capital gain and/or as ordinary income) differ depending on the type of property sold. The statutory categories of recapture property are: (1) Section 1245 equipment, (2) Section 1250 buildings, (3) Section 1252 farmland, (4) Section 1254 mines, and

(5) Section 1255 cost-sharing. Hence, for the business-use portion of Section 121-type property sold, there is no way to allocate the amount realized without first allocating the gross sales price. For this allocation, the proper B.U.F. is required.

As to the residential (personal use) portion of the property sold, only Steps 1, 2, and 5 above apply. Step 2 for both residential and non-residential uses is where each respective adjusted basis evolves. In revised terms, the Step 2 is acquisition cost, plus improvements, less detachments, plus expense of sale. Accordingly, the allocation factor [B.U.F. for business use; 1 – B.U.F. for personal use] has to be applied to each common component (cost, improvements, detachments, and expense of sale) before any amount of gain can be realized. Again, we point out that the *allocation mandate* applies only when the business-use portion of Section 121 property is *not within* the confines of the personal-use portion.

The "Within" Difference

Let's go back and acquaint you with the last two sentences of Regulation § 1.121-1(e)(1): *Allocation required*. Previously, we cited the third of its four sentences. Let's now add the fourth sentence and cite the two together. They read—

No allocation is required if both the residential and non-residential portions of the property are within the same dwelling unit. However, Section 121 does not apply to the gain allocable to the residential portion of the property to the extent provided by paragraph (d) [below].

The reference to "paragraph (d)" is: *Depreciation taken after May 6, 1997*, the last sentence of which reads—

Depreciation adjustments allocable to any portion of the property to which the Section 121 exclusion does not apply under paragraph (e) [above] *are not taken into account for* [exclusion of gain] *purposes.*

What does this regulatory language really say?

It says that, if you use your dwelling unit for business purposes — such as, for an office in home — all depreciation allowed or allowable is recaptured directly. It is recaptured as ordinary capital gain; not as Section 121 exclusionary capital gain.

To show the recapture amount, you report the Section 121 sale on Schedule D: *Capital Gains and Losses*. Before you can show the amount recaptured, you have to establish the full realized gain. From this gain, you subtract the allowable Section 121 exclusion. Then you add back the recapture gain. Using example figures, **Column (f)** on Schedule D would appear as follows:

Step 1: Gain realized $385,000

Step 2: Section 121 exclusion (single)   <250,000>

Step 3: Subtract Step 2 from Step 1   135,000

Step 4: Depreciation recapture   25,000

Step 5: Taxable gain (**Add** Steps 3 and 4) $160,000

Because the business-use portion is within your principal residence you get a computational break. No allocation of the gross sales price is required. No allocation of the adjusted basis (plus expense of sale) is required. The net effect is that your allowable Section 121 exclusion is *reduced* by the cumulative amount of depreciation that you have claimed for the building portion that you used for business purposes. Stating this another way, if you subtract the $25,000 of depreciation (at Step 4) from the $250,000 of exclusionary allowance (at Step 2), you wind up with the same $160,000 taxable capital gain [385,000 – (250,000 – 25,000)] as at Step 5 above. Instead of two separate sales (à la Figure 10.2), you have only one sale. But you do have depreciation recapture on your hands. This means having convincing records on the correct amount of depreciation "allowed or allowable."

Office-in-Home Depreciation

By far the most common business use of a dwelling unit is one's office in home. Ordinarily, an independent worker (whether an employee or nonemployee) needs some amount of office space within which to conduct his or her daily income-producing activities. He/she needs an office to house appropriate furniture, fixtures, and equipment, and as a place to meet with customers and clients. In such cases, one is allowed a prorata depreciation deduction for deterioration of the property structures within which he works. Let us illustrate in some detail.

Suppose you are a self-employed arson investigator who works exclusively out of your home. You have an office from which you conduct your business and prepare your reports. You also have a small shop where you examine structural parts and equipment of buildings deliberately set on fire by arsonists and domestic terrorists. You have a photo lab and storage space for chemicals used in testing the burned specimens. You have a vehicle (van) which is outfitted with fire extinguishers and probing tools; you garage it in your home. Altogether, you have four separate areas of your home allocated to business usage. A plan view of your business-use arrangement is presented in Figure 10.5. Note that we designate the four separate business areas of your home as A, B, C, and D. We also show the square footage of each of these areas, as well as that for the total business space and the total residence space.

It is very helpful to prepare a diagram of your home, showing all the rooms, storage areas, hallways, and garage (if attached). If the garage is not attached, diagram it separately if any part is used for business. Shade all business areas, and show doors that open to the outside. If your home is multi-story, provide an elevation view showing how your clients would get to your office from the street. If the access space is used primarily for business, include it as such.

Variants of Figure 10.5 could apply to a studio-in-home for a commercial artist, to a parsonage-in-home for an ordained clergyman, to a shop-in-home for a free-lance repairman. Assume that indeed the spaces indicated are used for bona fide business purposes. Customers, clients, and parishioners can come and go, by appointment during normal business hours. There is no personal or family living in those spaces whatsoever.

If the in-home business is day care services provided to minor children, the measuring quantity is *hours*: not square feet. This is because personal and family living spaces are customarily used. Small children scamper all over the place. It would be too impractical to try to confine them to a designated space.

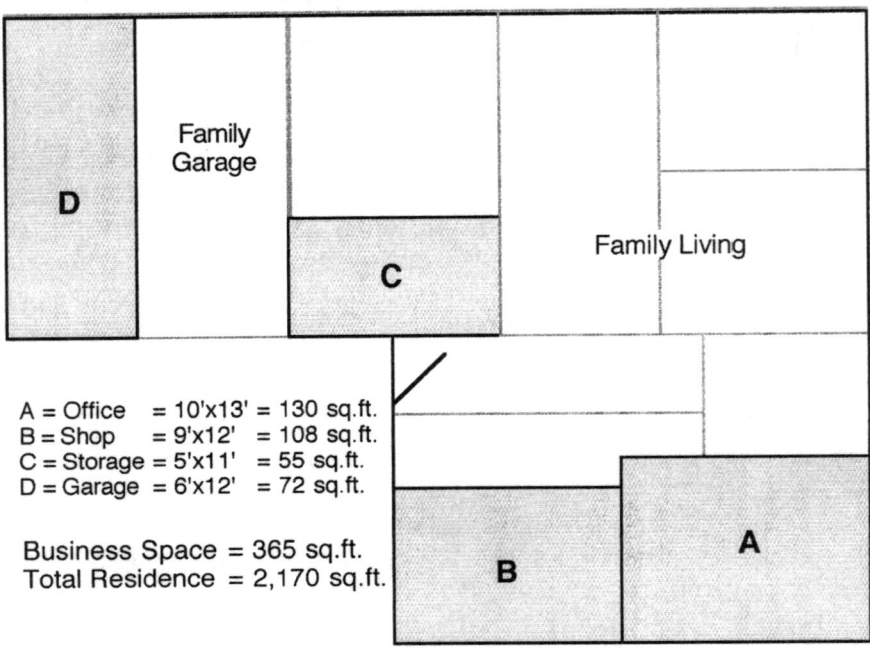

A = Office   = 10'x13' = 130 sq.ft.
B = Shop   = 9'x12' = 108 sq.ft.
C = Storage = 5'x11' = 55 sq.ft.
D = Garage   = 6'x12' = 72 sq.ft.

Business Space = 365 sq.ft.
Total Residence = 2,170 sq.ft.

Fig. 10.5 - Measurement of Space: Business Use of Home

The first step in the prorata allocation process is to measure all business spaces: length and breadth. Hint: measure to the *outside* of the walls To do this, measure inside then add the wall thickness to each dimension. The reason for using outside dimensions is that it is the building *structure* (including its fixtures and appurtenances) that depreciates: not the space of enclosed air. All items attached to the structure depreciate with it.

Identify each business space (as illustrated in Figure 10.5) and show its dimensions and square footage. Then measure the total residence space (personal plus business) and compute its square footage. Measure to outside surfaces if possible. Otherwise, measure inside, then add wall thickness. For residential construction, use 6" for each wall as being close enough.

Now Your Office Fraction

Next, compute the business space as a fraction or percentage of the total building portion of the residence. For example, suppose the total business space is 365 square feet, and the total building space (including garage) is 2,170 square feet. In this case, your *office* (for business) *use fraction* would be

$$\frac{365 \text{ sq. ft.}}{2,170 \text{ sq. ft.}} = 0.1682 = 16.82\%$$

The next step is to establish the cost or other basis of the building. This should be done up to the date that the business space was first used. The problem at this point is that the residence was acquired as building-plus-land as an integral purchase. We must separate out the land. It does not depreciate.

The taxpayer has the burden of establishing how much of the residence purchased is land, and how much is building. There are two ways of doing this. One, the County Assessor's Office usually assesses the land and building separately for property tax rate differences. If available, the assessor's information may be used. Otherwise, employ a professional appraiser to value the land and building for you.

For example, suppose the parcel of land (no excess acreage) on which your residence is built is valued at $126,000. And suppose the building separately is valued at $315,000. What is the building fraction of your total residence? It is—

$$\frac{315,000}{126,000 + 315,000} = \frac{315,000}{441,000} = 0.7142 = 71.42\%$$

Now, suppose the adjusted basis in your residence (land plus building plus improvements) up to the commencement of business is $326,000. What is the basis of your office in home for depreciation purposes?

Answer: $326,000 x 0.7142 (building fraction) x 0.1682 (office fraction) = $39,162.

Assuming that the building portion of your residence has a useful life of 30 years, your business-use depreciation would be

$$\frac{\$39,162}{30 \text{ yrs}} = \$1,305 \text{ per year}$$

Based on the facts above, $1,305 is the depreciation writeoff that you are allowed each year for business purposes.

Because an office in home is so common these days, a special IRS form is prescribed for computing **each year's** depreciation allowance. This is **Form 8829**: *Expenses for Business Use of Your Home*. Its Part III is where you compute the depreciation.

Part III (of Form 8829) duplicates much of what we have already presented. It does so, however, via two new concepts: (1) *business basis of building*, and (2) *depreciation percentage*. The business basis of building is simply the basis of your residential building times its business-use percentage. The depreciation percentage is 2.564% if your office in home was used the entire year for business. This figure derives from the expected useful life of a business use building being 39 years [1 ÷ 39 = 2.564%]. If you first start using the office — or cease using it — during the year, a reduced % for each of the 12 months is tabulated in the official instructions to Form 8829.

When your home is sold, you must "attach your own schedule" for showing the *cumulative* amount of depreciation taken since May 6, 1997. There is no provision on Form 8829 for doing this. This means that you jot down each year's separate depreciation, then add them all together at time of sale. On Schedule D (previously described) you show the amount of gain realized, and subtract your allowable Section 121 exclusion. Then ADD BACK the cumulative total office-in-home depreciation. This add-back feature recaptures the depreciation as ordinary capital gain. As you surely already know, capital gain tax rates are significantly lower than ordinary income tax rates.

11

INVOLUNTARY CONVERSION

Property That Is Destroyed In A Disaster, Or By Condemnation, Is Addressed By Section 1033. If ALL Reimbursement Proceeds Are EXCHANGED Into A Replacement Residence, No Gain Is Recognized. Proceeds That Go Into Nonresidential Items Or Money Are Taxable. Any Occupancy In A Temporary Residence, Pending Settlement Of The Reimbursement Process, "Tacks On" To Occupancy In The Converted Residence. You Have The Option Of Treating The Proceeds As An Exchange OR As A Sale. If An Exchange, No Section 121 Exclusion Of Gain Applies Until The Residence Is Sold.

There are situations in which one is compelled to give up his principal residence and seek another. No sale or exchange takes place involving the free choice or will of the owner. He disposes of his residence under compulsion and conditions over which he has no control. These dispositions are tax-termed *involuntary conversion* (without one's free will).

Involuntary conversion results primarily from destructive forces and condemnation powers. These are not dispositional "sales" in the ordinary sense. It is for this reason that special tax treatment applies. Since there is no special tax form that can be used to report the conversion, a taxpayer-designed "statement" attached to one's return is required.

Conversion by destruction covers all cases of physical damage caused by violent and external means. Examples are lightning, storm (tornado, hurricane), flood, earthquake, volcanic eruption, landslide, tidal wave, fire, and the like. Conversion by condemnation (or under the threat thereof) is the taking of property for public needs such as for freeway construction, airport expansion, public housing projects etc. The resulting destruction or condemnation may not be 100%. But it must be of such magnitude as to render a residence no longer habitable: beyond ordinary repair. Usually, restoration/replacement funds are sought through insurance claims and disaster loans from the government.

An involuntary disposition of one's residence may result in conversion into a replacement residence, or into money and other property. Whatever the cause, there is possibility of gain. This is due to the excess of awards, proceeds, and/or reimbursement over basis in former residence. Whenever there is a gain — whether under compulsion or not — there is accountability for tax.

Establishing the amount of gain under involuntary conversion conditions is tricky and time consuming. Insurance companies and government agencies do not pay promptly. Any reimbursement you get is quite unlike the closing escrow process in an ordinary sale. It usually takes several years before the full amount of the realized gain is known. Explaining the rules for establishing this gain is what this chapter is all about. Once your realized gain is known, the Section 121 exclusion benefits apply.

What Section 121 Says

Section 121 is intended for principal residences which have been sold or exchanged in the ordinary course of one's family living and occupational activities. When unusual circumstances occur which are outside of the general intent of new law, provisions must be made to encompass old law where relevant. The relevant old law for purposes of this chapter is Section 1033: *Involuntary Conversions*. Section 1033 was enacted back in 1950 and has been amended numerous times since then. It applies to all forms of destroyed/condemned property called: "converted property." Such property has capital gain potential.

In the case of one's principal residence, Section 121 has its own special rule with the same title words. It is Section 121(d)(**5**): *Involuntary Conversions*: *Application of Section 1033*.

As to subparagraph (A) of Section 121(d)(5), the statutory wording is—

*For purposes of this section, the destruction, theft, seizure, requisition, or condemnation of property shall be treated as the **sale** of such property.* [Emphasis added.]

The term "this section" refers to Section 121 in its entirety. Thus, the $250,000/$500,000 exclusionary amounts apply.

The phrase "shall be treated as [a] sale" means that, after the amount of conversion gain is established, if any, the exclusion of gain benefits apply (if so desired). Obviously, Congress did not intend that one be deprived of his exclusion benefits in those unfortunate circumstances where his principal residence is involuntarily converted. By treating the conversion as a "sale," one can wrap up his tax accounting at that time, and start over in a new or restored residence of his choice.

In addition to destruction and condemnation, subparagraph (A) includes reference to "theft, seizure, requisition." Stealing, seizing, and requisitioning a personal residence would be rare events. Yes, fraudulent titlings, unconscionable lawsuits, mortgage company foreclosures, tax liens and seizures, and requisitions by disaster authorities for emergency command centers could occur. Should any of these "takings" actually occur, no sale-like proceeds would be derived. Unless gross proceeds are involved, there is no possibility of establishing any realized gain. There could be realized loss, but losses are not the domain of Section 121.

Therefore, in this chapter we focus only on those destructive forces and condemnation processes that lead to involuntary gain. The point where "gain" begins requires special knowledge of its own. There is no way that we can convey this knowledge until you are more acquainted with Section 1033 and its provisions.

Introduction to Section 1033

A special tax law addresses the treatment of gain from involuntary conversion. This is Section 1033(a) of the Internal Revenue Code. Its two key general rules are: (1) *Conversion into Similar Property*, and (2) *Conversion into Money*.

Section 1033 is not exclusively applicable to personal residences. It applies equally to residences, nonresidences, business property, farm assets, livestock, excess acreage, outdoor advertising displays, maritime vehicles, aircraft, and so on. It is not a well written law. It is the patchwork of numerous amendments since its enactment more than 50 years ago. It consists of more than 3,500 statutory words. Like all patched-up laws, it has its own tax traps, gimmicks, and loopholes.

Its general rule (1) reads in pertinent part—

If property . . . is compulsorily or involuntarily converted . . . into property similar or related in service or use to the property so converted, ***no gain shall be recognized.*** [Emphasis added.]

General rule (1) under Section 1033(a) is similar in concept to the nonrecognition of rollover gain permitted formerly under Section 1034(a) [Rollover of Gain on Sale of Principal Residence]. Under repealed Section 1034(a), there was a 2-year replacement period within which the nonrecognition was valid. Under Section 1033(a)(1), there is no designated replacement period. The replacement period is whatever time it takes to process insurance claims, lawsuits, and government assistance programs. Settlements in these matters take easily three to four years or more. The costs for attorneys, appraisers, and consultants can be substantial. These costs have a direct effect, ultimately, on the amount of gain realized.

General rule (2) is more complicated than the above. Its preamble words read—

If property . . . is compulsorily or involuntarily converted . . . ***into money or property not similar or related in service or use*** *to the converted property, the* ***gain (if any) shall be recognized*** *except to the extent hereinafter provided.* [Emphasis added.]

The "extent hereinafter provided" covers another 800 words of special conditions. One of these conditions, subparagraph (A), permits a taxpayer to replace his residence, then "elect" to have any excess proceeds over replacement cost be treated as recognized gain. A second condition, subparagraph (B), requires that one start computing his gain—

2 years after the close of the first taxable year in which any part of the gain upon conversion is realized, or
at the close of such later date as the [IRS] *may designate on application by the taxpayer.*

Gain starts to be realized the moment one recovers his full capital basis in the property converted. For example, suppose the adjusted cash basis in your converted residence was $250,000. And, further, suppose that the fair market value of your property at the time of its destruction or condemnation was $600,000. After suing the insurance company or whomever, you are awarded $500,000 as compensation for the conversion. The moment you receive $251,000 you come under the *conversion to money* rule of Section 1033(a)(2). Every payment you receive thereafter has to be accounted for in the tax domain as "realized gain." The amount of gain *recognized* is the extent by which the compensation award exceeds the purchase cost of a replacement residence.

In Figure 11.1, we present an overview distinction between subsections (a)(1) and (a)(2) of Section 1033. The real substance of Section 1033 is its rule (2) within which rule (1) is the nonrecognition part. The replacement residence may be higher or lower in value than the residence converted.

"Threat or Imminence" of Condemnation

Section 1033(a) includes a parenthetical phrase which we excluded above. The excluded phrase is: "If property—

*(as a result of its destruction in whole or part, . . . or condemnation or **threat or imminence** thereof)*

is compulsorily or involuntarily converted . . ." The emphasized phrase raises the question: What constitutes the "threat or imminence" of condemnation?

The *threat or imminence* provision requires that the adversary party (usually a government agency)—

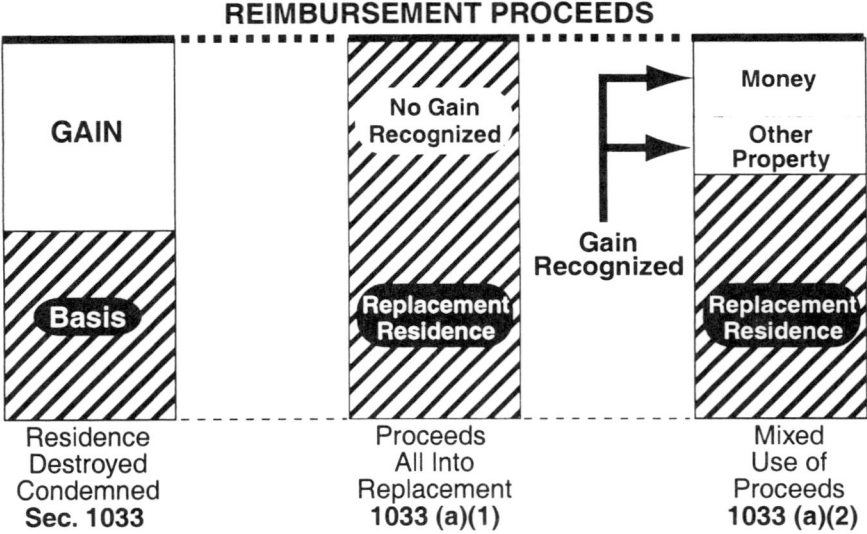

Fig. 11.1 - Treatment of Sec. 1033 Gain from Reimbursement Proceeds

1. Must have the legal power to condemn or to requisition, and

2. Must, in fact, make a threat of condemnation or make it known that condemnation is indeed imminent.

The disposition of one's residence under the above two conditions qualifies as an involuntary conversion. This is so regardless of whether condemnation proceedings, if undertaken, would be successful. The factual threat by a government body with the power to enforce its threat is sufficient. Once there's a "threat of condemnation" out there, one's property is at risk.

Condemnation is threatened or imminent when a homeowner is "informed," orally or in writing by a representative of a governmental body or by a public official authorized to acquire property for public use, that such body or official has "decided" to acquire his property. Some verification of the decision via an official memorandum or minutes of a public hearing is required. Based on such information, together with news reports and notices in public media, the homeowner has reasonable grounds to believe that condemnation will begin unless he sells voluntarily.

If condemnation is merely being "considered," rather than having been decided, there is no threat or imminence. Considerations and deliberations (of condemnation) go on all the time in the public arena. It is not until specific decisions have been made that threat or imminence looms.

If a homeowner has any doubt about whether condemnation has been decided, he should seek written confirmation from the condemning authority itself. Actually, getting confirmation may be difficult because of political and legal posturing.

If, in fact, threat or imminence does prevail, it is sometimes better to dispose of one's residence prior to its actual condemnation. The politics of condemnation, the inertia of bureaucracy, the greed of attorneys, and the delays of justice, can result in net proceeds to the homeowner much less than a pre-condemnation "sale."

Unfortunately, it is often difficult to "negotiate" with a condemning authority. Such an authority can be arrogant and intimidating, especially if some sharpie legal firm has been engaged to do the negotiating. As a precaution against being completely taken, *two* independent, impartial, professional appraisers (not attorneys) should be employed by the homeowner. Both appraisers should be present at the negotiating conference. Their fees are treated as part of your (deductible) selling expenses.

One of the likely benefits of a negotiated sale to a condemning authority is that the monetary proceeds may be available immediately upon transfer of title. If so, this can save valuable time and anguish in seeking a replacement residence. One can treat the settlement as an ordinary sale, subject to Section 121 benefits. Claiming such benefits now is better than doing so later.

Back to Section 121(d)(5)(B)

Earlier, we outlined the contents of Section 121(d)(5): Special Rules; Involuntary Conversions. We cited then subparagraph (A) and explained it. Now, we want to cite and explain subparagraph (B). Its title words are: ***Application of Section 1033***. We had to provide some introductory background on Section 1033 before you fully appreciate how it is umbrellaed into Section 121.

Subparagraph (B) reads as follows:

In applying section 1033, the amount realized from the sale or exchange of property shall be treated as the amount determined without regard to this section, reduced by the amount of gain not included in gross income pursuant to this section.

We again point out that the term "this section" refers to Section 121. It does not refer to Section 1033. Section 1033 is a "stand alone" irrespective of what Section 121 says. Separately, Section 1033 allows *all* conversion gain to be deferred.

So, what is the subparagraph (B) rule saying?

It is saying two things. First, you have to determine the net amount of gain that you realize from the total of all reimbursements that you receive from insurance and other sources. You establish this gain under the rules of section 1033(a). Secondly, if you qualify under the ownership and use rule of Section 121(a), you may then reduce the gain realized by the exclusion amount of Section 121(b). In other words, there is no requirement that you get a replacement residence (as required by Section 1033) if the amount of gain realized is $250,000/$500,000 or less. Any gain in excess of the exclusion is, of course, taxable.

How do you determine the amount of reimbursement gain?

First off, unlike closing an ordinary sale in escrow, all reimbursement proceeds are not processed at one time. Instead, said proceeds come from different sources (insurance companies, government agencies, and lending institutions) at different times. This means that you have to closely monitor the receipts, record each source, and make inquiry to each as to what additional payment, if any, can be expected. It is only after you have possession of all proceeds, set aside into a separate financial account of their own, that you are ready to determine the true extent of any reimbursement gain.

In Figure 11.2, we present a depiction and outline of the process involved. In this figure we particularly call to your attention steps 2 and 4. Step 2 is where you collect all of your expenses for getting the gross reimbursement in step 1. There will be fees and costs for attorneys, appraisers, contractors, accountants, and others who assist you in preparing and following up on your claims for reimbursement. These are like selling expenses when closing an ordinary sale. They are deductible against the gross proceeds before any gain can be established.

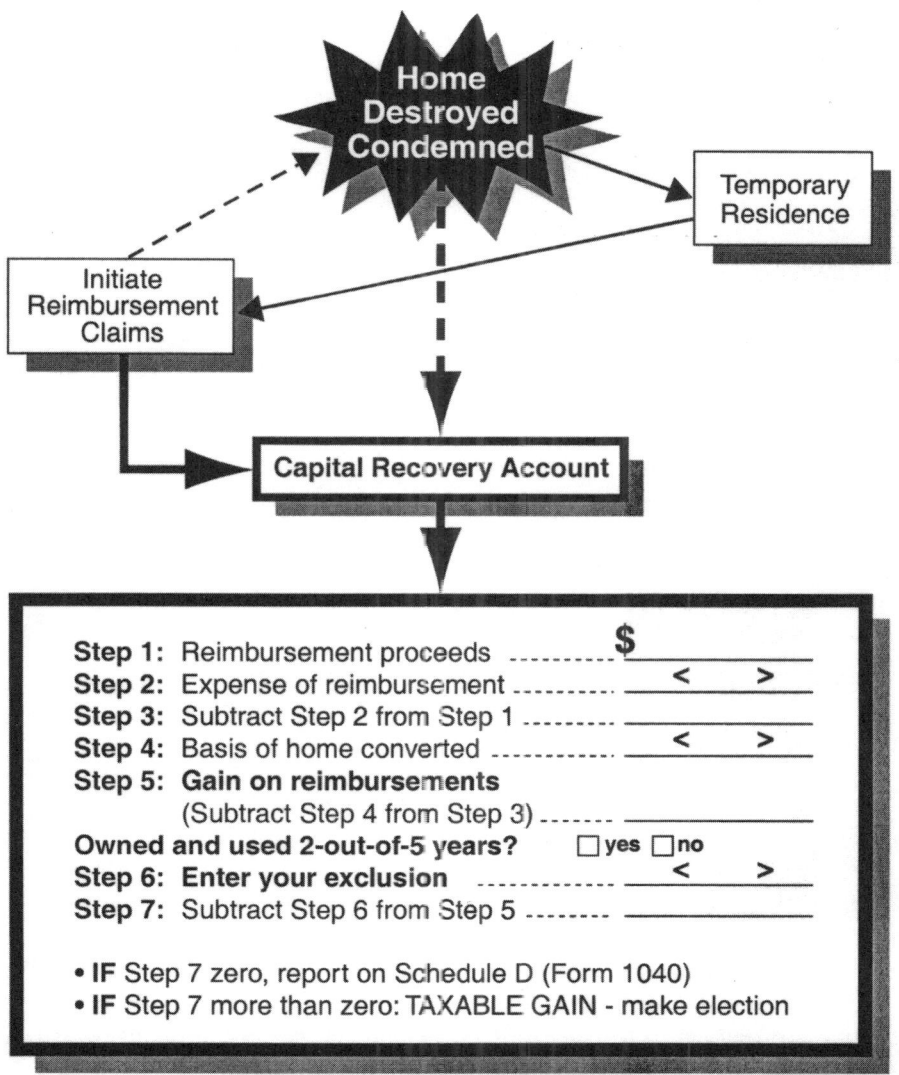

Fig. 11.2 - Establishing Reimbursement Gain When Home Destroyed

Step 4 (in Figure 11.2) is the tax basis in the home that was converted (involuntarily). If your home was destroyed by fire, flood, earthquake, or storm (instead of condemnation), there's a good chance that your tax basis records will have been destroyed also. If this is the case, you'll have to reconstruct your records from memory the best you can. (Recall Chapter 6: Basis of Residence Sold, for pointers in this regard.) Surely, from memory, you can recall your approximate acquisition cost, any prior gain deferred through exchanges and rollovers, costs for major improvements, and so on. If you make no such effort whatsoever, you are stuck with treating your tax basis as zero. From step 4 on, follow the computational sequence that we show in Figure 11.2.

Holding Period Tack-On

Note in Figure 11.2 the checkbox question that appears between steps 5 and 6. This is the ownership-and-use rule of Section 121. You might want to pause here for a moment and think about the intent of "ownership and use." Would not an involuntary conversion, as previously described, be treated as an unforeseen circumstance?

Yes, it would. Our point is that you may be able to count the time that you owned, *but could not live in*, your previous home because it was destroyed or condemned. The assumption is that you lived elsewhere temporarily, until the reimbursement process is settled. Your ownership of the converted home continues until you convey its title to the primary reimbursing entity. After that, you have the holding period (use rule) to consider.

The general holding period rule is Section 1223: ***Holding Period of Property***. It consists of 15 different subrules, the first of which relates to involuntary conversions. Accordingly, subsection (1)(A) reads in part—

> *An involuntary conversion described in section 1033 shall be considered an **exchange** of the property converted for the property acquired, and . . . there shall be included the period for which the taxpayer held the property exchanged. . . .*

Be aware that, whereas Section 121(d)(5)(A) treats your converted residence as a "sale," Section 1223(1)(A) treats it as an "exchange." A sale implies that some specific dollar amount is at hand. Independently, an exchange implies that the period of ownership and use *continues* from one property to another. Indeed, the continuation of ownership and use does apply to a converted residence, irrespective of whether a replacement residence is acquired or the funds for such a residence are received. The applicable concept here is presented in Figure 11.3.

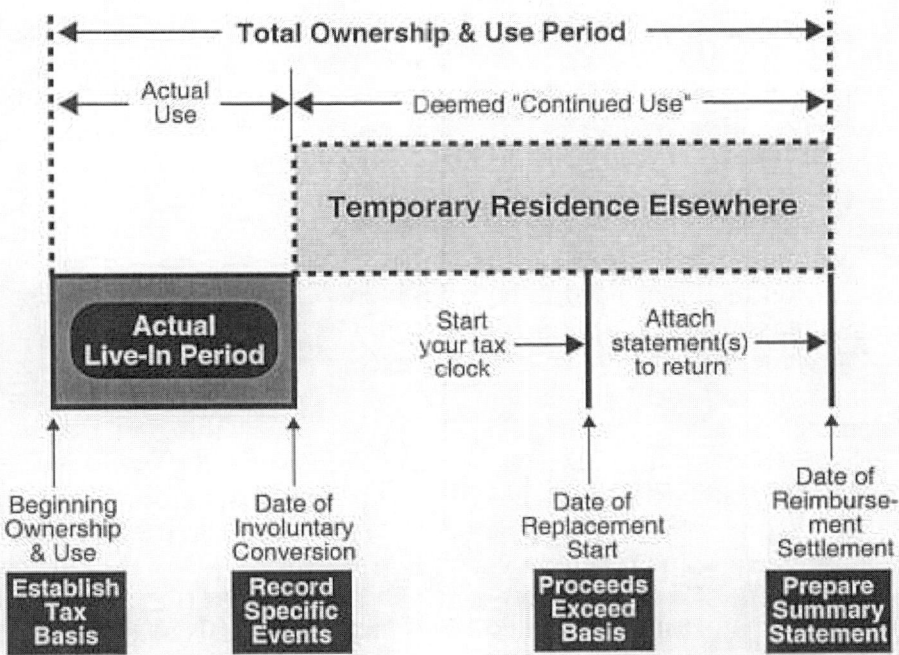

Fig. 11.3 - Use Period "Tack-On" When Forced Into a Temporary Residence

For example, suppose you bought and lived in your principal residence for one day. The next day a lightning storm struck your home and it burned down. In all likelihood, it would take more than two years to collect your insurance or other settlement proceeds. If you lived in a temporary residence (rental or with family or friends) during that time, that period of living in "a residence" would count as part of your use time of the converted residence. After all, if your home is destroyed or condemned involuntarily, you remain the owner of the property until all settlement proceeds are received. The fact that you were "forced" to live elsewhere is a bona fide exception to the 2-out-of-5-year rule. Both your ownership and use continue.

Election to Replace . . . or Not to

Without the exclusion-of-gain of Section 121, a converted residence has to be replaced within two years after the close of the first taxable year in which any part of the gain is realized. If the net realized gain is less than the applicable Section 121(b) amount, why go through the basis adjustment and tax accounting aspects of nonrecognition of gain with a replacement residence? If, after claiming the $250,000/$500,000 exclusion, there is no residual taxable gain, there is no basis adjustment to be made. Claim the exclusion, then start your cost accounting from scratch when you acquire another residence.

If, on the other hand, after tentatively claiming your exclusion amount, you have a net taxable gain, you have an election to make. You can elect to pay the tax on the excess-of-exclusion gain. **Or,** you can roll the whole gain over (*before* exclusion) into a replacement residence and basis adjust accordingly. In other words, you treat the converted residence replacement process as an exchange, rather than as a sale. This way, you postpone any tax on the excess gain until further downstream years when the replacement home is sold, voluntarily.

Section 121(d)(5)(C) recognizes this replacement option. The option is construed in the title and statutory words which read: ***Property Acquired After Involuntary Conversion***—

> *If the basis of property sold or exchanged is determined (in whole or part) under section 1033(b) (relating to the basis of property acquired through involuntary conversion), then the holding and use by the taxpayer of the converted property shall be treated as holding and use by the taxpayer of the property sold or exchanged.*

The title of Section 1033(b) is: ***Basis of Property Acquired Through Involuntary Conversion***. Here, the term "through" conveys a clearer implication than the term "after" in Section 121(d)(5)(C). The term *through* clearly means that the replacement residence and the converted residence are tied in to each other for purposes of basis accounting. This theme is also picked up in the last clause of Section 121(d)(5)(C) which carries through the holding and use period of the converted residence into the replacement residence. This is the tack-on concept depicted earlier in Figure 11.3.

Presidentially Declared Disasters

The replacement period for a converted residence begins 2 years *after gain*, if any, is realized. But if the conversion is brought about through widespread destruction in a disaster area — designated as such by the President — the replacement period (after gain is realized) is extended to four years. This additional time is necessary because, when so many residences are destroyed at the same time, the insurance and construction industries are overwhelmed. A "Presidentially declared disaster" is where federal assistance under the Disaster Relief and Emergency Assistance Act is warranted.

Section 1033(h)(1)(A) is the specific rule on point. The successive title words are:

(h)   Special Rules for Property Damaged by Presidentially Declared Disasters
(1) Principal Residences
(A) Treatment of Insurance Proceeds

Section 1033(h)(1)(A) reads in part as—

*If the taxpayer's **principal residence or any of its contents** is compulsorily or involuntarily converted as a result of a Presidentially declared disaster . . . **no gain shall be recognized** by reason of the receipt of any insurance proceeds . . . [if used to purchase] any property which is similar or related in service or use to the residence so converted (or contents thereof).* [Emphasis added.]

The fine points of Section 1033(h) go on to provide that the insurance proceeds may include reimbursement for personal household items as well as reimbursement for the residential building and its appurtenances. This is the significance of the above-emphasized phrase: ". . . or any of its contents." Thus, the insurance funds can be used to acquire not only a replacement residence but also its contents. This is a major departure from the regular residence replacement rules of Section 1033(a).

Another departure from Section 1033(a) is that Section 1033(h) also applies to renters. If a rented residence would otherwise qualify as the occupants' principal residence if they owned it, they are treated the same as an ordinary homeowner. No potential gain is tax recognized until the "pool of funds" from all disaster-related insurance claims exceeds the cost of getting a replacement rental.

Section 1033(h) is a very special rule indeed. It applies only to area-wide disasters such as floods, hurricanes, typhoons, earthquakes, and firestorms, where multiple properties are destroyed simultaneously. It is an exception to the ordinary provisions of Section 1033(a). These "ordinary provisions" address only the single property or single residence replacement situation, whether caused by accident or condemnation.

All forms of involuntary conversion of a principal residence qualify for the Section 121 exclusion-of-gain benefits. If said benefits are claimed, the reimbursement proceeds have to be tax reported. The reporting is done on Schedule D (Form 1040) as we discussed previously in Chapter 8: Claiming Your Exclusion. Particularly recall Figure 8.3 on page 8-12. The only reporting difference is that, instead of "Sale of residence," you describe its disposition as—

Converted residence: Sec. 121(d)(5)

After claiming the proper amount of exclusion, assign that amount to your tax-free accumulation account. Keep a copy of your converted residence Schedule D as part of your permanent records for supporting your accumulation of nontaxable "wealth."

Whether you change your principal residence voluntarily or involuntarily, Section 121 is truly a nest-egg opportunity to behold.

12

NEST EGG COMMENTARY

Section 121 Provides Unprecedented Opportunities To Amass Large Sums Of TAX FREE Money For Retirement. Over Your 30 To 50 Years Of Home Ownership, You'll Probably Make Between 5 And 8 Sales. With The Potential Of A $250,000 EXCLUSION OF GAIN Per Sale, You Could Amass Between $1,000,000 And $2,000,000. The "Key" For Doing So Is Rolling Over ALL Exclusion Amounts Into Each Successive Replacement Home, Until All Mortgages Are Paid Off. Target This For Age 55. Thereafter, Assign Your Sale Exclusions To A Municipal Bond Fund, Where All Interest Earned Thereafter Is Tax Free.

Our position is that there was tax and financial wisdom in old law that is not present in current law. Under repealed Section 1034 (Rollover of Gain), the idea was to cumulatively parlay the gains from residence to residence as one's occupational advancements and family needs grew. Because the rollover aspects were mandatory — not elective — they became a form of forced savings into an increasingly more expensive home. This continued from one's youth up into his retirement years, at which time, Congress offered a once-only tax bonus.

In principle, the cumulative rollovers were to culminate when the homeowner/taxpayer reached retirement age. Once over age 55, one could *elect* to use the $125,000 exclusion of gain under former Section 121. Or, one could defer the election (by continuing the rollover process) until he was truly ready to retire.

Then, the $125,000 exclusion election became a golden nest egg. In those earlier years, that was a lot of money.

Under current law (Section 121 effective May 7, 1997), we no longer have the old law mandatory nest egg feature. Now, when a residence is sold, the "up to" $250,000 exclusion of gain can be claimed. Unless there are excess gains over this amount, the tax accounting is closed. There is no option to roll over any of the gain; there is no election to defer any of the allowable exclusion. One can spend, disburse, invest, or fritter away the exclusion money in any way he/she/they see fit. The acquisition of another residence starts the exclusion process over again.

Each sale of one's principal residence now represents tax free money . . . when there is a gain. This fact opens up unique opportunities to build a quite substantial nest egg for one's retirement. By "substantial," we mean approaching $1,000,000 or more. The amount of buildup will depend on the number of sales in your home ownership lifetime, the extent of property value appreciation in the local area, and on the extent of improvements made by you as the owner. In this, our final chapter, we want to present a plausible rationale and methodology for truly "capitalizing" on the exclusion benefits of Section 121. The entire Internal Revenue Code consists of approximately 1,800 sections of tax law (actually, as of the end of 2005, the count was 1,831 sections). There is no other section where one single event can produce (potentially) up to $250,000/$500,000 in pure TAX FREE money. In a lifetime of home sales, there can be *multiple* such tax free events. The benefits of Section 121 are truly unprecedented.

Section 121 (Exclusion) Revisited

For refresher purposes, let's go back and recite the dominant rule of Section 121. The title of this section, recall, is: *Exclusion of Gain from Sale of* [your] *Principal Residence*. Its subsection (a) reads in full as—

> *Gross income **shall not include** gain from the sale or exchange of property if, during the 5-year period ending on the date of the sale or exchange, such property has been owned and used by the taxpayer as the taxpayer's principal residence for periods aggregating 2 years or more.* [Emphasis added.]

Based on this citation alone, do you agree that whatever amount of gain is excluded from gross income is statutorily tax free? If you agree, we then raise the question: What will **you** do with your tax free money?

We suspect that your answer will depend on the amount of exclusion money involved: $10,000; $100,000; $250,000; or $500,000. Not every sale in your lifetime will produce the maximum allowable exclusion amount.

What is the maximum allowable exclusion amount per sale? Subsection (b)(1): *In General*, says—

The amount of gain excluded from gross income under subsection (a) with respect to any sale or exchange shall not exceed $250,000. [Emphasis added.]

This is a pretty clear statement that the exclusion applies to ANY (meaning: each separate) sale of your principal residence throughout your lifetime. Except for the time interval between sales, there is no limitation on the number of sales that can be made. This is the *genetic seed* behind our rationale for parlaying your gains into a substantial retirement nest egg.

Subsection (b)(2): *Joint Returns*, sets forth the conditions whereby a husband and wife can exclude up to $500,000 per sale event. The conditions are:

(A) The spouses must make a joint return for the year of sale,
(B) **Either** spouse meets the **ownership** requirements of subsection (a),
(C) **Both** spouses meet the **use** requirements of subsection (a), and
(D) Neither spouse has claimed his or her exclusion within the past two years, ending on date of sale.

Subsection (b)(3) says that the exclusion amount applies to only one sale every 2-plus years. The exact statutory wording does not say "2-plus"; it says—

Subsection (a) shall not apply to any sale or exchange by the taxpayer if, during the 2-year period ending on the date of such sale or exchange, there was another sale or exchange by the taxpayer to which subsection (a) applied.

We prefer the frequency concept of 2-plus years, where the "plus" means two or more *days* beyond the two years.

With such a huge and unprecedented exclusion potential ($250,000/$500,000), it is much too risky to "knife-edge" the 2-year count. The exactness of the two years has yet to be judicially determined. What about leap years; what about weekends; what about time of day? Does two years mean: two consecutive 365-day years, or two consecutive calendar years, including leap year (if any)? Must the beginning year and ending year days be full 24-hour days? Our position is "Yes." If a leap year is involved, the frequency of sale interval is 731 (365 + 366) 24-hour days. To miss a $250,000/$500,000 exclusion for being one hour short of a knife-edge technicality, borders on reckless inattention. Because of the large tax free amount, count on the IRS to confirm the legal 2-year period with painstaking scrutiny.

No Gimmick Tax Accounting

For once in a tax law, there are no gimmicks. If you meet the ownership and use requirements of subsection (a) and the frequency of sale requirements of subsection (b)(3), tax reporting and accounting for the sale is almost a no brainer. Note that we do say, "almost." You still have to keep records on the acquisition basis (purchase, exchange, gift, inheritance) of your home, improvements thereto, and other adjustments to your cumulative capital investment. Once you do so, the preparation and filing of Schedule D (Form 1040), covered in Chapter 8, are quite straightforward.

From the gross proceeds of the sale, you subtract the following amounts in the order listed:

1. Expense of sale
2. Adjusted basis of residence sold
3. Your allowable exclusion amount

What could be simpler than this?

If your gain realized, after subtracting items 1 and 2, is less than your allowable exclusion, you have what we call an *accuracy tolerance* in your favor. For example, if your allowable exclusion is $250,000 and your gain realized is $200,000, your accuracy tolerance is $50,000. This means that the combination of items 1 and 2 can be overstated by as much as $50,000 and still there would be no tax to pay. The less the gain realized on each sale, the greater your accuracy tolerance for that sale.

Regardless of recordkeeping accuracy tolerance, you want to isolate and set aside your allowable exclusion amount from each sale. We suggest you do so by establishing a **HSERA** plan: **H**ome **S**ale **E**xclusion **R**etirement **A**ccount. Think of your HSERA as a "parlaying" retirement plan which, unlike IRAs, 401(k)s, SEPs, TSAs, ROTHs, etc. is not subject to IRS rules and restrictions. The only HSERA restriction is your own self discipline to not squander your exclusion money. As to "investing" said money, we suggest (and urge) a two-pronged conservatism:

[1]   Successive mortgage buydowns, and
[2]   Tax free municipal bonds, or
[3]   Top grade corporate bonds.

If your gain realized is more than your allowable exclusion, you have taxable gain. This means that if you owned the residence more than two years, you pay tax at a favorable 15% capital gain rate. This is better than paying tax at your regular rate (which could be on the order of 25% to 35% for tax year circa 2006).

If you do have *taxable gain*, you have the option of reporting the sale via the installment method (Form 6252). This spreads the capital gains tax over 5, 10, or more years. We do not recommend the installment method until your last or next-to-last homesale. When close to your "final sale," if you follow our urgings herein you will have your mortgage paid off or nearly so. When closing the sale, you become the primary mortgage holder. You collect the commercial interest rates on the mortgage which is secured by the property you already know about (your own prior home).

In Figure 12.1, we summarize in a schematic way the simplistic aspects of reporting an ordinary (no business use) home sale. Once you get this pattern down, and you repeat it a number of sale times, you'll begin to realize how you can amass a quite considerable sum of tax free money over your lifetime.

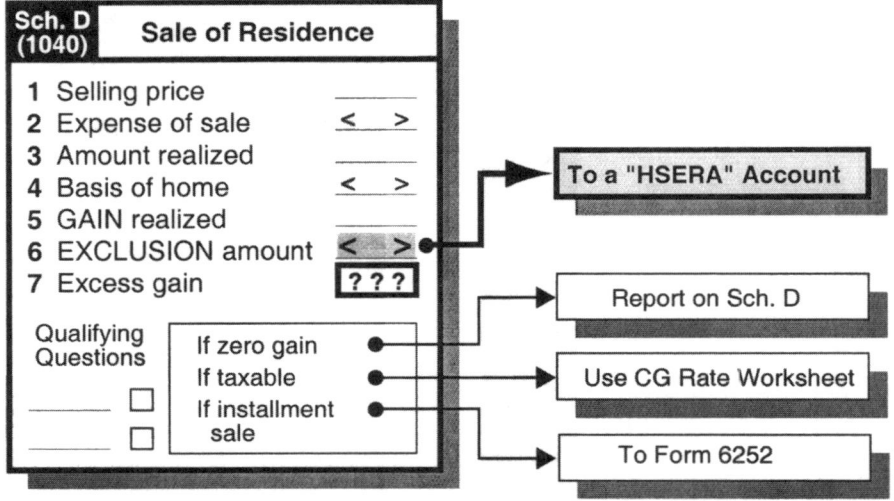

Fig. 12.1 - Simplified Version of the "Mechanics" of a Homesale

Three Bad Examples

We indicated earlier that it is possible to formulate a "plan" for saving your homesale exclusion money. Saving money these days is not as popular as spending it. Having tax-free money causes a form of hypnosis that deadens one's sense of self-caution on money matters. We offer three real-life examples on how the Section 121 exclusions were squandered.

In Case X, the husband and wife couple were hard-working Russian immigrants. They gathered their savings and borrowed enough money from personal friends to purchase a home in a rural area of California. It was a fixer-upper and they were intent on improving the home for its Section 121 sale. This was their first home in America and they loved the entrepreneurial spirit for making money. When the home was sold several years later, they realized approximately $300,000 in capital gain (all tax free). After paying off their credit cards and personal loans, they had $180,000 tax free to save or spend as they desired.

What did they do with that $180,000 tax free?

Answer: They took a vacation to Las Vegas, Nevada and its various gambling casinos. In just five days' time, they lost every penny! They had to borrow enough money from friends to get back to their jobs in California.

In Case Y, the husband and wife homeowners were insatiable credit card purchasers. They purchased every car, boat, vacation, and entertainment event imaginable Their seemingly endless source of funds was the equity in their appreciating $600,000 home. They refinanced, re-refinanced, and got repetitive extended lines of credit. Things got to the point where they could no longer refinance. Anxious creditors started to hound and pound. The couple decided to sell their home, pay off all debt, and start fresh in a new home. The house sold for $690,000 and they tax claimed their full $500,000 capital gain exclusion. BUT, after paying off all mortgages, all credit card debt, and all taxes outstanding, guess what! They were left with only $1,000 in cash! They totally committed to others $499,000 of their tax-free money.

In Case Z, the homeowner was a single man age 63. He had been married twice, divorced once, and widowed once. He had three grown children. He was laid off from his job and had to figure out what to do until his social security benefits kicked in at age 67. He attended several investment seminars and became intrigued by the wealth amassing prospects in Section 1256 *Contracts and Straddles*. His intrigue focused on the 60% treatment of any day-trading gains as long-term capital gains. He had nearly $200,000 in retirement savings and, thus, began dabbling in day-trading in Section 1256 contracts.

> *Editorial Note*: A "Section 1256 contract" requires that all settlement prices and margin adjustments on all contracts involving securities futures, commodities futures, foreign currencies, options, and straddles be established on a *daily basis* called "marketing-to-market." At the end of the year, "marked-to-market" tax rules apply. The result is that 60% of capital gains and losses are treated as long-term and 40% are treated as short-term. Thus, regardless of actual holding period, 60% of the contracts are **long-term** and 40% are short-term. Long-term capital gains are much more tax favored than are short-term capital gains.

Within about three months, he had dissipated $212,000 of his retirement and other savings. He had no choice then but to sell his home. He had paid $185,000 for it, including all improvements thereto. After selling expenses, his realized capital gain was $360,000. He sold early in the year. All of his homesale proceeds were sale-year "reinvested" in Section 1256 contracts.

Can you sense what is coming?

On his homesale-year Schedule D, we reconstruct his reportings as follows:

Exclusionary gain	$250,000
Taxable gain	110,000
Section 1256 <loss>	<285,000>
Net tax-free gain	$ 75,000

After working some 40 years, the Case Z homeseller had only $75,000 for his retirement nest egg. Fortunately, one of two sons was well to do, and insisted that his dad move in with him permanently.

One Rare Good Example

We also offer a rare good example of Section 121 behavior. An 80-year-old couple bought their only home more than 50 years ago. They raised four children, one of whom was killed in a hang glider crash. The couple were physically fragile, chronically ill, and needed walkers and wheelchairs to get around. One day, a "family meeting" was convened to discuss what to do with the house: sell it or keep it for the children and grandchildren. While a consensus opinion was evolving, the couple, at the urging of elderly friends, visited several full-service retirement homes. They took a fancy to one in particular, a rather expensive facility for $6,000 per month.

Because the residential real estate market was very hot at the time, the couple decided to sell. They originally paid less than $50,00 for their home and added, over the years, some $100,000 worth of improvements. Within three days after the home was put on the market, it sold for — can you guess how much? — $1,350,000! That's one million 350 thousand dollars.

Their realized gain over basis ($150,000) plus selling expenses ($100,000) was $1,100,000. Of this gain amount, $500,000 was totally tax free. The remaining $600,000 gain was taxable, for which they paid $150,000 in taxes (federal and state). Their net/net cash out of the deal was $50,000 (basis minus selling expenses) *plus* $500,000 (tax free) *plus* $450,000 (after tax) . . . for a grand total of $1,000,000 (precisely).

Excluding their social security benefits, nonimpressive pensions, IRA drawdowns, and tax-free earnings on their nest egg, they could expect a comfortable twilight lifestyle for a minimum of 15 years . . . to at least age 95.

Lifespan of Home Ownerships

We don't know what a "typical homeowner" is — age, economic level, frequency of sales, etc. — yet, we'll assume that there is such a human icon. Probably, the age of earliest home ownership is in the range of 25 to 30 years. If one marries within or before this age span, the desire to acquire and live in one's own home, rather than renting, is a basic instinct of nature. This is especially true, if the housing of children and other family members (parents, siblings, etc.) is contemplated.

Once one acquires the experience of home ownership — the responsibilities and the benefits — the natural path is to continue the experience well into one's retirement years. At some point in retirement, the physical and financial burden of ownership becomes unsatisfying. At such point, a "final sale" is made. After this sale, one then lives in a "close community" type arrangement. The age likelihood of one's final sale? Probably in the 75- to 85-year-old range. We say this because people of reasonable health and occupational success live longer these days.

Actuarially, a male at age 60 is expected to live to around age 78: a female to age 82. At age 80, a male is expected to live to age 87: a female to age 89. Other actuarial life expectancies between the ages of 50 and 95 are presented in Figure 12.2.

Theoretically, therefore, the "average" lifespan of home ownership is between 40 and 50 years: 25 to 65, to 70, to 75. During this lifespan, how many sales are likely to occur? We say somewhere between five and eight: maybe less, but seldom more.

AGE AT RETIREMENT	LIFE EXPECTANCY			
	MALE		FEMALE	
	Actuarial Factor	Age at Death	Actuarial Factor	Age at Death
50	25.5	75.5	29.6	79.6
55	21.7	76.7	25.5	80.5
60	18.2	78.2	21.7	81.7
65	15.0	80.0	18.2	83.2
70	12.1	82.1	15.0	85.0
75	9.6	84.6	12.1	87.1
80	7.5	87.5	9.6	89.6
85	5.7	90.7	7.5	92.5
90	4.2	94.2	5.7	95.7
95	3.1	98.1	4.2	99.2
/////////	IRS Reg. 1.72-9 : Annuity Tables			/////////

Fig. 12.2 - Life Expectancy From IRS's Actuarial Tables

Most occupationally active persons tend to reach their professional peaks by around age 55. After this age, they are treated as "over the hill" by their associates. They are within 10 years or so of normal retirement. Each subsequent year, they become more preoccupied with retirement planning than with professional planning. If they don't retire normally at age 65 or so, they surely retire at age 75 (or so).

From our observation of those "climbing the professional ladder," the average frequency of home sales between the ages of 25 and 55 . . . is about six sales. This is one sale, on average, every five years. This is about the way it is in these days of frequent job changes and technology changes. In some upwardly mobile occupations, especially where involved in international commerce, a home sale every three years or so is not atypical. In the 55 to 75 age range, the frequency of home sales drops markedly. One's upward professional mobility slows down, and tends to flatten out altogether. During this 20-year period, there may be at least one or two sales, but rarely more than three.

In the most general of generalizations, we submit that the nominal frequency of home sales in one's lifetime is between five and eight. With this number of sales, there is potential for cumulatively amassing between $1,000,000 (1 million) and $2,000,000 (2 million) in PURE tax free money (8 sales x $250,000 potential exclusion per sale). Surely, you could retire sensibly on this amount of money.

Maximizing Your HSERA Goal

Whether you are buying (or acquiring by other means) your first home . . . or your 10th home, here are some suggestions that may help you towards your HSERA goal [HSERA = Home Sale Exclusion Retirement Account]:

One. If you can, buy in an area where property values have a reputation for steady appreciation. Usually, this is an area of new homes, upscale living, and in the path of urban population growth. As of the end of 2000 (latest census), official estimates of the U.S. population stood at 298,439,000 people. Our "population bomb" is still ticking away with no end in sight. At least for the foreseeable future, this is your assurance that your home will sell, when you are ready to sell.

Two. Make quality improvements to your home. Talk to local real estate agents concerning the types of improvements that generate enhancement value. An "enhancement" improvement is of the type that, for every dollar you put in, you get $2 out when you sell. This has nothing to do with the appreciation in property values of the area at large. Some improvements, such as remodeling the kitchen, adding an extra bedroom or bath, extending the garage, relandscaping, and others, add value to your home over and above that of your neighbors. If the improvement is of a type you can do yourself, or mostly yourself, so much the better. You are converting your personal services into exclusion-of-gain income. This is a rare tax opportunity in itself.

Three. Sell when the opportunity arises or when necessity requires. Job changes, family changes, schooling needs, age and physical stamina, and other factors influence your frequency of sales. Sell as often as is prudent. In your younger years, sell frequently; in your older years, sell less frequently. After age 70 or 75, plan your "final" sale. By that time, your expenditures for health care and long-term needs will accelerate. The money you saved over the years will be needed.

Set Goal to Pay Off Mortgage

As you sell each home and acquire another, reinvest part or all of each exclusion amount into your new home. Do not direct the exclusion money to other uses. Think of it, if you will, as putting that money under your mattress. You'll know where it is at all times. You can protect and enhance it by continuing your program of selected improvements to each new home that you acquire. This is the way you test your own self-discipline. Each exclusion is not fritter-away money; it is mortgage paydown money.

Set as your goal having all home mortgage debt paid off by age 55 . . . or absolutely no later than age 60. That is, use the cash proceeds from each sale as down payment on your next home. The "cash proceeds" will consist of: (a) your initial out-of-pocket down payment, (b) your return of capital in the adjusted basis of home sold, and (c) your allowable exclusion of gain. This is what we call: *Mortgage Self-Buydown*. We depict this concept for you in Figure 12.3. Owning your home free and clear by age 55 is quite doable . . . if you set your mind to it.

Why do we pick age 55 as your goal of total mortgage payoff/ buydown? There are several reasons actually.

As we stated earlier, by age 55 you will have probably reached your professional and occupational peak. Your children, if any, will be adults. You likely will have reached the home value and size with which you are content. You are vulnerable to corporate downsizings and layoffs. And, if you are fortunate enough to have an employer-sponsored-and-paid pension plan, you are vulnerable to being forced into "early retirement." Established companies routinely do this as a means of curtailing their ongoing pension benefit liabilities. If you are self-employed — or forced into self-employment by corporate downsizings — having your home fully paid off is a security blanket of its own. It's that "money under the mattress" feeling. You will have the money available when needed, and, when not needed, it will not vanish into thin air.

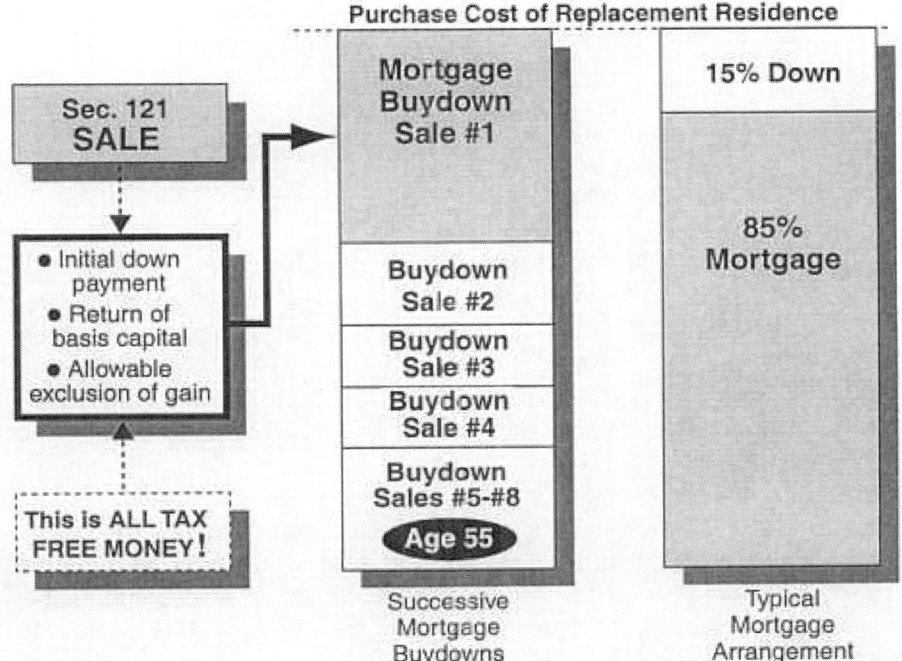

Fig. 12.3 - Concept for Achieving Total Mortgage Pay-Off by Age 55

For those who argue that home mortgage payments are tax deductible, let us review the facts of life. First off, only the mortgage *interest* (not principal) is tax deductible. It is deductible only on Schedule A (Form 1040): ***Itemized Deductions***. There it is subject to further diminution depending on your filing status and gross income level.

For every $1,000 you pay out in mortgage interest, you save approximately $350 in federal income tax (at the top individual rate of 35%). You spend $1,000 to save $350; this means that you are cash out-of-pocket by $650. In contrast, if your mortgage were paid off, you'd pay about $350 tax for each $1,000 of nondeductibles. Thus, your savings after tax would be $650 for each $1,000 of would-be mortgage interest you did not pay. It is these savings that you can use for other expenditures in your life.

If our above frequency-of-sales scenario is applicable to your case, you will have made between five and eight sales in the 30-year period ending when you reach age 55. By this age, conceivably, you could have boot-strapped yourself into a $1,000,000 (1 million) home. Being fully paid off, that $1,000,000 would be ALL AFTER-TAX MONEY. Think seriously about this as your goal!

Selling & Buying Lower

Once you are in the "typical" retirement age spread: 60 to 70, it is a good idea to make one intermediate sale before the final sale of your home. Sell and get yourself (and spouse) a smaller, lower priced home. You probably have no further need for the larger home that you have cumulatively acquired during your pre-retirement years. Target the smaller home at about 60% of the selling price of your current home. Not only do you want to reduce your day-to-day home expenses, you also want to take some of that tax free exclusion money out from under the mattress. You want to test putting that mattress money into continuing tax free investments, namely: *municipal bonds*. While the yield rates are not spectacular (3% to 5% range), the principal is relatively stable over long periods of time.

On the subject of municipal bonds, Section 103: *Interest on State and Local Bonds*, says—

Except as provided in subsection (b), **gross income does not include** *interest on any State or local bond.* [Emphasis added.]

Subsection 103(b) focuses on "private activity bonds" (shopping malls, sports stadiums) for which the alternate minimum tax (AMT) applies.

Talk to your broker, mutual fund, or other advisor about a portfolio of municipal bonds . . . with *checkwriting* privileges. This could become the "new excitement" in your life: experiencing and using tax free exclusion money to earn tax free income.

To illustrate the amount of money initially available for tax free investing, consider that the net selling price of your home (after selling expenses) was $825,000. A 60% replacement residence would come to about $500,000 (825,000 x 60%). This would still be a comfortable home for your initial retirement years.

The amount of cash out of the transaction would come to around $325,000 (825,000 – 500,000). Suppose you had saved cumulatively $600,000 prior Section 121 sales. At a muni bond interest rate of 5%, say, your $925,000 could generate about $46,000 in tax free income each year. We doubt that your social security benefits would ever approach this annual figure.

As we see the potentials for you, we profile your lifetime of home sales in Figure 12.4. The unshaded area (to age 55) is where your exclusion money is used to buy down your mortgage. What you don't use for buy down, you save. Admittedly, the pattern presented is a "scenario." Yet, we want you to see the growth in your home values over the years and how the exclusion of gain rules (Section 121) and adjustments to basis rules (Section 1016) can help you achieve truly tax free financial independence. Even so, you still have one last sale to make.

Your "Final" Sale

At this point in our Figure 12.4 scenario, you are living in a $500,000 home. It is your final home and is fully paid off. Now, you need that money under the mattress (or much of it) to pay for rising medical costs and long-term twilight care. Thus, you must make your final sale.

One arrangement for disposing of your last home is via an installment sale. This method permits you to pay any capital gains tax over an extended period of time: 5 years, 10 years, or whatever. The central feature of this stretching-out of tax payments is the establishment of a **GPP** (Gross profit percentage) for the sale overall. The GPP is applied to all payments on principal in the year of sale, and to all payments (on principal) annually thereafter. The mechanics for computing the GPP are prescribed on Form 6252: ***Installment Sale Income***. There is a reminder on the form that it is strictly for payments on principal (for which a capital gains tax is due). If no capital gains tax is due, no Form 6252 is required.

If you acquired your final home for $500,000 and you held it two years before sale, it is highly unlikely that you would have any taxable gain. To have taxable gain in excess of your exclusion amount, your home would have to appreciate *more than* 25% each holding year. We doubt that this would happen. Therefore, no tax on the final sale of your home is likely.

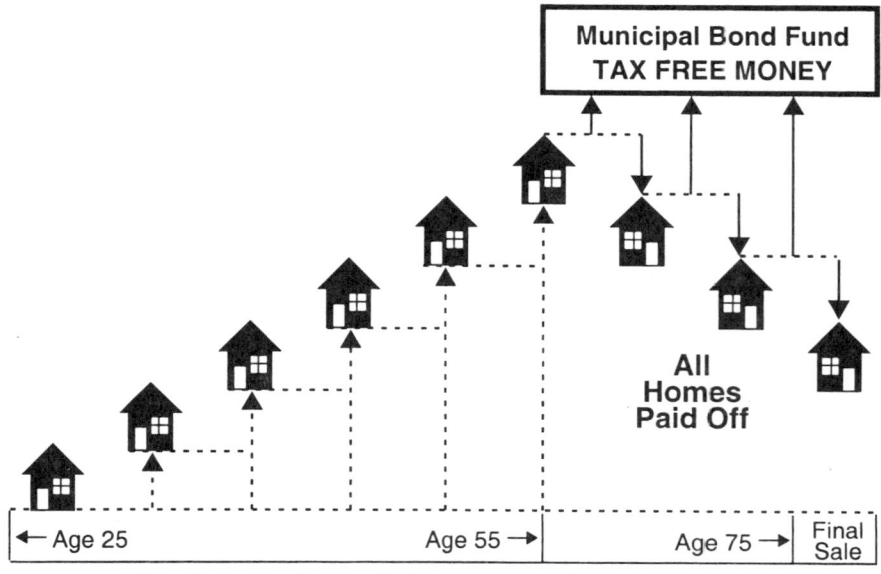

Fig. 12.4 - Likely "Profile" of Your Lifetime of Home Sales

In this case, then, there is a different benefit to an installment sale. You could be the sole mortgage holder on the property sold. As such, you would be entitled to the going commercial rate of interest . . . whatever that rate may be. On a $500,000-plus mortgage, the principal and interest received could provide a quite comfortable source of income. Regard this as a supplement to your other retirement sources. The interest earned, however, would be taxable, but your principal would not be taxed.

Limit your final installment arrangement to five years. Insist on a balloon payment with all principal due and payable at the end. Take the final cash money and assign it to your municipal bond HSERA account (which is nontaxable). After all, your twilight years are approaching fast. You want to simplify matters for yourself . . . and for your heirs.

ABOUT

THE AUTHOR

Holmes F. Crouch

Born on a small farm in southern Maryland, Holmes was graduated from the U.S. Coast Guard Academy with a Bachelor's Degree in Marine Engineering. While serving on active duty, he wrote many technical articles on maritime matters. After attaining the rank of Lieutenant Commander, he resigned to pursue a career as a nuclear engineer.

Continuing his education, he earned a Master's Degree in Nuclear Engineering from the University of California. He also authored two books on nuclear propulsion. As a result of the tax write-offs associated with writing these books, the IRS audited his returns. The IRS's handling of the audit procedure so annoyed Holmes that he undertook to become as knowledgeable as possible regarding tax procedures. He became a licensed private Tax Practitioner by passing an examination administered by the IRS. Having attained this credential, he started his own tax preparation and counseling business in 1972.

In the early years of his tax practice, he was a regular talk-show guest on San Francisco's KGO Radio responding to hundreds of phone-in tax questions from listeners. He was a much sought-after guest speaker at many business seminars and taxpayer meetings. He also provided counseling on special tax problems, such as divorce matters, property exchanges, timber harvesting, mining ventures, animal breeding, independent contractors, selling businesses, and offices-at-home. Over the past 25 years, he has prepared well over 10,000 tax returns for individuals, estates, trusts, and small businesses (in partnership and corporate form).

During the tax season of January through April, he prepares returns in a unique manner. During a single meeting, he completes the return . . . *on the spot!* The client leaves with his return signed, sealed, and in a stamped envelope. His unique approach to preparing returns and his personal interest in his clients' tax affairs have honed his professional proficiency. His expertise extends through itemized deductions, computer-matching of income sources, capital gains and losses, business expenses and cost of goods, residential rental expenses, limited and general partnership activities, closely-held corporations, to family farms and ranches.

He remembers spending 12 straight hours completing a doctor's complex return. The next year, the doctor, having moved away, utilized a large accounting firm to prepare his return. Their accountant was so impressed by the manner in which the prior return was prepared that he recommended the doctor travel the 500 miles each year to have Holmes continue doing it.

He recalls preparing a return for an unemployed welder, for which he charged no fee. Two years later the welder came back and had his return prepared. He paid the regular fee . . . and then added a $300 tip.

During the off season, he represents clients at IRS audits and appeals. In one case a shoe salesman's audit was scheduled to last three hours. However, after examining Holmes' documentation it was concluded in 15 minutes with "no change" to his return. In another instance he went to an audit of a custom jeweler that the IRS dragged out for more than six hours. But, supported by Holmes' documentation, the client's return was accepted by the IRS with "no change."

Then there was the audit of a language translator that lasted two full days. The auditor scrutinized more than $1.25 million in gross receipts, all direct costs, and operating expenses. Even though all expensed items were documented and verified, the auditor decided that more than $23,000 of expenses ought to be listed as capital items for depreciation instead. If this had been enforced it would have resulted in a significant additional amount of tax. Holmes strongly disagreed and after many hours explanation got the amount reduced by more than 60% on behalf of his client.

He has dealt extensively with gift, death and trust tax returns. These preparations have involved him in the tax aspects of wills, estate planning, trustee duties, probate, marital and charitable bequests, gift and death exemptions, and property titling.

Although not an attorney, he prepares Petitions to the U.S. Tax Court for clients. He details the IRS errors and taxpayer facts by citing pertinent sections of tax law and regulations. In a recent case involving an attorney's ex-spouse, the IRS asserted a tax deficiency of $155,000. On behalf of his client, he petitioned the Tax Court and within six months the IRS conceded the case.

Over the years, Holmes has observed that the IRS is not the industrious, impartial, and competent federal agency that its official public imaging would have us believe.

He found that, at times, under the slightest pretext, the IRS has interpreted against a taxpayer in order to assess maximum penalties, and may even delay pending matters so as to increase interest due on additional taxes. He has confronted the IRS in his own behalf on five separate occasions, going before the U.S. Claims Court, U.S. District Court, and U.S. Tax Court. These were court actions that tested specific sections of the Internal Revenue Code which he found ambiguous, inequitable, and abusively interpreted by the IRS.

Disturbed by the conduct of the IRS and by the general lack of tax knowledge by most individuals, he began an innovative series of taxpayer-oriented Federal tax guides. To fulfill this need, he undertook the writing of a series of guidebooks that provide in-depth knowledge on one tax subject at a time. He focuses on subjects that plague taxpayers all throughout the year. Hence, his formulation of the "Allyear" Tax Guide series.

The author is indebted to his wife, Irma Jean, and daughter, Barbara MacRae, for the word processing and computer graphics that turn his experiences into the reality of these publications. Holmes welcomes comments, questions, and suggestions from his readers. He can be contacted in California at (408) 867-2628, or by writing to the publisher's address.

ALLYEAR Tax Guides
by Holmes F. Crouch

Series 100 - INDIVIDUALS AND FAMILIES

BEING SELF-EMPLOYED .... T/G 101
DEDUCTING JOB EXPENSES .... T/G 102
FAMILY TAX STRATEGIES .... T/G 103
DIVORCE & ITS TAX IMPACT .... T/G 104
CITIZENS WORKING ABROAD .... T/G 105

Series 200 - INVESTORS AND BUSINESSES

CAPITAL GAINS & LOSSES .... T/G 201
BEFORE STARTING A BUSINESS........................... T/G 202
THE PROS & CONS OF LLCs .... T/G 203
MAKING PARTNERSHIPS WORK .... T/G 204
SMALL C & S CORPORATIONS.............................. T/G 205

Series 300 - RETIREES AND ESTATES

DECISIONS WHEN RETIRING .... T/G 301
LIVING WILLS & TRUSTS...................................... T/G 302
ORGANIZING YOUR ESTATE .... T/G 303
YOUR EXECUTOR DUTIES .... T/G 304
YOUR TRUSTEE DUTIES .... T/G 305

Series 400 - OWNERS AND SELLERS

RENTAL REAL ESTATE .... T/G 401
TAX-DEFERRED EXCHANGES .... T/G 402
FAMILY TRUSTS & TRUSTORS.............................. T/G 403
HOME SALES UNLIMITED..................................... T/G 404
SELLING YOUR BUSINESS .... T/G 405

Series 500 - AUDITS AND APPEALS

KEEPING GOOD RECORDS .... T/G 501
WINNING YOUR AUDIT .... T/G 502
DISAGREEING WITH THE IRS .... T/G 503
CONTESTING IRS PENALTIES .... T/G 504
GOING INTO TAX COURT .... T/G 505

For information about the above titles, contact
Holmes F. Crouch
Allyear Tax Guides
Phone: (408) 867-2628   Fax: (408) 867-6466